Andrew Young

Andrew Young in his garden at Stonegate in the 1950s

Andrew Young
Priest, Poet and Naturalist
A Reassessment

Richard Ormrod

(L)
The Lutterworth Press

The Lutterworth Press
P.O. Box 60
Cambridge
CB1 2NT
United Kingdom

www.lutterworth.com
publishing@lutterworth.com

ISBN: 978 0 7188 9513 6

British Library Cataloguing in Publication Data
A record is available from the British Library

First published by The Lutterworth Press, 2018

Copyright © Richard Ormrod, 2018

Cover images:
(front) John Gay, *Andrew John Young*, 1948
© National Portrait Gallery;
(back) *Andrew Young as a young man*
© Ruth Lowbury

All rights reserved. No part of this edition may be reproduced,
stored electronically or in any retrieval system, or transmitted
in any form or by any means, electronic, mechanical,
photocopying, recording, or otherwise, without
prior written permission from the Publisher
(permissions@lutterworth.com).

Dedicated
to the memory of Alison Young,
who wanted me to write this book;
and
as ever, to my wife, Shirley,
for her love, support and patience!

There is always a living face behind the mask.
W.B. Yeats

Man is explicable by nothing else than all his history.
Ralph Waldo Emerson

If we owe regard to the memory of the dead, there is
yet more respect to be laid . . . to truth.
Dr Samuel Johnson

Contents

Part 1
The Early Poet and the Priest

Part 2
The Later Poet and Priest

PART 3

THE NATURALIST AND TOPOGRAPHER (1945-1967)

PART 4

REASSESSMENT

LIST OF ILLUSTRATIONS

Aknowledgements

I am indebted to the following for their help and assistance:

The British Library
Jeremy Dore Book Search
Lambeth Palace Library
The National Library of Scotland, Edinburgh
The National Portrait Gallery
The Wealden Group, Hawkhurst, Kent.

And to the following people:

Basil Dowling (deceased)
Leslie Norris (deceased)
Rosemary Sutcliff (deceased)
Alison Young (deceased)
Ruth Lowbury, Andrew Young's Literary Executor

INTRODUCTION

The title of this book, *Andrew Young: Priest, Poet and Naturalist,* is taken from the memorial tablet erected by his parishioners in St Peter's Church, Stonegate, East Sussex. To them, naturally enough, he had been primarily a priest; but the second person of this trinity, the poet, was not only first chronologically but was more basically the linchpin of his personality. He was a priest by choice and a naturalist by habit, but he was, from the beginning, an *inevitable* poet.

When he went up to Edinburgh University in 1903, he read for a general arts degree which included Fine Art, Latin and Greek, Natural Science, Logic and Metaphysics, Archaeology, and Moral Philosophy: an incredibly (and nowadays untenably) wide spectrum of knowledge. 'Edinburgh University was to me a true Alma Mater, Kind Mother,' he said many years later, and when he finally left, having extended his three-year course to four, it was for the equally safe, 'motherly' confines of New College, Edinburgh, for four years' theological training. Few poets in the English language, with the obvious exceptions of Milton and T.S. Eliot, have had as much formal academic education as Andrew Young. Understandably, he was later described as being formidably well read.

'A faded photograph shows me as a child with curls riding a hobby horse,' he recalled at the age of 82, and added: 'I have been riding hobby horses all my life and, while I have kept on changing horses, a favourite hobby has been with words.'[1] To relegate words to the status of 'a favourite hobby' is to totally underestimate their real importance in his life, yet such a throwaway phrase is typical of the man whom his daughter Alison remembered wearing, 'the amused, half-mocking smile of one who reveals little of his inner thoughts,'[2] and whom Richard Church called, 'wry, witty, epigrammatic, shrewd, and finally, *elusive.*'[3]

1. Andrew Young, 'Early Days' from *New Poly-Olbion*, 1967.
2. Said to the present author in 1983-84.
3. Richard Church's essay in *Andrew Young: Prospect of a Poet*, ed. by Leonard

Yet if Andrew Young is to be found anywhere, it is in his words. As F.R. Leavis said of the archetypal poet: 'He is a poet because his interest in his experience is not separable from his interest in words; because, that is, of his habit of seeking by the evocative use of words, to sharpen his awareness of his ways of feeling,' and, in Young's case, ways of thinking, 'so making these communicable.'[4]

'Evocative' and 'communicable' are perhaps key words here: though not principally an innovator, like Hopkins or Eliot, he strives to be 'evocative', precise and original in his imagery (who could forget 'those hidden *ventriloquists* . . . singing in the wood / Flinging their *cheating* voices here and there' [my italics]) and to make his viewpoint 'communicable' to others, as he rarely did directly. This 'displacement' activity may have been a psychological prop to a man intrinsically introverted and often socially inept (e.g. he had no small talk) but it also helps to push him into Ruskin's, 'first order of poets, who feel strongly, think clearly and see truly.'[5]

It is the central contention of this book that Andrew John Young (1885-1971) is still seriously undervalued amongst twentieth-century poets, principally because he has been over-anthologised – and by implication, dismissed – as yet another 'nature' poet of the Georgian ilk, and because he was outside the mainstream 'movements' and innovations of his own time. Indeed, he actively disliked innovators such as Yeats, Auden and Eliot, preferring Spenser, Hardy and Edward Thomas. Yet in the seven volumes of poetry published between 1920 and 1931, there are clear signs of change and development towards a more individual, spare, less ornate 'period' style. Paradox and a deceptive simplicity were becoming his hallmarks. By 1933 he had taken the advice he later gave when adjudicating a poetry competition: 'When writing poetry, try not to be too poetical.' By 1939 he was writing his best collection of short poems, *Speak to the Earth*, in which his originality is not in his verse forms but in his conceits, imagery, paradoxes and verbal tropes. Ironically, by 1952, *Into Hades* opens with an almost Eliotian line: 'One midnight in the Paris Underground'.

A reassessment is long overdue: Roger Sell's 1978 *Trespassing Ghost: A Critical Study of Andrew Young* (Åbo Akademi, Finland) began the process by labelling him 'a major poet', but he is arguably a *great* poet, a modern metaphysical, a poet's poet, whose idiolect is distinctive and whose 'individual talent' both links to yet subtly changes literary 'tradition'.

Clark, 1957.
4. F.R. Leavis, *New Bearings in* English *Poetry*, 1932.
5. John Ruskin, *Modern Painters*, vol.3, 1843-1860.

If, as Pope observed, 'the proper study of mankind is man', then it is also of 'man in his circumambient universe'; interlinked, one with the other, where the physical and moral universes meet. Young sees and shows the relationship between external nature and human nature, often through the prism of pathetic fallacy, symbolism, paradox or metaphor, as when he asks, rhetorically, in *Dead Crab*:

Or does it make for death to be
Oneself a living armoury?

Young had no illusions about nature, human or animal, and no sentimentality about either: he was a meditative observer; something of a moral philosopher; a theist and a pantheist; an ironist and wordsmith. Many of his poems may be seen as meditations on mortality and immortality, themes which come together in his final, major poems, *Out of the World and Back*. These themes are present from his earliest poems (perhaps they were an occupational hazard) but reach their full fruition in the Stonegate years, from 1941 to 1959, along with his tendency to juxtaposition, irony and wit:

I had seen Death at last:
He had ridden past me, not on his pale horse,
But on a cycle with the *Sunday Times*.

It is clearly not always true that Young's is essentially a landscape without people, but it often is. Like Hardy, a poet he both admired and learned from, 'he was a man who noticed such things' as birds, beasts and flowers, on his long walks in the Sussex countryside, when he visited outlying parishioners, then sat silent when he arrived. On one such occasion he was offered a book, which he duly sat and read, then went home!

Andrew Young was, by any standards, an eccentric; a loner, introvert, perhaps misfit; a distant, detached family man who insisted on eating alone; a moody, chauvinistic patriarch who expected to be respected and obeyed. Perhaps he was more himself on the page than ever he was in person; yet he inspired great devotion in those who loved him, such as his long-suffering wife, Janet. The widow of writer Leslie Norris admitted after Andrew Young's death that although 'he was a terrible man', she had 'wept buckets when he died' in 1971.

He was himself as much of a paradox as any creature he ever wrote about. His daughter Alison and her husband Edward Lowbury, in their biography of the poet (*To Shirk No Idleness*, University of Salzburg, 1997) comment on 'his lack of interest in or understanding of other people', which probably places him somewhere at what we would now call the Asperger's end of the autistic spectrum. It must also have been a professional handicap in a priest.

Writing was a lifelong habit with Young from about the age of eight onwards, and allowed for the expression of a range of thought and feeling not expressed anywhere else in his life, except perhaps occasionally in sermons.

In some ways, Young played truant 'on principle' *all* his life, not just as an errant schoolboy at Dalmeny. Like Blake, Young spent much of his life not quite in this world, and he takes this to its logical conclusion in the two long, whimsical, Dantesque spiritual autobiographies on which his reputation ultimately rests. They link him in a line of descent from the medieval dream vision poets, Langland and the unknown 'Gawain poet' through Bunyan, Blake and Wordsworth. They are both Christian and classical pagan; using the 'conversational' blank verse of Shakespeare, yet unmistakably modern. Like Young himself, they are complex, paradoxical and multi-layered.

A wry, whimsical, observant, engaging persona is also clearly evident in Young's prose works, particularly in the two flower books, *A Prospect of Flowers* (1945) and its companion volume, *A Retrospect of Flowers* (1950). Both books are rich potpourris of anecdote, information, history and reminiscence, written in the tradition of the great English prose stylists such as Sir Thomas Browne and W.H. Hudson, whom he often reread. Yet they are not imitative but uniquely his own; the irony is, perhaps, that the genial, amusing and companionable persona evident in these volumes bore so little relationship to the man, as usually perceived.

In *New Poly-Olbion* (1967), a gentle take on Michael Drayton's 1613 poetic original, Young's prose is once again sparkling, amusing and full of literary references and conceits: 'Crocuses in gardens were awake, stretching themselves and yawning; if daffodils are the spring's trumpets . . . every garden had its brass band . . . even violets shivered in their purple hoods.' (*Cold Cotswolds*)

As well as combining poetic and natural observation, there is also a certain amount of carefully selected and controlled autobiographical reference, especially in the chapter 'Early Days'. Along with the unpublished and unfinished autobiography *My Life*, we have Young's reconstructed version of events to compare with the primary testimony of others and the 'internal' testimony of the poems themselves.

To write so well in poetry and prose is itself quite remarkable. Young had been elected a Fellow of the Royal Society of Literature in 1944, and after *A Prospect of Flowers*, honours came thick and fast: he was made a canon of Chichester Cathedral in 1947; in 1951 he was given an Honorary LLD from Edinburgh University; in 1952, after the publication of *Into Hades*, he was awarded the Queen's Gold Medal for Poetry; and in 1961 he won the Duff Cooper Memorial Prize for *Collected Poems*.

In his later years, he enjoyed the friendship of other writers such as Christopher Fry, Leslie Norris, Richard Church, Basil Dowling and Rosemary Sutcliff, and befriended younger poets such as Norman Nicholson and James Kirkup. Even Philip Larkin, a modernist if ever there was one, remarked of Young that 'his works are in no danger of being forgotten'. May these words prove not just prophetic but an underestimate of a truly remarkable voice in English poetry.

Part 1
The Early Poet and the Priest

Chapter 1
The Boy and his Background
(1885-1902)

This is not that impossibility, a *definitive* biography; nor is it an academic thesis on Young's writing. But it *is* an attempt to re-examine the inter-relationship between the man and the works and the apparent discrepancies between the two; and it *is* a critical reassessment of his place in the 'canon' of English literature. Neither of these tasks is easy!

Biography at its most basic level, like the novel, has plot, characters, themes and style, and is a form of fiction based on facts – an attempt to reconstruct imaginatively from a basis of evidence. But as Virginia Woolf observed, 'The novelist is free; the biographer is tied.'[1] He is: firstly to externally verifiable fact and secondly to interpretative truth. There is no primary creation; he does not have to invent plot or character. Because of this, Virginia Woolf and others have maintained that biography 'is lived at a lower degree of tension' than poetry or fiction. I suspect that few working biographers would agree.

The unwritten brief of the biographer is to present, with authenticity and accuracy, a sympathetic and fully rounded portrait of his subject's life and personality. His art is akin to that of the portrait painter rather than the photographer, and its primary requisite is respect for 'warts-and-all' truth. Biography emphasises, indeed actively celebrates, *individuality* – those very aspects of a person which make them unique. Something of that uniqueness always defies complete definition and eludes the most earnest endeavours to pin it down. One can never capture the *real person* between the covers of a book: only, at best, an approximation. That is the fascination, and the frustration, of biography: perhaps one has to be something of a masochist to enjoy it.

It may be argued that 'contemporaneous' biographers, who knew their subjects during life, such as Boswell with Johnson, or Forster with Dickens, have distinct advantages and insights over 'later

---

1. Virginia Woolf, 'The Art of Biography' essay in *The Death of the Moth and Other Essays,* 1942.

onset' biographers, to whom their subjects are, at least initially, dead 'strangers'. It is, of course, something of a double-edged sword: a balance between subjectivity and objectivity. As Leon Edel remarked in *Literary Biography*,[2] the biographer 'must be warm, yet aloof, involved yet uninvolved'. I am glad, therefore, never to have known Andrew Young personally. He was, in any case, difficult to know: reserved, moody, often uncommunicative. I must rely then on the primary testimony of those who *did* know him, as family, friends, parishioners or fellow writers; and on the published – and unpublished – work, letters, accounts, reviews, and so on.

Although a very private man, Andrew Young did leave two accounts of parts of his life, or rather aspects of it: 'Early Days', published in *New Poly-Olbion* (1967), and the unpublished and unfinished *My Life,* begun two years before his death. However, by far the most dangerous and potentially misleading material for the biographer is that written by the subject himself, especially memoirs and autobiographies. Comparing Richard Church's autobiography[3] with his diaries (all unpublished) covering the same period of his life, I was amazed by the distortions, omissions and misrepresentations in the former. Mary Lou Kohfeldt made a similar point about Lady Gregory's autobiography, which, as well as muddling chronology, was 'a ragbag of . . . anecdotes, unconnected snippets from letters and diaries, brief insights and trivia.' In addition, 'The parts she did not put in her final version are usually more interesting than those she did'. She eliminated all trace of her adulterous affair with Wilfrid Blunt because 'her deepest instinct was to hide'.[4] Autobiographies simply cannot be taken at face value and the biographer does well to regard them with a healthy scepticism. Like confessions to psychiatrists or priests, they tend to be highly selective, partial accounts in which memory and fantasy intermingle. The autobiographer is inevitably an image-builder who wishes not to accuse but to justify himself; to create sympathy rather than antipathy. We all have 'selective' memories and much of what we write, or even recall, about ourselves is partial, subjective and impressionistic in a way biography can never be. The apparent frankness is itself a mask behind which much is hidden; even 'admissions' tend to be self-aggrandising, whereas the biographer deflects attention away from himself on to his subject and, generally speaking, has no personal *angst* to grind comparable to the autobiographer, who is, at best, an unreliable narrator.

2. Rupert Hart-Davis, 1957, p.7.
3. *Over the Bridge*, Heinemann, 1955.
4. Andre Deutsch, *Lady Gregory: The Woman Behind the Irish Renaissance.*

Andrew Young was fond of saying, for instance, that he was descended from a long line of illiterate shepherds, but this was not the case: his ancestors had been farmers, maltsters, papermakers and grocers; in other words, mainly literate producers of goods and services. He also embroidered his truanting, omitted almost everything about his family relationships and later repeated much of what was already in print elsewhere. Often, of course, what is *not* said is more telling than what is said.

In the eighteenth century, novels were often written like biographies (such as *Joseph Andrews*), whereas now biographies are often written as straight narratives like novels (such as Matthew Hollis' *Now All Roads Lead to France: The Last Years of Edward Thomas*),[5] with little direct quotation. I have tried to steer a middle way between the more traditional and modern methods.

Edward Thomas was one of the poets admired by Andrew Young and could be said to be a literary 'forerunner' of his, being long dead by the time Young's mature work began to appear between 1933 and 1958. It raises a question: Why is it that so much has been written about Edward Thomas and so little about Andrew Young? Part of the answer is that Thomas is easier to warm to, identify with; he also died in a war with so many other fine poets, so there is a sense of tragically unfinished business. Yet both wrote feelingly and originally about animals, birds and landscapes; both treated their devoted wives selfishly and were often indifferent to their children. Both show more engaging personas in their writings than in their lives. Hollis' book is in keeping with the changed ethics of biography (beginning perhaps with Froude's *Carlyle* and Holroyd's *Lytton Strachey*): a 'warts-and-all' approach which suits contemporary sensibility, which demands 'the whole truth and nothing but the truth', whatever it is. I have taken an essentially *holistic* view of Andrew Young, the man and the writer, looking at the related aspects of his intellectual, social, emotional, religious and literary lives. After all, biography at best is a species of revealed truth and, as Pope observed, 'The proper study of mankind is Man.'

* * *

According to child psychology, the dynamics of personality are set early on, so it is pertinent to ask what forces and factors in Young's childhood went towards producing the man, with his particular, often paradoxical nature.

---

5. Matthew Hollis, *Now All Roads Lead to France: The Last Years of Edward Thomas*, Faber, 2011.

He was a man with a 'lack of interest in or understanding of other people', he was 'intensely self-centred', and had an 'enjoyment of mockery which verged on the sadistic', according to his daughter Alison: all serious indictments. On the more positive side, he was a keen sportsman, a voracious reader and a man of deep religious conviction. He was also, from a very early age, fascinated by words, their meanings and derivations, and used them to express his thoughts, observations and feelings. Writing was both a creative and a therapeutic outlet in which he was able to reinvent himself through a number of personae. If, as the comic poet Stevie Smith suggested in one of her many serious moments, 'Nobody writes or wishes to / Who is one with their desires', it is worth asking what the 'irritant' factors were which produced the 'pearls' in this particular 'oyster'?

One of the most formative influences on Young's life was his father, another Andrew John Young, born in 1845 at Almondbank in Perthshire, to a grocer, David, and his wife Jane Small. They had nine children, of whom Young's father was the second, but eldest son. He was himself a very devout product of 'an ultra-conservative branch of the Presbyterian Church' known as the Original Seceders (Old Lights). They had been governed by articles in the 'Westminster Confession of Faith' from the seventeenth century, which emphasised the fellowship of believers, direct access to grace without need of priests or bishops. Their ministers and elders were democratically elected, as set down in the first and second 'Book of Discipline'. But in 1732 an 'Act of Assembly' was passed which limited the rights to elect ministers to the Assembly itself if a vacancy was longer than six months. Several members, including one Ebenezer Erskine, protested, were censured by the Synod, and then suspended from all ministerial functions. In response, they constituted themselves as a Presbytery with Erskine as Moderator. After this, there was a rapid growth in the Secession Church, who were finally 'excommunicated' by the Synod. By 1820 the breach had ended, with the United Church taking the title The United Associate Synod of the Secession Church. Later, in the 1840s, The Free Church of Scotland came into being, and after failing to unite with the United Presbyterian Church in the 1860s, there was a Declaratory Act in 1892 which softened the 'asperities of Calvinism' and led to the formation of the United Free Church of Scotland in 1900, into which Andrew Young was later ordained.

Scottish Presbyterianism is linked to the Calvinist theological tradition through John Knox, with a strong emphasis on scriptural authority, strict observance of the Sabbath and the reception of grace through practising of the faith and, of course, through good, moral behaviour. The Seceders believed firmly in the doctrines of the elect (i.e. that there were a fixed number of people pre-chosen for salvation) and predestination.

Presbyterian organisation was through councils of elected elders, with regional and national assemblies. There were no priests or bishops but the office of elder was supplemented by the offices of pastor and deacon. There were only two sacraments: baptism and the Lord's Supper. Doctrine was learned through catechisms and enforced by habit and preaching. Services usually consisted of Bible readings, prayers and hymns, with a (longish) sermon as the main event. The meeting houses (they were rarely called 'churches') were plain and sparsely furnished, the focal point being the pulpit. There was no stained glass, nor icons, statues or crucifixes, as these were seen as unnecessary distractions from the main business of worship, without which hellfire and damnation loomed. Andrew was 53 before he felt able to break out of these strictures and embrace the more ritualistic and liberal Anglicanism to which he had long been attracted. By then, he had been a Presbyterian minister for twenty-six years, both in Scotland and England.

In this atmosphere, where grace was said before meals and there was family worship on each night except Sundays, Andrew and his three elder siblings were raised: David, who was five when Andrew was born; Margaret, who was three; and William, who had died within a year of birth three years earlier. Their mother Maria, nee Adams, daughter of a clerk in Glasgow, had been an orphan when, living in Elgin with two aunts, she married Andrew senior in 1875. Despite an education which included a knowledge of Latin, Andrew senior, like Maria's father, had been a clerk for some years. By the time their fourth child, Andrew, was born in 1885, he had been stationmaster at Elgin for eleven years. When Andrew was two, the family moved to Edinburgh where his father worked at the head office of an insurance company. Within two years, he had been promoted to secretary (equivalent to deputy manager) with a fairly affluent £250 a year salary. A pair of good leather shoes cost about 4/6d; and it was said that on £400 a year, a London man could keep a wife, children, three to four servants and a carriage, so the Youngs in Edinburgh were far from poor. They were, however, 'careful' with money; for example, Andrew never remembered having 'bought' toys, although there is a photograph of him, aged two to three, astride a rocking horse.

Within the family at this time, the father was often a stern, patriarchal figure whose word was law. Andrew himself became such a figure in his turn; and his ambivalent relationship with his own father, in turn, translated into an ambivalent relationship with his own son, Anthony.

Andrew was in awe of his father into his maturity; for example, delaying becoming an Anglican for some years in fear of his father's reaction, and not leaving Scotland until six years after his father's retirement. It is not sufficient simply to say that Victorian family life *was* authoritarian and austere, incorporating, as it did, family prayers, corporal punishment, emotional distance and rigid standards of behaviour. It is hardly surprising, however, that, as his daughter Alison observed, 'he had a greater affection for his mother than for his father'.[6] She was more tolerant and gentle towards him, such as in allowing him to 'play' (forbidden on the Sabbath) when his father was out at evening prayers, which Andrew was then too young to attend. She took the children for seaside holidays in August, and Janet, Andrew's wife, always maintained that she was in the habit of 'spoiling' Andrew, as is often the way with the youngest child.

The family went to morning service on Sundays where they occupied a pew in the front row. Andrew liked the sermon best, because as it began, his father handed a bag of sweets down the pew, presumably to keep the children quiet! Andrew's first reading, apart from the Bible, was in his father's small library, which contained Bunyan, Scott, an expurgated Shakespeare, as well as volumes about the saints. Andrew stated, late in life, that he was 'naturally religious', quite apart from being 'religiously brought up'.[7] Be this as it may, there is no doubt that Andrew was profoundly influenced, both obviously and more subtly, by this upbringing and more especially by his father's insistence on self-discipline, routine, temperance and respectability. The father figure, like God himself, inspires awe, fear, devotion, and must be placated at all times to ensure approval.

One of his earliest memories was saying his prayers at his father's knee, over which he was also sometimes chastised.

* * *

Family myths and skeletons live in the same cupboard marked 'Private: Keep Out'. But the biographer must disregard this imperative and unlock it with his truth-seeking key. There are several of each in the Young family. To begin with the myths: the first was Andrew's sister Margaret's contention that the family were related to Carolina Oliphant, Lady Nairne, a Scottish lyricist well known in her day (1766-1845) for 87 mainly Jacobite songs. She had lived in Gask, Perthshire, a few miles from Almondbank, before marrying and moving to Edinburgh. The second

6.   Edward Lowbury and Alison Young, *To Shirk No Idleness* (Salzburg: University of Salzburg Press, 1997).
7.   Essay 'Early Days' from *New Poly-Olbion*, 1967.

family myth was that the family were either related to, or descended from, Robert the Bruce, through the marriage of Gabriel Small, Andrew's great-grandfather, to a Mary Bruce. Neither connection could be proven. The family skeletons are more serious: one concerning Andrew himself, the other his elder brother David (See Chapters 2 and 5).

* * *

Presbyterians generally, and Andrew's father particularly, placed great importance on education, including what we now call 'lifelong learning': principally, of course, the study of religious doctrine, scriptural and theological writing, in order to understand the faith and to put it into practice. There was no question of critical free-thought or making up one's own mind in such matters. Andrew declared that his father began to teach him Latin when he was four years old, that is, before he went to boarding school aged five, so presumably he had already learned to read and write in English. The pupils wrote on slates with slate pencils, and when neither reading nor writing, sat bolt upright with their arms folded. At eight, he was sent to James Gillespie's fee-paying school, where he continued with his Latin. It was at this time that Scottish history and poetry came together for Andrew, in the form of one of his first poems, *The Battle of Bannockburn*, most of which is now lost, apart from a fragment he remembered much later:

> They fell, they fell,
> Till there were few to tell
> How the great battle ended.

It was also about this time that he began his lifelong study of dictionaries, which he continued into his eighties; so already it was clear that he had both a sense of cadence and a great interest in the effects words could achieve.

From James Gillespie's, where he spent four years, Andrew won a scholarship to The Royal High School in Edinburgh, which he later referred to as 'my kind stepmother', stressing its nurturative aspects. This was, after his *formative* influences, the first *transformative* influence on his life: it was here that he became a good athlete, a sportsman and a keen naturalist. He must also have been a good scholar, although he downplayed this later, saying that he was 'not . . . clever', and that he 'did not enjoy' his schooldays. However, he did enjoy the lessons of his English teacher, Mr White, who used rote learning of poetry and mnemonic devices, although Andrew later claimed that he lost interest in poetry when he discovered novels.

He records losing his scholarship several times for playing truant 'on principle', without ever saying what the principle was; neither does he record his father's reaction to these misdemeanours. Given that his father was cautious with money and would have had to pay the school fees until, through hard work, Andrew had regained the scholarship, it is curious that he does not mention it, to say nothing of his father's disapproval! Obviously truancy was a form of self-assertion.

Andrew may have been influenced by the fact that a previous famous pupil, Sir Walter Scott, also played truant from the school; or it may have been some innate perversity, or desire for risk-taking. He took more than one risk too, recording that he often took the train from Edinburgh to Cramond, to trespass into Dalmeny, the estate of the Earl of Rosebery. These adventures were reconstructed later in *A Prospect of Flowers*, and probably embroidered for effect; yet there seems little doubt that his almost obsessive interest in wild flowers began here and led indirectly to two classics of English prose in the wake of Drayton, Walton and White. His love of walking also began at this time: three miles each way to school and back daily, in addition to other sports and excursions, including climbing the Lion's Head mountain overlooking Edinburgh. For three years running, he won the 100 yards in the school sports day.

'One of my troubles at school,' he recalled later, 'was due to my habit of arriving late'. He could have taken a tram but preferred to walk, by devious routes, and to linger in Princes Street. Many years later, after his *Collected Poems* (1950) and his honorary Doctor of Laws degree from Edinburgh University (1951), his life and works were reviewed in his old school magazine, *Schola Regia*, which declared that his achievements were 'ample justification for pride in a school that shared . . . the privilege of educating him'. No mean accolade.

Andrew was well grounded in the Classics and English and Scottish literature, philosophy and history, and became 'addicted to novels', including detective fiction. He was described later as prodigiously well read. He seems to have been a good all-rounder at school, so it is not perhaps surprising that when it came to university at eighteen that he opted for the multi-disciplinary general arts degree. At this time, when he walked past the Law Courts, he had 'an idea that one day I might wear a wig'.[8]

His elder brother David graduated with an MB from Edinburgh in 1901, when Andrew was sixteen, then had to submit a thesis for his MD in 1902. Although this was successful, David was not allowed to receive the MD for another two years, until he was twenty-four, after

8.   Chapter 1 of his unpublished and unfinished autobiography, *My Life*.

which he became a house physician at Edinburgh Royal Infirmary. Their sister Margaret had become an art student and, like Andrew, would later continue her studies in Paris. It is clear that Andrew senior took pride in sending his two surviving sons to university, an opportunity he had never had himself; and he seems ahead of his time in recognising that education was good for his daughter too.

Andrew's 'kind stepmother' was about to be superseded by his next transformative experience, at his 'Alma Mater, Kind Mother', Edinburgh University, which he entered in 1903, aged eighteen.

CHAPTER 2
STUDENT DAYS
(1903-1911)

Andrew was, as a student, in the shadow of a brilliant elder brother, not always a comfortable place to be; and on his own admission, he did not stand out as in any way exceptional in his own right. He still lived at home at 2 Morningside Park, and was therefore still both financially dependent on, and subject to, his father's authority.

The range of his studies was a wide and inclusive arts degree, incorporating: Latin, Greek, English literature (with the famous Professor George Saintsbury, whom he admired), logic and metaphysics (with Professor Pringle-Pattison, whom he liked), and fine art. The course was normally a three-year one, but Andrew managed to extend it to four (he erroneously said later, five)[1] by winning a fine art prize of £15 ('a substantial sum in those days', he remarked later), which, supplemented by an allowance from his father, enabled him to spend several summers in Paris, 'lodging in the Latin quarter' and continuing his fine art studies at the Louvre and elsewhere, in the company of a male French art student, to whom he had been introduced. Andrew's father seems to have been fairly indulgent when it came to educational expenses.

Andrew was keen, as Milton had been, to organise his own extracurricular studies (or what he called 'my own education'), which included wide reading (from Lao Tze to Baudelaire to Scottish ballads), writing poetry, studying Christian mysticism (particularly John of the Cross and St Teresa of Avila), and sorting out his allegiance, or otherwise, to various philosophers. He declared himself 'a Berkeleian', adhering to Berkeley's form of *idealism* which maintains the essential individuality of entities created by the infinite mind, not the absolute idealism of Hegel, in which all finite persons are absorbed into an *Absolute*, which transcends personality. (This clearly links to aspects of Buddhism.) This was Andrew's first real freedom of mind and action; along with his studies, he made time for many excursions into the Border Country, which he grew to love.

1. *My Life,* unpublished.

His studies were divided into upper and lower divisions, with some lectures common to both, such as those on constitutional history, antiquities or literary history. In his first year, he studied Virgil, Martial, the *Ars Poetica* and undertook Latin prose composition. There was a fortnightly verse composition, metre, 'or some other special subject', and, twice yearly, in December and March, 'written examinations on the work done in the class'. In the summer, he began readings in the Greek authors: Homer, Aeschylus, Sophocles, Euripides, Plato and so on. 'Greek Verse Composition' was voluntary, unlike translation of 'unseen passages'. During the winter of 1904, he studied Aristotle's *Poetics* and Aeschylus' *Agamemnon*, passing his Latin and Greek exams that year. He passed logic and natural philosophy in 1905; English and fine art in 1906, and moral philosophy in 1907.

Recalling this time 60 years later, Andrew observed wryly: 'I look back on examinations as I look back on mountain mists, wondering how I came through them all'.[2] but in April 1907 he finally graduated with an 'Ordinary Degree of MA' in arts.

Little detail is known of his two summers in Paris, presumably in 1906 and 1907 (although his daughter Alison thought it was 1907 and 1908), as he had won the prize money which helped to finance it, in 1905. Internal evidence, however, suggests that as well as soaking up painting, sculpture and architecture, he also visited theatres and other places of amusement but strove to maintain his moral purity and chastity ('starved myself'), living as 'a St John the Baptist in the Latin Quarter'.

That the art, beauty and freedom of Paris impacted positively on Andrew is clear: it was a formative, perhaps transformative, period in his life. He wrote; he thought; he walked and explored; he became almost obsessed with Strauss' *Salome* (based on Oscar Wilde's play), in which sadomasochism raises its head, linking desire with death. In the summer of 1907, when it was performed in Paris, he saw five of its six performances.

His future was still undecided during this 'timeout' period between graduation and taking up a place at New College in 1908. Poetry was an ambition but not a means of livelihood. *City of Night* was probably written at this time:

Each light is like a flashing gem
Within her guilty diadem;
The night is shed on her like hair
That hides a face's dark despair.

---

2. *My Life,* unpublished.

The deadly river, too, glides by
Like some swift tiger, stealthily,
Its sinuous back all painted bright
With quivering bars of golden light.

And far above the city's jars
The ancient army of the stars,
That in a quiet, reproachful mood
Keep watch from God's own solitude.

Strongly visual, it personifies Paris as a woman wearing a 'guilty diadem' of lights, hiding her 'face's dark despair' behind her hair. Even the river Seine is 'deadly', its reflected lights likened to a tiger's bright yellow stripes. The stars are keeping a 'reproachful' watch over the city's activities, on God's behalf. Despite its conventional AABB verse structure, the poem's imagery is a graphic promise of things to come, as is the solemn mood. Here we see a young poet experimenting with imagery and tone, but also detect the moral distance he wishes to keep between himself and the city's vices.

Although he appears to have wanted to enjoy the moment and delay any decisions about his future as long as possible, circumstances were to force his hand: 'I hesitated a long time before deciding to enter the Church; the idea of the law was still in my mind; it was this hesitation that kept me five [*sic*, four] years at the university. What helped me to decide in the end was the case of my father. He had *somehow assumed* I would become a minister' (my italics).[3]

There was more to it than that, which Andrew omitted in his autobiographical writings, merely mentioning that: 'my brother had gone as a doctor to Singapore; he wrote home each week, till suddenly the letters ceased'.[4]

It was one of the skeletons in the family cupboard which remained there until his daughter Alison revealed it in 1997. It seems that David had left Scotland in 1905 to become a medical partner to a Dr T. Murray Robertson, in Singapore. All went well until 1907, after Andrew's graduation and second trip to Paris. When David's letters home stopped so abruptly, he was reported 'missing', but there was more to the story: in December 1907 he was mentioned in a court case involving the illegal dispensing of large amounts of morphine and forged prescriptions; then he was sacked by his employer, Dr Robertson, who put a dissociation notice to that effect in *The Singapore Free Press* in January 1908, five days

3. *My Life,* unpublished.
4. Ibid.

running. He obviously wished to publicly cut all connections with Dr David Young. In addition, it transpired that he was also wanted by the police about share transactions and 'other serious matters', according to the *Penang Gazette* of 8 January 1907.

Whatever the truth was, no one ever heard of or from David again. It seems unlikely that he committed suicide, since no body was ever found; but more likely that he escaped from Singapore, adopted a new identity and lived a new life somewhere else.

The effect of his disappearance on his mother was profound, and it was said that she never fully recovered from it; but his father apparently hoped that he might turn up in Paris, a city he loved. The Youngs had now effectively 'lost' two of their three sons, which put subtle pressure on Andrew to fulfil his father's wish for him to enter the Presbyterian ministry. It would also extend his student years by another four, giving him some extended freedom. In addition, he had been previously influenced by the preaching of Dr Alexander Whyte, of Free St George's, on Sunday evenings, and Whyte had a close association with New College, Edinburgh, which had been founded in 1850 as 'the Free Church's theological showpiece'.[5] Dr Whyte became its principal from 1909 to 1916, during three of Andrew's four years there.

Whyte was a remarkable man: very widely read amongst theologians of all persuasions, the poets and philosophers, and with an exceptionally ecumenical mind. His correspondents included Cardinal Newman and General Booth. He enjoyed close relations with his students, which included retreats, evenings in his study, and the foundation of the 'Alexander Whyte Theological Literature Prize' in 1897, to encourage the reading of theological literature by students, and essay writing. In his inaugural address as principal of New College, on 13 October 1909, which it is likely that Andrew attended, he chose to speak about his five predecessors as principal: Messrs. Chalmers, Cunningham, Candlish, Rainy and Dods.

Marcus Dods had been appointed Professor of the New Testament in 1889, and Whyte had been involved in the resulting controversy about the divine inspiration of scriptures and their 'sacred' nature. A generation earlier, Dods, a Professor Bruce of Glasgow, and Robertson Smith had been tried for 'heresy' in the General Assembly. Whyte had put up a spirited defence: 'Speaking broadly, we have on the one side . . . the conservative caution and sensitive reverence of the Church, and on the other, the keen, restless, insatiable spirit of modern critical

5. A.C. Cheyne, *The Transforming of the Kirk: Victorian Scotland's Religious Revolution*, St Andrew's Press, Edinburgh, 1982.

inquiry . . . the world of mind does not stand still. And *the theological mind will stand still at its peril*' (my italics).[6] Whyte was deeply concerned with the principle that inquiry should be free, and that 'the authority of scripture should find a more secure basis than the old, rigid theory of literal inspiration'.[7]

This had led, by the time that Andrew entered New College, to a more liberal theology, concentrating on the 'historical Jesus' and His teaching about the Kingdom of God. The arguments had hung on whether the first five books of the Old Testament (the Pentateuch), traditionally ascribed to Moses, were historical, supernatural or poetic. By 1908-09, it was widely accepted that Moses had *not* written the Pentateuch, nor David most of the Psalms, nor the Apostles most of the Gospels. Much of this new thinking and 'de-Puritanisation' of Presbyterianism had led to a revival of Christian philanthropy as well: between 1901 and 1914, the Scottish Christian Social Union was formed, partly as a result of crofters' grievances, unrest and agitation, and partly out of social conscience about slum housing, child welfare and unemployment. These concerns were indirectly political: a statement on 'The Social Teaching of Our Lord', put out by the Church Life and Work Committee in 1908-09, concluded: 'the mind of Jesus condemns all oppressive, unjust and alienating conditions of life and labour, and favours the more equal distribution of happiness and opportunity'.[8] This was quite radical thinking for the time.

Other movements were also afoot as Andrew entered New College: liturgical reform, an emphasis on sacraments and ministry, a new breed of Scottish biblical theologians, such as A.B. Bruce and James Denney. It is not stated what Andrew thought of any of this, but he must have discussed it with some of the lifelong friends he first met at New College, principally John and Donald Baillie, who both became professors of theology later; John Laird, who became a professor of philosophy; and Cecil Simpson, with whom Andrew spent a holiday in Germany. They were all keen talkers and walkers, who discussed theological issues, mysticism, poetry, and presumably much else besides.

Andrew perhaps learned his love of Dante, Thomas Browne and St Teresa from Dr Whyte, who lectured them and of whom Andrew remarked later: 'His sermons were powerful, but he was the best sermon himself.'[9] His wife, Jane Whyte, was an educated woman with an interest

6. Ibid.
7. Ibid.
8. A.C. Cheyne (as previously).
9. *My Life*, unpublished.

in literature, including poetry, and met Andrew at New College, inviting him several times to 'the Sabbath Supper'. On one of these occasions, Andrew remembered meeting the sister of W.B. Yeats (spelt 'Yates' in his manuscript), a poet he never liked.

More importantly, on another of these Sundays, he was invited at the same time as Miss Janet Green from Glasgow, who was staying with the Whytes for the weekend, and to whom Andrew was, by this time, engaged. Andrew had first met her through her brother, Harry Green, a friend of a friend, to whom he was introduced some time in 1909, in his first year at New College.

Andrew's pursuit and courtship of Janet seems to have been both rapid and unconventional. She was in her middle twenties, described as being tall, with a graceful figure, brown eyes, who wore her hair in a bun. She still lived at home, at 36 Princes Street, Regent Park, Glasgow, with her widowed mother, four sisters (Elizabeth, Alice, May and Margaret) and two brothers (Harry and Gresley). She occupied a semi-basement room in which she studied and slept. Andrew, being less than sociable, soon discarded the niceties of ringing the front doorbell and being shown down, for simply tapping her window and being let in that way! She had been courting a John Scott until Andrew's appearance. Scott eventually married Janet's sister Margaret, so the former rivals became brothers-in-law.

Janet's background was far more cosmopolitan than Andrew's: she had been born near Cape Town in 1883, the daughter of an architect and builder, Robert Green, originally from Belfast. Before moving to Glasgow in 1889, the family had also lived for a time in Cheltenham. According to her daughter Alison, Janet's had been 'an exceptionally lively and intellectually stimulating household',[10] so it is perhaps strange that Andrew took steps *not* to be part of it! Unusually for the time, Janet had entered Glasgow University in 1900, taking an honours degree in French and German language and literature in 1903. She then took an MA in Literature, Moral Philosophy and History in 1906, so she was better qualified than Andrew. The university calendar for 1903-04 shows her listed twice as a prize winner: in French Language and Literature, honours class, third prize, and in German Language and Literature, equal first prize, with two others. She was clearly a woman of some intelligence.

By the time that Andrew met her, she had just become a lecturer in English at Jordanhill College of Education in Glasgow. Writing about this period of his life over 60 years later, Andrew conceded that Janet's

---

10. Edward Lowbury and Alison Young, *To Shirk No Idleness* (Salzburg: University of Salzburg Press, 1997).

mother 'may not *altogether* have approved of my entering the house in such a way; *perhaps* her father would have disapproved' (my italics, showing Andrew's poor perception of his effects on other people). [11] Robert Green had died in 1904 but had been very strict about his daughters' male visitors! But Andrew, characteristically, was not to be deterred.

They talked about literature and in the summer, when there were no classes at New College, or presumably at Jordanhill, they 'took a train or bus somewhere',[12] to beauty spots, or went hillwalking, or perhaps sailing. Their shared interests were mainly literature, outdoor life and sports. During term time, Andrew was granted the special concession of leaving the class of Dr Mackintosh, Professor of Dogmatics, fifteen minutes early, at 12.45pm on Fridays, in order to be able to catch the one o'clock train to Glasgow.

Whilst at New College, Andrew became (but did not remain) a vegetarian, presumably on some principle of animals' right to life. Other than that, he had two main problems at New College: one was an initial inability to learn Hebrew; the other, with trying to overcome his 'nervousness in the pulpit',[13] on 'preaching practice' in various churches. This is rather surprising in a man who had previously contemplated a career as a barrister! However, sermons at this time often lasted thirty to forty-five minutes. His first service was in a village in Fife; and in his final year at New College, he spent the whole summer in charge of a village church on the island of Mull – apart from a few visits to Glasgow – whose wildlife and fauna he greatly enjoyed. Along with the poet and the churchman, the naturalist in Andrew Young was a developing aspect of his psyche, as it had been from his Dalmeny days.

During his time at New College, his first book of thirty-one poems, *Songs of Night* (dedicated to his mother), was privately published, paid for by his father at the cost of £16, a goodly sum in those days. Although Andrew later said that they had been written whilst he was at university (i.e. between 1903 and 1907), several of them were probably written in 1909, the year he met Janet Green. For example:

Her Hair.
Believe me, Love, that I am tired
Of flowers that blossom on a grave:
All that I thought too sweet to have,
And all that once I most desired.

---

11. *My Life,* unpublished.
12. Ibid.
13. Ibid.

As one that in dim water dips
His hands, so I would feel the strands
Of thy hair rippling through my hands
And cool the fever of my lips;

And cease from all the strife and care
And interchange of song and sin,
And hide my hands and lips within
The sweet oblivion of thy hair.

Janet's was dark and abundant, though usually fixed up in a bun, but perhaps she took it down for Andrew?
  Or perhaps this:

> *Merchandise.*
> I would not give thy coloured lips
> That Love has crimsoned with his dyes,
> For all the pomp of merchandise
> That purpled seas in Tyrian ships;
>
> Nor those deep eyes that overflow
> With love, for all the lights that gem
> And weave for Death a diadem
> About his pale, imperious brow,
>
> No gold dust out of distant lands
> Nor all their wealth of woven ware,
> Could buy this weight of lavish hair,
> I hold like water in my hands.
>
> But not thy lips nor languid eyes
> I love, nor yet thy loosened hair,
> But that sweet soul that dwelleth where
> Stars slumber in wide azure skies.

One of the night-themed poems in the collection shows a clear link between the two 'loves', human and divine, especially in the second line of the third verse:

> *At Night.*
> This living darkness is to me
> As thy dim-shadowed hair,
> And in my heart the thought of thee
> Is holy as a prayer.

For but to gaze into thine eyes
Or but to touch thy hand,
Stirs in me deeper mysteries
Than I can understand.

The sanctity of love is such
At thy lips' eucharist,
That other Love I seem to touch,
That filled the heart of Christ.

The word 'eucharist' is doubly unexpected here, given his churchmanship where the 'Lord's Supper' was a rare event, and the clear linking of *eros* and *agape*. A similar linking occurs in *Night Thought*:

O gracious Lips that I have kissed
And tasted in the Eucharist,
With you alone an answer is,
And yet no answer but a kiss.

This may also perhaps hint at his decision to be ordained, since the 'Spirit of God's Love', like his father's, was 'more a falcon than a dove', from which there was 'no hiding place'. This poem also reveals unconscious literary echoes from his reading:

A little while, and I shall be
At one with earth and air and sea

is reminiscent of one of Wordsworth's 'Lucy' poems:

rolled round on earth's diurnal course
with rocks and stones and trees

As a collection, *Songs of Night* is in some ways typically 'Georgian': mainly descriptive, especially of flowers (snowdrops, roses and daisies), landscapes and seasons. He uses conventional rhyme schemes, archaisms such as thee, thy, thine, O, art, thyself, fain, givest, and so on; along with some clichés: 'dizzying height', 'monstrous birth' (with its unconscious echo of *Othello*); and the sentiments can be bland and predictable. However, there are some arresting images, such as:

like a wound the sunset bleeds ('Landscape');

the scentless flowers of frost ('Winter');

and the use of pathetic fallacy (here, almost erotic):

And in the night an amorous moon
Sings to the sea a tender tune,
And all the star-encrusted sky
Shivers with silent ecstasy.

Personification and paradox are also apparent, as they were to be later:

Twilight folds her hands ('Nocturne')

The Leaf.
Sometimes an autumn leaf
That falls upon the ground,
Gives the heart a wound
And wakes an ancient grief.

But I weep not that all
The leaves of autumn die,
I only weep that I
Should live to see them fall.

Andrew clearly saw this himself – keeping only nine of the thirty-one poems to be reprinted in the *Collected Poems* during his lifetime, and also adhered to by his editors in the posthumous edition of 1985. The rest, he must have discarded as 'juvenilia' or apprentice pieces for the master craftsman he later became. Of the twenty-two poems later discarded, a number were on religious themes: *The Star in the East, The Passion, Prayer, The Sea,* amongst others. One of the simplest of these echoes George Herbert, a poet he admired, and is worth quoting in its entirety:

Vision.
Say not my Lord is dead;
Last night I saw Him in the flesh,
His wounds were red and fresh
The thorns about His head.

'These limbs of ivory,
And precious drops of sacrifice,
Rubies and pearls of price,
My Son, I paid for thee.'

I saw His pale lips move,
And His bright eyes were like a sword;
I cried, 'Have pity, Lord,
Thou woundest me with love.'

Other influences were clearly at work too: in *Song*, Andrew adopts a world-weary pose reminiscent of the Romantics:

> Wild grass and flowers that fall
> And winds and rains that weep,
> For I am tired of all
> Sweet things save only sleep.

A review in *The Gambolier*, in Edinburgh, dated 12 May 1910, notes that:

> *Songs of Night* is commendable not only as the work of an undergraduate, it is a book whose appeal is to everyone of refined taste in verse, whose ear is trained to the more hidden subtleties of melody and metre. Artistically conceived, artistically fashioned, soft with delicate half-tones, strong with the lustre of passion, Mr Young's is difficult to characterise.

Characterising Andrew's work was certainly to remain 'difficult'. Yet despite the 'rills/hills' rhymes, the vocabulary of death and constant references to things 'oppressive' and 'desolate', the collection shows a good sense of rhythm, repetition, and some experimentalism with literary devices and imagery. It is possible to sense, in the best lines, the poet to come.

CHAPTER 3
CAREER AND MARRIAGE: EARLY YEARS
(1912-1920)

In 1912, Andrew was ordained as a minister in the United Free Church of Scotland, then in 1913 he was appointed as assistant minister (rather like a curate) at Wallace Green Presbyterian Church in Berwick-upon-Tweed, where he lived in lodgings. The work did not sound too arduous, being mainly taking or assisting at Sunday services, and pastoral visits to the elderly, sick or needy, where he would listen to and/or pray with them. He commented later that he felt 'it was easier to speak to God than to them'.[1] This was to remain the case throughout his ministry: his strengths were never pastoral, as he had little real, deep interest in other people.

However, he was quietly devout and was to become an effective preacher. It is likely that the teaching of Dr Alexander Whyte also influenced Andrew's ministry: 'Prayer and work. All great and true and eminently successful ministers from Paul's day downwards bear the same testimony: prayer and work'.[2]

Whyte was a powerful advocate of Christian unity, which was discussed at the United Free Church Assembly on 28 May 1912, then again the following year, when the possibility of uniting with the Church of Scotland was in the air. After all, the United Free Church itself had only come into being in 1900 – when Andrew was fifteen – with the amalgamation of the Free and United Presbyterian Churches. Whyte had also advocated wider, interdenominational understanding, ahead of his time: 'When we have humbled ourselves to admit that some other Churches have things of no small moment to teach us and to share with us . . . then the day of a reconstructed Christendom will have begun to dawn, at least for ourselves'.[3]

Certainly for Andrew, an admiration of Anglicanism had 'begun to dawn', as he acknowledged later: he was drawn, even as a student, towards

---

1. *My Life,* unpublished.
2. Part of his opening address as Moderator of his church.
3. As 2 above.

its relative ritualism and emphasis on the sacraments, but he was to serve a total of twenty-six years as a Presbyterian minister before he finally changed his affiliation.

On a more personal note, he seems to have become engaged to Janet in his last year at New College and continued his courtship from Berwick: on Saturdays, he would meet her at the railway station, she equipped with 'a small leather bag with sandwiches and a half-bottle of port wine'.[4] Sometimes they went south – making several trips to Durham Cathedral – at other times north, for example to Melrose Abbey, or explored the Borders countryside. Their daughter Alison was to comment later:

It is not surprising that the Greens were unenthusiastic about Janet's engagement. Andrew had swept her off her feet, and was showing a tendency to dominate and monopolise her. . . . They were piqued . . . by Andrew's avoidance of their company. . . . Andrew, for his part, continued to take no interest in the Greens *and even discouraged their visits later on when he and Janet were married* [my italics].[5]

After a year in Berwick, Andrew was 'elected' minister of the United Free Church at Temple, a small village on the River Esk, in Midlothian, on 29 May 1914. He must have had to preach a sermon as part of his assessment for the post, where he was installed on 2 July, and was to remain until 1920. It was about fifteen miles from Edinburgh and Andrew often cycled in to visit his parents as his father had retired that year.

Andrew now having a secure job with a house meant that the engaged couple could marry, which they did on 8 September 1914, in Glasgow. Janet was thirty-one (old for a woman to marry in those days) and Andrew was twenty-nine. Alison commented that: 'Janet must have realised that her acceptance of Andrew would lead to some severance from her own family, but she responded with warmth to Andrew's possessive love, . . . admired his self-possession, directness, vitality and highly individual good looks.'[6]

Early photos show a strong yet sensitive clean-shaven face with an aquiline nose and brown hair, parted in the middle, a style he never changed. They shared a love of music, literature and the outdoor life. They honeymooned briefly in Paris and Chartres, then went boating, or rowing, in Oxford, Windsor and on the Norfolk Broads. It seems that the pattern of their future emotional and domestic lives was set at this

---

4. *My Life*, unpublished.
5. Edward Lowbury and Alison Young, *To Shirk No Idleness* (Salzburg: University of Salzburg Press, 1997).
6. Ibid.

time, with Janet henceforth 'devoting her gifts and energies totally to the fulfilment of Andrew's wishes and aspirations'.[7] She was a highly educated, capable woman, with a college career behind her, but who seems, upon her marriage, to have totally abdicated from 'selfhood', from any personal ambitions or desires, content to be, not just a wife and mother, but a general dogsbody. In later life she told her daughter that 'if she had taken a firm stand' on her honeymoon, 'things might have been different'.[8] That she did not may have stemmed from her own family experiences: her father, Robert Green, had been 'severe and forbidding' so that 'we stood in awe of him', she told her brother-in-law John many years later; so when Andrew behaved similarly, Janet was hardly surprised.

As it was, Janet soon set about keeping house at the manse a few weeks after the war had started, writing to her sister, May in October 1914: 'I have been very busy, domestically and socially. As never before, I wish the day were three times as long'. As well as having no labour-saving devices, or help in the house, they kept chickens, a pig, and grew their own vegetables as food became scarcer. To save the expense of an organist, Janet, who was really a violinist (like her future granddaughter, Pauline Lowbury) played the harmonium in church on Sundays. As the minister's wife, Janet was welcomed by the congregation, and Andrew remarked later that she had many invitations out to tea, (some of which she must have found tedious). They appear to have been well liked by their parishioners.

By early December, Janet was pregnant. In February 1915, after one of her sister May's rare visits, Janet wrote to her, admitting: 'I appreciated your many sisterly attentions very much – you know they are a luxury now. I only wish I could enjoy them oftener'. Anthony was born on 8 August 1915, and Andrew told his friend John Arlott later (as he awaited the birth of a child) how pleased he had been by the birth, saying, 'Those were wonderful days'. But Andrew was to prove a difficult, demanding father, especially to Anthony. To Alison later, he was, by her own account, rather a distant, indifferent father, so that their experience of him, as children, was rather different. But marriage was certainly a 'transformative' experience to Andrew: it began a regulated, work/home life, with all his needs serviced by an increasingly devoted wife, with built-in periods of solitude for writing or walking.

However, although inclining to pacifism, Andrew, like Edward Thomas, felt that he had to enlist; but the 'office bearers' or elders of his church 'contrived' to have him released *before* he was called up. He was not exactly

7. Ibid.
8. Ibid.

in a 'reserved occupation' but it was not until 'an old, retired minister' could be found to fill his position that Andrew was posted abroad: not in a combat capacity, like Edward Thomas, but as the superintendent of a YMCA Rest Camp, near Boulogne, first in 1917 then again in 1919. Soldiers from the front line were taken to the rest camp for a week at a time, and according to Alison later, Andrew was responsible for their programme of activities, as well as Sunday services, like any other military padre.

Andrew remarked later that 'death staring them in the face, the men felt the need of religion'.[9] Luckily for Andrew, an old friend from New College days, the Rev Donald Baillie, was in charge of another nearby rest camp, so when the camps were relatively empty, they found time to walk and talk together. They also shared knowledge of the death of a mutual friend who had also been with them at New College, Cecil Barclay Simpson, who had been blown up by a shell exploding at his feet while inspecting a trench. Alison said that the horror of this event haunted Andrew all his life, although he had no other direct connection with the realities of trench warfare. Edward Thomas, whose poetry Andrew was later to much admire, died in similar circumstances to Simpson, in the same year, 1917.

Donald Baillie and Andrew combined together in a tribute to Simpson, published the following year as *A Memorial by Two Friends*. Baillie wrote the prose and Andrew the poetry, *Memorial Verses, 1918*. This was a new departure for Andrew: the longest, at twenty-six eight-line verses, to date; the first in a predominantly elegiac mode; and in seven decasyllabic iambic lines, followed by a final alexandrine or twelve-syllable line, rhyming ABBABCCA. Like his previous mentor, Dr Whyte, Andrew was a lifelong admirer of Dante, sharing with Whyte the view that his writings were 'a treasure house of truth and beauty'.[10] There is a clear link between Dante and Andrew's mature, long poetry (*Into Hades*, and *Out of the World and Back*) but it is seen here for the first time: like *The Inferno*, which begins with the traveller entering a bewildering 'great forest' in which he 'had lost the way', Andrew's persona 'sank / By a deep path to where the alders grew / Black in the darkness'. Like Dante's traveller, Andrew's is helped by 'moonlight in the trees' and 'stars' which soon becomes 'the Star of Love' which leaps 'Out of the sepulchre of the deep-buried sun'. It is not until verse five that there is any overt reference to the subject, Cecil Simpson, brought to mind by the, 'bridge, half-broken', from verse one, where they had often stood and talked, but now he had 'taken thy dark, uncompanioned way

9. *My Life*, unpublished.
10. G.F. Balfour, *The Life of Alexander Whyte*, Hodder & Stoughton, 1924.

alone' (verse 6). Andrew marvels that at the very moment of Simpson's death, his friends were unaware of it:

> Were we then
> Asleep or waking? Or perhaps we dreamed
> Or smiled, so thoughtless of the shell that screamed
> Between the two thunders of the hoarse throats of war.

More positively, Andrew wonders if:

> thou, in dying for thy soldier's vow,
> Foundest something more than death . . .
> for so we deem
> That sacrifice sufficient to redeem
> Thy spirit from the dread autocracy of death.

Or again:

> Or shall we think it was more wisely plann'd
> For thy life's beauty that swift Death should steal
> Thy May-time bloom than that thy age should feel
> The Winter's bloody stab on its deciduous leaf?

There are some unexpected and unusual images in places:

> But heavier than the weight of pyramids
> Sleep lies upon thy head . . .

> the lightning's bright unlidded eyes . . .

> heavy brown-eyed sunflowers

The sea even:

> mourns, and bids the wandering moon to throw
> On thy French grave her whitest fleur-de-lys

In verse 24, the poem becomes a prayer, said on the bridge in the moonlight, as he began. He imagines Simpson watching and waiting:

> with quiet heart, until
> The universe should break apart in pain,
> And earth and sun and moon and stars again
> Be mixed and shaken out of their kaleidoscope.

The last verse has a verbal vigour which forms a fitting end, and without the stylised, often archaic diction of many of the verses, sounds both more modern and foreshadows his maturer style:

XXVI.
Here all was wild: leaves swirled about my knees
And, running, pattered on the road like rain:
And wood and gale were wrestling in the strain
Of violent war; the great winds surged in seas
Against the elms: the branches creaked in pain
And waved wild signals; all the ground was strewn
With broken twigs: the wind's ally, the moon,
Splintered a thousand lances in the thundering trees.

Despite its obviously 'dated' language and sentiments, *Memorial Verses* is more succinct, controlled and accomplished than the poetic poses and 'Georgian' excesses of *Songs of Night*. We see that the discipline Andrew applied to himself – and to those near him – he also applied to his verse. He mixes genuine emotions, ideas and natural imagery in a tightly controlled verse form.

* * *

Whilst Andrew was away in France, Janet kept in close touch with her mother, brother Harry, and sisters May and Margaret, remarking to May in June 1918: 'the strawberries are a mass of blossom . . . a fine crop. The hens are also laying and we have begun to get fresh butter, so things are not so bad'. She tried to be positive, especially as she was bringing up Anthony alone in the manse, whilst the retired minister conducted services and ran the parish. According to Alison, the mother-son bond became particularly close, not surprisingly; yet Andrew's return in 1919 was to cause a seismic shift as his dominance over her reasserted itself, and relationships had to be readjusted. This must have been true of many wartime families but it was to cast a long shadow across the Youngs.

In Chapter 3 of *My Life*, written nearly fifty years after the event, Andrew recalled his welcome home:

'my wife was not the first to welcome me, though the door was opened as soon as I opened the gate. The first to welcome me was a tiny boy who toddled towards me to fall into my arms'. This idyllic picture is in marked contrast to the family life and relationships described by Alison later, although in all fairness she was not yet born at this time; but she did remember Anthony telling her that his earliest memory was of, 'lying outdoors in his pram; his father pointed upwards and said, 'What is that?' 'The sky,' answered Anthony, but Andrew scoldingly said, 'You silly boy, it's a cloud!'[11]

---

11. Edward Lowbury and Alison Young, *To Shirk No Idleness* (Salzburg: University

Like many returning home after the war, Andrew became restless, and on his own admission 'was feeling an ambition for a larger scope of life and work'[12] than was available in Midlothian. He was thirty-five and feeling hemmed in by his circumstances. This feeling coincided, a few months later, with a letter from a friend, the Rev James Reid, who was minister of the Presbyterian Church in Eastbourne, telling Andrew that there was a vacancy at the Presbyterian Church (later renamed St Cuthbert's United Free Church) in Hove. Reid was the Moderator and invited Andrew to apply for the post, which, as usual, involved preaching a sermon to the congregation. The church (pulled down in 1985) stood near the Sussex County Cricket playing field, which perhaps helped to clinch it for Andrew (who was later given a season ticket for the ground by a member of the congregation). Andrew's sermon clinched it with the Moderator and the congregation too, so Andrew was offered and accepted the post.

The Youngs left Midlothian in February 1920, after six years, intending to return to Scotland at some future date. They were given gifts and a good send-off by a grateful parish. In Hove, there was no official manse, but the church bought them 'a small, charming house' at 15 Bigwood Avenue, off the Old Shoreham Road. Later, in the mid-1920s after Alison's birth, they were given a larger house, 'Seamark' in Lloyd Road, where they were to spend their last ten years in Hove.

The move south cut Janet off more or less completely from her family, whose rare visits were unwelcomed by Andrew. However, she remained a lively letter writer, known as 'Jintie' to her mother and siblings, commenting on family and outside events, showing concern and offering advice when she felt it necessary, e.g. exhorting May to, 'go to bed early – and don't rush about – . . . and also you must think of your looks. They are very important even though you are in an office, and every nice man you ever knew is buried in France'.

On annual holidays to Scotland, apart from walking, sailing and other outdoor activities, Andrew visited his ageing parents in Edinburgh, but it is less likely that Janet was allowed to visit hers in Glasgow. We know little about Janet's views on the move to Hove, as there are no extant letters between 1919 and 1922, but it appears that they soon settled in. They particularly enjoyed the nearness to the South Downs, although Andrew later described them as being 'nearer molehills than mountains'. In addition, their – or certainly Andrew's – cultural life was about to expand, and his writing was about to take new turns.

---

of Salzburg Press, 1997).
12. *My Life,* unpublished.

PART 2
THE LATER POET AND PRIEST

Chapter 4
The Move South
(1920-1937)

'Hove has no architectural interest; it is even said to have the ugliest town hall in England,' Andrew wrote fifty years later in his unpublished *My Life*; yet St Cuthbert's was 'a local landmark, a dignified red building with a tall steeple and an impressive though austere interior'.[1] It enjoyed a good reputation in the town. The mayor and corporation visited it occasionally and Andrew soon became a member of the town's education committee. There was also a thriving church literary society, which Andrew chaired, spoke at, and where he met other writers.

During this time, Andrew must have been writing odd poems here and there, many on Old Testament subjects, as within a few months of arriving in Hove, *Boaz and Ruth and other Poems* was published under the imprint of J.G. Wilson, an old friend, and printed by the Cliftonville Press in Hove, which was run by one of Andrew's new parishioners. Wilson became important to Andrew as he was to publish six books of poetry and two verse plays by him between 1920 and 1931.

The immediate motive for the quick publication of *Boaz and Ruth* was to help shore up church funds, which had been depleted by buying the 'manse' in Bigwood Avenue. The book sold at two shillings a copy and made a total of £15. One of the 150 copies sold was favourably reviewed by the *TLS* on 21 July 1921. Dedicated this time 'To My Father', the book had a marked religious tendency in at least half of the twelve poems, both long and short, which would certainly have pleased his father and seemed becoming in a minister. *Creation* is an amusing take on the usual story:

God plucked a golden quill
From Michael's wing:
The host that had before been still
Began to sing:

---

1. Edward Lowbury and Alison Young, *To Shirk No Idleness* (Salzburg: University of Salzburg Press, 1997).

He spread a sheet of light
Before Him; then
Deep down into the pot of night
He dipped His pen.

Earth and the sea and air,
Sun, moon and stars,
All things of power and beauty were
His characters.
The mighty word was penned
Age after age;
And, each age coming to an end,
He turned a page.

And last, to make all sure,
(Read it who can!)
He set thereto His signature
And called it Man.

showing a fluent, less stilted style, with some apt imagery: 'a sheet of light', 'the pot of night' and the extended metaphor of the written page, ending with 'His signature'.

   On the Cliff, with its alliterative and assonantal line, 'Sings the incessant sea', ends like a prayer:

Lord, in the weakness of my words,
Let all these pray for me,
The broken cliff, the crying birds,
And the foam-mottled sea.

Many of the other, shorter poems, are about sleep, dreams, unidentified pains/troubles, nightfall, moon and stars, in landscapes with 'flowery wells', 'asphodels', 'leaf-dripping dews', pastoral rather than realistic, with occasional echoes of other poets, for example Keats with 'no bird singing' in *Sonnet*. The directly religious poems *Chorus from Jephthah* and *The Death of Eli* are deliberately stilted and archaic, presumably to stress the distance of the past:

Crush the brazen cymbals on high
And leap, ye priests, on a nimble foot
(*The Death of Eli*)

Some of *Jephthah* has a visual richness, colour and rhythm which succeeds in conveying opulence and 'otherness':

And camels come from Havilah by the road to paradise
With mountain gold and cassia, spikenard and sweet spice,
And bring from Sheba silken scarfs and blue-lipped Negresses
Perfumes and dyes and singing dwarfs, incense and golden mice

But overall, these poems are hard for a modern reader to appreciate, and although Andrew had a habit of 'mining' from previous poems, he seems to have regarded most of these as juvenilia, since he omitted them from his *Collected Poems* of 1950. However, *Jephthah*, *The Death of Eli* and *Morning Hymn of the Hebrew Shepherds* were resurrected in the posthumous editions of 1974 and 1985.

The one poem which was directly personal, rather than a poetic pose, was *To A— (On his third birthday)*, a tribute to Anthony, who was three in 1918:

The Christmas day that you were born
December snows were far away,[2]
For in the time of flowers and corn
You made a second Christmas day

neatly links the two births, suggesting that Anthony's was second in importance only to Jesus' for Andrew. He continues the metaphor in a touchingly personal manner, rare for him:

Six times has Christmas come since then,
To us six times, if to none else;
Three we observed with other men,
But three came with no church bells.

The ABAB rhyme scheme requires 'else' to be pronounced 'ells'. By the end, however, Andrew has reverted to a more conventional personification:

Alas, can summer hope to save
The sweets her rippling roses shed?

Yet there is, in this poem, a hint of the more relaxed, naturalistic poetic voice to come.

In 1921, the twelve poems in *The Death of Eli and Other Poems* (dedicated once again to his mother) was published, which shows that Andrew was now writing on a regular basis. The subjects were his now familiar ones: flowers (violets, daisies, clematis); seasons (mainly autumn); night, divine love, beauty, death. Pathetic fallacy and personification abound, as do the archaisms 'thy/thou' and the suffix -est, as in 'touchest', 'speakest', and so on:

---

2. He was born on 8 August 1915.

O pilgrim in thy purple hood,
That stayest late into the year
(*To a Violet in Autumn*)

Where Time wrote with his iron pen
The things that may not come again.
(*Youth*)

A Blakean note occasionally creeps in:

For where the folded daisies are
In every one I see a star.
(*Daisies*)

In *Love,* a twelve-line poem, the effect is spoilt by line eight ('Is of too fine a sky') and the word 'dear' at the beginning of verse three:

In giving love you gave me all,
Your hand, your heart, your soul;
If other women give in part,
Yet you have given the whole.

If then you ask me how I know
We shall not wholly die,
I answer that that love of yours
Is of too fine a sky.

A love of such dimensions, dear,
So long, so deep, so broad,
Is such a love as sure must share
Eternity with God.

It as though the rhyme – scheme has partly dictated the content – presumably relates to his wife Janet.

In the two autumn poems, there are some arresting images:

where the catkins swung their tails
Like caterpillars on the trees . . .

the rose's sepulchre
(*Autumn*)

And:

The clematis grows old and clings
Grey – bearded to the roadside trees
And in the hedge the nightshade strings

Her berries in bright necklaces.
(Song for Autumn)

It has to be said that by the early 1920s, when he had been writing poetry for over a decade, Andrew had still not outgrown the 'poetic diction' and archaisms of the nineteenth century, nor had his subject matter gone much beyond the conventional themes of nature, love, religion and death. He was, to all intents and purposes, still stuck in the 'Georgian' era of de la Mare, Masefield, Bottomley, Elroy Flecker, and so on. Despite some occasionally startling and original imagery, his style was stilted and he remained outside contemporary developments: by this time, T.S. Eliot, three years Andrew's junior, had published *Prufrock and Other Observations* (in 1917) when he was twenty-three. The settings were urban, urbane and modern; the language hesitant, repetitive, visual, unassailably twentieth century:

Then how shall I begin
To spit out all the butt-ends of my days and ways?
And how should I presume?
(The Love Song of J. Alfred Prufrock)

The winter evening settles down
With smell of steaks in passageways.
Six o'clock.
The burnt-out ends of smoky days.
(Preludes)

Poems of 1920 had followed, with *Gerontion*, the Sweeney poems and a more cosmopolitan, continental awareness. The poems of Edward Thomas, who had died aged thirty-nine, in 1917, were published in a collected edition in 1920. His poems had broken with the Georgian formality and predictability, and were more naturalistic, especially the 'dialogue' poems, *Up in the Wind, The Chalk Pit, As the Team's Head Brass*:

T'would have been different,' the wild girl shrieked, 'suppose
That widow had married another blacksmith and
Kept on the business. This parlour was the smithy.
If she had done, there might never have been an inn
(Up in the Wind, 1914)

Thomas' many nature poems were, like Andrew's, about seasons and animals, such as *Sedge-Warblers, Old Man, Fifty Faggots*, yet they were not merely descriptive but questioning, insightful metaphors for other things:

I have mislaid the key. I sniff the spray
And think of nothing; I see and I hear nothing;
Yet seem, too, to be listening, lying in wait
For what I should, yet never can, remember:
No garden appears, no path, no hoar-green bush
Of Lad's – love, or Old Man
(*Old Man,* 1914)

Andrew's earlier poetry cannot compare to such poets at the same stages of their poetic lives: but it does later, in the 1930s, by the time he is writing poems such as *The Dead Crab, The Swans* and *The Ventriloquists.*

Yeats, twenty years older than Andrew, and a poet whom, for some reason, he disliked, was writing *The Wild Swans at Coole* (1919) and *Easter 1916* (1921) contemporaneously with Andrew's *Death of Eli and Other Poems.* Again, it shows the distance in subject matter, thought and style. Andrew's poetic maturity came late in his poetic life, and he disliked poets like Yeats, Eliot, Hopkins, Auden – 'modernists', experimenters and innovators. He *did,* however, like Edward Thomas, Hardy, Clare, Swinburne, Spenser and his own contemporaries W.H. Davies, de la Mare and John Freeman.

Every year, Andrew took his family to visit his parents in Edinburgh, and occasionally at other times. One of these was the marriage of his only sister Margaret in April 1921 to a widower called Percy Debnam, an Anglican. This was expected to be difficult, as their father was such a staunch Presbyterian, but he was brought round to accept the situation by the fact that Mr Debnam was a churchwarden, an office held in high regard. This acceptance of an Anglican within the family was a precursor to Andrew's eventual change of religious allegiance and his father's acceptance of it; but it is doubtful that this occurred to Andrew at the time.

In the late autumn of 1921, Janet became pregnant with her second child. Anthony was then six and the house in Bigwood Avenue was already quite cramped, with Andrew having to double up his study with the sitting room. Finances were none too plentiful on a pastor's stipend and when Janet was sent some money by her sister May in January 1922, she replied that, 'I am going to buy some luxury for myself'. There would have been few opportunities to do that; however, she did have a maid/nanny called Bertha at this time, who looked after Anthony and was 'willing to do all she can for me'. She added that, 'I actually had two mornings in bed last week' and also that, 'after tea (I) simply long for bedtime: I feel sickly and all at ease then. But that will pass off no doubt. . . . It isn't so long till the beginning of June'.[3]

Janet was obviously finding her pregnancy rather arduous and longing for it to be over. On a lighter note, she tells May in the same letter: 'When I asked Anthony what he wanted for Xmas, he said he would like a little brother – or a football. He has the football – and you can imagine what the house is like'.

In February, when Janet had finished marking university papers (which she seems to have done for many years, presumably in order to have some money of her own), they planned a ten-day holiday, 'not very far, only into the hills of Surrey', (she and Andrew were great walkers), as 'the doctor says it is all right if I am careful'.[4]

By 5 June, Janet wrote to May, 'This is Sunday morning and still nothing has happened – I hope it won't be long delayed, for nurse is due to come in on Tuesday and I don't want her to sit down cooling her heels!'[5] On money matters she remarks, 'My money has come – a godsend. I have been paying . . . bills and debts beforehand, so as to be in bed with an easy mind,' which suggests that she organised the family accounts, as well as their domestic life. Returning to the imminent birth, Janet comments matter-of-factly: 'Anthony (and Andrew, I hope) are doing a church excursion tomorrow to Arundel – it would fit in nicely, *if it could be got over* some time during the day. . . . Andrew will send you news at once when there is any' (my italics).

Janet is nothing if not practical!

Three days later, on 8 June, their daughter Ruth Alison was born, though for some reason she was always known as Alison. The dedication verses to Andrew's *Thirty-One Poems* published that year, however, includes her first initial:

> J.Y., A.J.Y., R.A.Y.,
> Dears, take this little book;
> Taking it make it ours;
> Here runs a thin-voiced brook
> Enskying some few flowers.
>
> And when from the last hill
> Fades the flame-coloured light
> Dears, will you hear it still
> Singing across the night?

3. Letter from Janet to May, January 1922.
4. Letter from Janet to May, 27 February 1922.
5. Letter from Janet to May, 5 June 1922.

It is clear that Andrew, at this time, had a strong sense of a compact family unit sharing a common life. There are five child-centred poems in this collection, and two which mention, or are addressed to, his wife: *Waiting*, about the coming of spring (and presumably Alison's birth), changes from 'My love and I' to 'My wife and I' in the last verse. In *At Owley*, Andrew admits:

> Dear, I wished you had been there;
> It was almost a pain to bear
> The beauty of that place alone;
> One needed a companion.

The last verse, however, changes its tone, becoming a paradoxical, rhetorical question, and therefore more typical of his later style:

> And I remember came the thought
> Should God by act of death be brought
> Nearer than now, might I not die
> Slain by my immortality?

This thought links to the last verse of *The Dead Sparrow*, and foreshadows dead moles, sheep and other birds to come:

> That sparrow asks no man
> To dig for it a grave;
> Gentle is death, I thought, that can
> Both slay and save.

A Child Sleeping, begins with a conventional enough simile:

> She is like the sorrel's white bud
> That grows in a sun-watered wood

This extends to:

> Quickly her slender head is bowed,

at the end of the day. But in the last verse there is a very amusing metaphor:

> And sluggish and enormous trees
> Pull their green smocks down to their knees

which also suggests the older, dressed child.

In *A Child's Voice*, it is not so much a human's as a number of newborn lambs' 'voices' which he recalls through 'a small voice crying' later.

In *Child Love*, the father tries in vain to communicate his love to the child:

> But love, I say to her
> Taking her by the hand;
> But will she smile? Or will she stir?
> She does not understand.

A similar idea emerges in *To a Child*:

> When I take your two hands in my two hands
> And speak to you, you are as one who stands
> A traveller in new-discovered lands
> That cannot break to meaning native words.

There are, as usual, poems about autumn, cuckoos, shepherds, ploughmen, trees, birds and animals, with a few neat touches:

> Our Mephistopheles
> Singing at ease,
> Cuckoo . . .

> So through the night walked three of us
> By earth and air and sky,
> Dim shadow and moon luminous
> And in between them, I.
> (*Full Moon*)

The final verse of *The Snail* shows Andrew's growing ambition as a poet:

> Flesh, sinew, blood and bone,
> All that of me is strong,
> Blithely would I bury in one
> Short-lived immortal song.

In *To A*—Andrew exhorts his growing son to love nature as he does:

> Be thou thy father's son
> True to thy blood and birth
> Not in one single thing but one
> The love of God's sweet earth.

At times, Andrew is able to dispense with archaisms and grammatical inversions for a more natural- sounding speech:

> Today I saw a bird
> Lie upturned on the ground;

It seemed as though I found a word
That had no sound.
(*The Dead Sparrow*)

An almost Hardyesque note is achieved in *Song*:

With every sweet apostle
That spread the news of spring,
Linnet, lark and throstle,
Blackcap and redwing,
I too began to sing

This manages to weave in both religious imagery and colour. The opening verse of *Sand Strapwort* conveys colours, seasons and the oxymoron 'dying birth':

When colour lifting from the earth
Catches from trees a dying birth
And in the ivy's yellow bloom
Wasps and blue flies make angry hum

In the same year, Eliot published *The Waste Land*, his vision of the post-war, arid world, the 'dead land' which Andrew would neither have understood nor shared. Yet some of Eliot's imagery was not too far from some of Andrew's:

stirring
Dull roots with spring rain.
Winter kept us warm, covering
Earth in forgetful snow, feeding
A little life with dried tubers
(*The Burial of the Dead*)

On 14 September, Janet wrote to her sister Mary from Kingsbridge in Devon, where they were holidaying, describing her new baby: 'I can see the expression in my baby's clear, bright eyes. . . . She is a dear – she has brown eyes, but promises to be better-looking than her mother', adding, 'I am feeling stronger now, but not fit to do a washing', which in those days was a feat that took hard work over several days with copper and mangle.

Whilst Janet was immersed in motherhood, housekeeping, aspects of church organisation, writing to friends and family, and so on, Andrew made time, outside his ministerial duties, to both write and have some social life with a small group of fellow writers, whom he sometimes met in London. The Brighton Belle made London accessible within the hour. His main friend and fellow writer of the time was John Freeman, a 'Georgian' poet, through whom he met W.H. Davies, a poet he admired, J.C. Squire and Conrad Aiken, amongst others. Nearer home, Andrew sometimes went to the Sussex Poetry Society, or the Hove branch of the Poetry Society, where he met Alfred Noyes (of *The Highwayman* fame) and John Drinkwater, another anthologised 'Georgian' poet, whose work, like that of W.B. Yeats, a guest speaker in 1922, Andrew did not like. As his daughter Alison later observed: 'Andrew was at this time taking an active part in the social side of literature – something he avoided in later years'.[6]

Despite some time conflicts between ministry and writing, Andrew managed to keep them in tandem, even increasing the congregation in his early years in Hove. The Youngs were popular with the congregation, who treated them with generosity, as Janet told May on 31 December 1923: 'They were all so good to the children – *they* at least have had a lovely Xmas, and we, of course, by reflection'. She continued this letter with a little snapshot of their family life:

> You would like my little girl, I know. She is very strong-minded, and independent and promises to be capable – She is a regular little woman – adores dolls, and all living creatures: loves dusting. . . . She is learning to talk too: at breakfast a napkin fell in somebody's porridge – one of the boys (i.e. Anthony or Andrew!) said, 'Dash' and she repeated it so sweetly . . . it is as well bad language is not current in the house. . . . Anthony is a great big boy at the Grammar School – a voracious reader. . . . We gave him *Treasure Island* and *The Jungle Book* – but they are just a little beyond him.

Contrary to his initial nervousness in the pulpit when a theology student, Andrew, at Hove, developed into a powerful and popular preacher, with addresses on the Church, the saints and figures in the Old Testament. He also frequently brought literary topics in, with titles like *King Lear,* a study in suffering, or *Macbeth,* a study in sin. Milton, Dante, Bunyan and the nineteenth-century poets were also frequently mentioned. His daughter Alison recalls: 'He spoke with a quiet authority and always preached from memory with a minimum of gesture, using few, if any, notes. . . . The number of sermons he memorised over the years was astonishing'.[7] It was almost inevitable that this would lead to the writing

---

6. Edward Lowbury and Alison Young, *To Shirk No Idleness* (Salzburg: University of Salzburg Press, 1997).
7. Ibid.

of religious verse plays: four between 1923 and 1937, beginning with *The Adversary*, an encounter between Job and Satan, which has echoes of Pepys ('up betimes'), Keats, Marlowe's Mephistopheles, and Milton. It contains some memorable lines:

> (Satan). He said that at my fall
> A tear fell from the great Father's face
> On heaven's burning pavement; such a star
> Might compass the salvation of a world,
> And yet it scalds my heart . . .

> When God made man He made a fool . . .

> while silent night
> Nails down her coffin with a thousand stars.

Also in 1923, came *Ritzpah*, on the theme of atonement between David, Saul and the Gibeonites. Ritzpah is the mother of two of Saul's sacrificed sons. Unlike *The Adversary* which had only two speakers, *Ritzpah* has choruses and several semi-choruses to push the action forward and give various viewpoints, reminiscent of Greek drama. Naturalistic they were not, and these days read as antiquated.

However, the final play, *Nicodemus* in 1937, brought him into contact with Bishop Bell of Chichester, and was to have profound repercussions.

* * *

With a growing family and a tight budget, Janet was considering applying 'for an examinership in Bristol' at the suggestion of her brother-in-law, Leonard Russell, her sister Alice's husband. It involved marking English literature papers 'equivalent to the University Prelim',[8] she told her sister May. She was worried about being able to supply 'testimonials' as her Jordanhill days were a decade earlier and she was not sure where particular potential referees were. Several months later, she told May: 'I am still in doubt, but think I will apply. I feel that if I did and got it, it would be for the best' not just financially but because, 'the discipline of preparing things . . . it would mean setting papers, I suppose – would be good for me. One gets terribly lazy intellectually in my job – though one's legs get plenty to do'.

Like many intelligent and well-educated wives and mothers, Janet felt stagnant and unstretched. The reference to using her legs a lot may be a veiled reference to Andrew's habit of ringing a bell and shouting, 'I say!' when he wanted anything!

---

8. Letter from Janet to May, 10 May 1924.

Janet regretted previous advice she had given to May, her unmarried younger sister, when she admitted: 'If I had known as much as I know now, I should certainly have encouraged you at that time long ago to go in for medicine – it was the money that frightened me then. But I see now you have to spend in order to get, and to take all sorts of risks. We were a timid crew, and too much inclined to play for safety'. Janet is rather self-judgemental here, especially as women's higher education and entry to the professions was hardly universal at the time. She adds, as though it is not too late, 'I would like to see you at Oxford or Cambridge if only for the fun of the thing!. . . Couldn't you learn typing and shorthand in the holidays? Or you might like to go out to Harry [their brother, who was working abroad]'.

Janet, articulate and thoughtful in her letters, is very aware of the pre-feminist problems women faced:

> Life for women who have their way to make is a hard business. In spite of my poverty, and hard work of a kind, I feel I have a soft job – though I dare not think much of the future and what we shall be able to do for our two children. . . . Sometimes I feel like being snuffed out – I have done so little with myself and what can I do now? These ten years since my marriage have gone in a dream. The only thing I have learnt to do is to make myself agreeable to commonplace people and cultivate some charity.

At the end of 1924, Janet's mother paid a rare visit to Hove but did not stay long as, 'The weekend is so very busy for me,' she told May, adding a character analysis of the children: 'Mother will have told you how the children are looking. As far as I can see, Alison will be able to hold her own in the world.[9] Anthony is more like us and I am trying to stiffen him up a bit. At least I understand where his weaknesses may lie'. He was aged nine at the time, and not getting on too well with his father.

As was usual for the time, husbands and wives had different priorities and demands on their time, but Andrew would certainly have been one of the demands on Janet, especially as he was often at home. If in some ways Janet felt trapped like a bird in a cage, Andrew's next poetry collection was called *The Bird Cage* (1926). He was working on it up to and including 1925, the year that Janet's mother died, unexpectedly. On 5 May, Janet wrote asking her mother for several days 'as Andrew will be away', adding, 'I am sorry not to say just come any time, but you will understand – it just takes me all my time to keep things going to everybody's comfort'.[10]

---

9. She was two and a half at the time!
10. Letter from Janet to her mother, 5 May 1925.

Alison comments, "'Everybody's' here obviously means 'Andrew's'. Andrew was most particular about his comfort, and would become sulky and cross if things were not to his liking."[11]

Unfortunately, Janet's mother never got to Hove, dying suddenly a few days later whilst staying with Janet's sister May on the Isle of Wight. She wrote to May on 12 May:

> I wish I could have been with you now: but I simply could not leave the children and Andrew with Nellie (the maid?) – Andrew and I discussed whether he ought to come to Glasgow (i.e. for the funeral) but we decided that, under the circumstances when he could do nothing, you would not wish him to spend the money.

Money was always a concern, but apart from that, Andrew had, quite deliberately, kept his distance from Janet's family from the beginning. Janet ended her letter by remarking: 'Let me know . . . all there is to tell. I had been looking forward to a quiet weekend with Mother – I do wish she had just seen the children again, and they her.'

But this was not to be the end of it: there were ongoing problems with debts, death duties and decision-making between the siblings. It appears that they decided to pool whatever money was left, but that Harry, who was working abroad, had borrowed money from their mother which he still had to repay. Janet refers to this in an undated letter to May later that year:

> I have written to Harry thanking him as well as I could, and telling him that if ever, within the next five years, he has a few odd pounds burning a hole in his pocket, just enough to buy me a new frock, I would accept them gratefully – but not more.' She added: 'We can't save a halfpenny – but if only I can equip the children decently for life that would satisfy me.

Once more, to this end, Janet had agreed to mark Higher Certificate literature papers the following Easter, 'just as many in number as the Lower, but much shorter and therefore less remunerative. But perhaps it is as well, for *it is a difficult job fitting them in between meals and family washing, etc.*' (my italics). Unfailingly loyal and practical, Janet's life was far from easy, yet she took a tolerant attitude to Harry's problems in another undated letter to May about this time: 'I am as cavalier about money as

---

11. Edward Lowbury and Alison Young, *To Shirk No Idleness* (Salzburg: University of Salzburg Press, 1997).

he (i.e. Harry) is even if Mother had advanced him money, I should have thought nothing of it, for she would have looked on it as a good investment and a means of saving —', but afraid she had offended Harry in some way, Janet remarked, 'I think I have made it all right with him', then suggested the proposed repayments of £10 a month 'could be spread over a longer period than ten months' and so ease his feeling of responsibility.

In October of the same year, 1925, it was Andrew's turn for a family drama: they had spent a week in Edinburgh in August when, after a trip to Cumbria, they had seen Andrew's parents. His mother Maria was 80 and his father 79. Both seemed well, but in October, Maria became suddenly ill and died on the seventeenth. Although Andrew rushed there when summoned, he arrived too late to see her alive. Consequently, he was not only grief-stricken but also guilt-ridden and remained so, to some extent, for the rest of his life. One of the poems in *The Bird Cage*, (1926), written in 1925, according to Alison refers directly to his mother:

> O blue-eyed one, too well I know you will not awake,
> Who waked or lay awake so often for my sake,
> Nor would I ask our last leave – taking to retake.[12]

It is possible that the delayed shock of his mother's death contributed to his' breakdown' eighteen months later.

The Green family money questions continued off and on: in the summer of 1926, it appears that Harry had invested £50 for each of his sisters in a coal mining venture. Janet commented to May that 'if it is a success it will be a fine thing'. Always careful herself, Janet advised May not to 'take risks' by investing any of her 'patrimony in South Africa' since one day she will want 'to retire on a modest competence without worry', (presumably Janet's dream too), *not* like the people in Hove who 'congregate from the ends of the earth . . . (in) shabby gentility and semi-starvation'. Janet adds revealingly, 'I pray continually that that may not be my lot'.

Before they went to the Channel Islands in mid-August, Andrew's widowed father paid them a rare visit, but Janet complained to May that 'having visitors in this tiny house is a great trial, and we don't do it often for that reason'. However, the account of Andrew's father is rather surprising: 'Grandpa is really a dear. The soul of kindness. He is off with Alison to the recreation ground with a ball – I am sorry for his old rheumaticky fingers. He took Anthony for a sea trip to Eastbourne last week and arrived home at midnight'. This seems far from the austere father he had been to Andrew as a boy.

---

12. Verse 6 of 'The Flood'.

Significantly, Janet comments on the two children's progress and interests, but never mentions Andrew or his relations with the children: 'Anthony is thriving – a huge boy[13] – was fifth in his form and is one of the very youngest – not bad, for it was quite without effort – he could do much better'.

The Bird Cage published in 1926 was dedicated 'To Anthony', and though divided into three sections (Spring, Summer, Autumn), contained forty-eight poems on his now usual subjects: birds (wrens, rooks, jays, cuckoos, martins, hawks, jackdaws, etc.); seasons; flowers (hellebore, Old Man, campion, burdocks); places and occasionally people: a woodcutter, Alison (aged four).

Published a year after Eliot's *The Hollow Men*, and just before the early poetry of Auden and the mature poetry of Yeats, it marks the beginning of a sea change for Andrew: a less stilted, more naturalistic, conversational tone as in:

> So thick a mist darkened the wood today
> My friend, the jay, flashed by two trees away[14]

This is along with the development of greater lyricism, wit, whimsical conceits and paradoxes. *The Young Martins* are described as being:

> Like skaters cutting figures on a pond
> High swifts that curve on tilted wings are drawing
> Vanishing circles

A rook's passing shadow is described as 'a black flying ghost' and the imagery is sustained until 'Like disembodied spirits' they flew away.

In *The Ventriloquists*, unseen birds are heard singing in subtly imitative verse:

> Yet everywhere those hidden ventriloquists
> Were singing in the wood,
> Flinging their cheating voices here and there

Here, the word 'cheating' being skilfully chosen and placed. Other examples of apt imagery are also seen in this poem:

> one white house shone sharply as a sail . . .

> The thick sky-scrawling branches of the wood . . .

And, as so often, pathetic fallacy:

---

13. He was eleven at the time.
14. 'January' (from *The Bird Cage*, 1926).

The rusty catkins crawling on the ground.

This is not always successful, and in *Rooks* becomes almost ludicrous:

Where silent grass gave a loud shout

Green Hellebore shows an unexpected use of religious imagery:

Green with the loss of blood,
No heavy head looks up,
But in this Easter wood
Hangs down an empty cup.

The Yellowhammers and *The Lane* show evidence of experimentation with assonance, alliteration and hyphenated words to give a 'clotted', almost Hopkinsian flavour:

Yellowhammers, gold-headed, russet-backed,
They fled in jerky flight before my feet[15]

shaggy-hoofed / Horse . . .

sharp-scarped hill . . .

this lane tree-roofed . . .[16]

In *Ghosts*, the 'white ghosts of flowers' are paradoxically described in the last two lines, as:

Taking from the glad earth
Their burial and their birth.

The poem *Findon* addressed to a dead 'dear love' is a mystery as it clearly does not refer to Janet:

Calling you now I call in vain;
Your absence works in me like pain
More poisonous than dull henbane . . .

Yet love remains and memory
Of God and you, of earth and sky,
All that is intimately I.

This is also a verse form departure similar to the villanelle but rhyming AAA (except the first verse, which rhymes ABA), and showing a rare emotional intensity. An equally personal but less intense poem is addressed *June – To Alison*, who was then aged four:

---

15. *The Yellowhammers*, verse 2.
16. All quotes from *The Lane*.

> Four years ago this day of June,
> Clear in the sky, a thread-thin moon
> I saw you first, you weak, I strong,
> As small tits cheep and thrushes song

The book's dedication to Anthony seems to make some concessions to his age in poems such as *Turkeys*, *The Spider* and the humorous *The Sign*:

> the ruffled turkeys pass
> As stately as dromedaries . . .

> When the merry carols are sung
> And those high-stepping turkeys are due
> To have their proud necks wrung. . . .

> From twig to twig a speckled spider
> Legged like a hermit crab, had tied her
> Invisible web with WELCOME
> For sign, and HOME SWEET HOME

The feminine rhymes (spider / tied her; past her / disaster) add to the humour of the first two verses. In the last verse, 'wingy' instead of 'winged' is skilful (reminiscent perhaps of Hopkins' 'roundy wells'), and 'deadly symmetry' seems an unconscious echo of Blake's 'fearful symmetry' in *The Tyger*. 'Geometric' is the perfect word perfectly placed:

> Now she weaves in the dark
> With no light lent by a star's spark
> From busy belly more than head
> Geometric pattern of thin thread,
> A web for wingy midge and fly,
> With deadly symmetry.

We see Andrew in complete control of his medium, using stylistic devices to good effect.

The Seeds has an almost Hardyesque, meditative quality, bringing in his characteristic preoccupation with seasons, birth and death:

> Puffing like smoke over the wood
> The old man's beard[17] is stained with blood,
> And strewn along the pathway lie
> Like small open sarcophagi
> The hazelnuts broken in halves
> By squirrels, and the old jay laughs.

17. *This was a dead clematis.*

The Sign is a neat little descriptive/narrative poem, with its own built-in humour. Soaked going through a thick wood, the narrator divests himself of the offending garments:

> My clinging coat I hung on a tree-knop
> And sodden shapeless hat I laid on top,
> Then went my way

When he describes the landscape in its 'aftermath of rain' including:

> the close-bunched keys
> Drooping like mistletoe from sycamore trees
> To show black glistening snails that strolled abroad
> Making soft shameless love on the open road

Later, returning, the narrator looks up:

> startled I stood
> To see a dead man hanging in that wood;
> Clear from the ground by two free feet of air
> By hat and coat I marked him swinging there.
> Who was that man? I lifted hasty eye;
> Heaven laughed to me from the blue-rifted sky.

His little self-deprecatory narrative tone would later be developed par excellence in his two 'flower' books, detailing his escapades whilst searching for rare wild flowers, such as the Martagon lily, and would also have amused the eleven-year-old Anthony.

In addition to book publication, Andrew was having some success in magazines, publishing poems in: *The Spectator* (*The Star, Walna Pass*), *The Weekly Westminster* (*The Lane*), *The New Leader* (*The Cuckoo, The Yellowhammers, The Teasels, The Woodcutter*), and *The London Mercury* (*The Track, The Hawk, August*).

He read prolifically, especially old favourites such as Hardy and Dante, Spenser's *The Faerie Queene*, but little fiction, apart from escapist detective stories. It is clear that he took poetic advice from friends such as John Freeman and his wife, Janet – though neither of them ever seemed to mention this fact. Their daughter Alison alludes to it and there are copies of Andrew's poems in Janet's handwriting. *The Bird Cage* seems to have been generally well-received, with the *TLS* describing it as 'a volume of nature poems of unusual distinction'.[18]

At the same time, Andrew's inner life was not so thriving: made 'Moderator of the South Coast Presbytery', he travelled widely, visiting

18. *TLS*, 27 January 1927.

other Presbyterian churches, evangelising, and writing and delivering lengthy sermons. As a result, he was frequently stressed.

Alison wrote over half a century later: 'He was often tired and his pent-up emotions erupted in outbursts of temper, with Janet the immediate victim. . . . Janet would react with tears and abject apologies. The outburst would be followed by a 'cold angry state', during which he sometimes retired to bed.' [19]

As she was only a child of four to five years old at the time, she must have been told this by Janet and/or Anthony later, but also to have experienced it herself, when older.

In early 1927, Andrew had a 'nervous breakdown' or what Janet described to May as 'an attack of brain fag',[20] and Andrew recalled in his autobiography *My Life*:

> in a Sunday morning service I broke down in the middle of a sermon my mind blank. I stood silent for a little time, then gave out the number of the closing hymn. That evening we had a visit from a member of the congregation, Mrs Watney of Watney's Pale Ale, and she presented me with a cheque for £100, suggesting we should go for ten days or so to the south of France; it would give me the rest I needed. I suggested the north of Scotland, and she willingly agreed.

They left the children with a friend, Mrs Baird, and headed north on the night train, going to Perth, Elgin and Braemar. Andrew described the 'attack' in more detail to John Freeman, saying he had been, 'very ill . . . (with) most morbid and depressing thoughts . . . when I came home I told my congregation I should have to take things more easily'.[21]

They must have taken this to heart, as the following year the family were enabled by the parish to move to a larger, more comfortable house, called 'Seamark' in Lloyd Road, where they were to remain for the next ten years.

* * *

When Anthony was twelve, in August 1927, Janet described him to May as 'a great big schoolboy – seven in boots he takes!'

Since Andrew's breakdown, both children getting whooping cough, continuing problems about Harry and money, 'it was a trying time' for Janet.[22]

---

19. Edward Lowbury and Alison Young, *To Shirk No Idleness* (Salzburg: University of Salzburg Press, 1997).
20. Janet to May, August 1927.
21. Undated letter, spring 1927.
22. Letter to May, 13 August 1927.

On their annual visit to see Andrew's father in Edinburgh, 'There would be conversation between Janet, the children and their grandfather, but *hardly any communication – during meals or at other times – between Andrew and his father*; they had almost no interest in common, and half-hearted attempts by the old man to make contact with his son *met with an offhand response*' (my italics).[23]

A similar situation was played out in Hove between Andrew and Anthony. Andrew would often read the paper or play patience at meals, to the irritation of Janet and the consternation of the children. There were scenes between father and son and increasing friction; Alison remarked later, 'in self-defence, Janet said that when she realised she had to decide between her husband and her son, she chose Andrew, because he had no one else but her'.[24]

As an indirect result, it was decided to send Anthony to boarding school and he sat the entrance exam to Mill Hill, being awarded a scholarship for the autumn of 1929, but more money was needed for his other expenses such as uniform and equipment, so, despite his 'distant' relationship with his father, Andrew asked for his help. As usual, where education was concerned, the old man obliged.

In March, Janet's brother Harry was invalided home from Pretoria with depression and anxiety, due to a new post and money worries. As there is a copy of a letter from Harry's wife Kate, to her sister May, in Janet's papers, May presumably sent her a copy, asking her advice, since she (May) had been accused of taking 'strong stands' on matters she knew little about. Janet went instantly into protective elder sister mode, reassuring May, 'I don't think you should worry about what Kate said: I felt very much as you did', yet she can be judgemental too: 'he (Harry) was worrying too much about his silly pension. He ought to have known what he wanted, and made for it, cost what it might to him.'[25]

Understandably, Andrew's state of mind was more of a worry to Janet than Harry's, which was to remain unchanged for several years in various hospitals. When she wrote to him, Janet was careful never to mention money, as that had contributed to his breakdown, joking to May, 'I never believed that a Green would find any way of getting rich quickly!'[26]

Kate wrote directly to Janet in May:

23. Edward Lowbury and Alison Young, *To Shirk No Idleness* (Salzburg: University of Salzburg Press, 1997).
24. Ibid.
25. Janet to May, 11 April 1928.
26. Janet to May, 20 April 1928.

I'm sorry to say the news is pretty much the same: he is . . . more controlled by far, but he has a strong inhibition against facing his work again and that is what the doctors are trying to overcome. He dreads the lab(oratory) and some of the people there; and all our efforts are to overcome the dread . . . (and) get him back to his old post . . . he went to work for a few days and then his worries overcame him again.

Whilst all this was going on, Andrew was back at his post in Hove and Anthony was at school. Andrew must have been writing occasional poems amidst all his other activities, since *The Cuckoo Clock*, a collection of thirty-five poems (dedicated to 'W.W. (Willy) Peploe, True Artist and Best of Friends') came out in 1928. This was the year in which the mature poetry of W.B. Yeats appeared (*Sailing to Byzantium*, *Leda and the Swan*, *Among School Children*, etc.), and the early poetry of W.H. Auden, who was twenty-one that year. His themes, unlike Andrew's, were often to be erotic or political, and it was said of him, by his 1979 editor, Edward Mendelson, that he was 'the first poet writing in English who felt at home in the twentieth century'.[27] But, like Andrew, Auden rejected aspects of 'modernism' and was influenced by Dante and the use of traditional forms of English prosody.

In *The Cuckoo Clock*, there is little of real note or merit, or indeed of development since *The Bird Cage* two years earlier. It bears all the hallmarks of someone *going through the motions* of writing verses for its own sake, almost as an existential exercise: the collection seems fallow, lacking the verve, imagination and poetic drive of two years earlier. This perhaps reflects the combined effects of his mother's death, his own 'breakdown', and ongoing family problems. He seems, at times, to have retreated into the 'safety' of archaic, often religiose language: 'But hark!' (*On the Beaulieu Road*); 'thou', 'O heart', and the three rhymes for 'forest', 'adorest', 'abhorrest' 'scorest' (*Good Friday*); the inversion 'crisp leaves *across it roll*' (*The Hanger*); 'Is it not thus and thus (*The Oak-Wood*).

Having said this, there are still occasional flashes of the poet of two years earlier and the poet to come:

White-cowled oast houses stare
And piled poles in hop gardens seem like hands
Whose fingers join in prayer.
(*Rother in Flood*)

27. Preface to *W.H. Auden Selected Poems*, Faber & Faber, 1979.

> The cuckoo's double note
> Loosened like bubbles from a drowning throat
> (*Cuckoo Bottom*)

> The wood shakes in the breeze
> Lifting its antlered heads
> (*The Old Tree*)

It is an entirely appropriate visual metaphor.
   A scarecrow is described vividly as:

> A sun-greened jacket on a pole
> Guarding the seeds from harm
> Salutes the wind with broken arm.
> (*The Hunger*)

> Pathetic fallacy, as usual, makes an appearance:
> Lighthouses wink,
> One winking slowly with a bloodshot eye
> (*Kilnaughton Bay*)

Perhaps most startlingly:

> cherries hung *like gouts of blood*
> Down the long aisles of whitewashed wood.
> (*The Shower*)

For the first time in Andrew's verse to date, there is a contemporary life
reference:

> All but one pterodactyl
> That hid in mist and rain
> High over Kingley Bottom
> Hums *like an aeroplane.*
> (*Kingley Bottom*)

Audley End, written in rhyming couplets, uses repetition and rhythm to
cumulative effect, each verse ending with:

> It's raining now at Audley End,

Including the last:

> high on the air
> A peacock screams (though none is there);
> It's raining now at Audley End.

It would be three years before another – his seventh – volume appeared, though not all of its forty-one poems would be new, due partly to Andrew's habit of re-vamping old poems, and the rapidity with which they went out of print. He also had far too many generic titles, such as *Autumn, Cuckoo, The Tree, Song* and variations on them, such as *Cuckoo in May* or *Autumn Seeds* and so on, confusing to the reader, and perhaps even to Andrew himself.

* * *

In June and July 1928, Janet was busy planning the move to 'Seamark', telling her sister May, 'The rooms are quite small – but I think if I manage well, they will do. There is a decent-sized garden (for Hove) and . . . we can see the sea. . . . We hope to grow a few vegetables etc. Still no spare bedroom, but that seemed to be too much to hope for.'[28] Janet was clearly a make-do-and-mend housewife, who often worried about money matters, was kept busy by the house, the parish, Andrew and the children.

As usual, they went north in the summer, this time to Oban, via Edinburgh:

> It is extravagant, but Andrew's father is an old man, and very
> good to us – it is sad that he sees so little of his grandchildren,'
> Janet told May, in the same letter, adding, 'you wouldn't know
> Anthony – he is past my shoulder and very strong-limbed. He
> is doing quite well at school – not brilliantly – but . . . finds
> the work quite heavy . . . he is good at English . . . because he
> reads so much.

Janet was always trying to predict her children's futures, saying of the thirteen-year-old Anthony: 'he is not the kind of person ever to make money, I am afraid. He will probably fall into one of the underpaid professions!'

In fact, leaving Mill Hill in 1934, he read Classics at Cambridge, then became a psychologist, perhaps proving his mother partly right.

Their first Christmas at 'Seamark' went off well, with the children receiving many presents, including money gifts from their Aunt May: Anthony was paying for his dog licence for an Aberdeen terrier he adored; Alison, recovering from bronchitis, loved to be read to by Janet or Nora, the new maid. The habit of reading at meals, possibly started by Andrew, but disliked by Janet, was 'the height of bliss' to the children. Apart from concerns about her immediate family, Janet felt a mixture of worry and guilt about her brother Harry, writing to May:

28. Janet to May, 7 June 1928.

> Margaret tells me that Harry arrives[29] on 7 January (1929) – I
> do hope he will improve in a new atmosphere – but I am afraid
> he will not like our winter. . . . I wish I could do something to
> help, but this house is no place for a nerve-racked body – I
> could not give him the peace and comfort he would need.[30]

She does not say so, but trying to provide 'peace and comfort' for Andrew
was probably job enough; especially as, at the beginning of 1929, he had
'a kind of reoccurrence of the trouble he had two years ago –' for which
he was apparently taking Sanatogen tonic wine, before they went away
somewhere at the end of the month. Significantly, Janet added: 'If only
Harry hadn't neglected himself, and had allowed his wife to feed him up
and look after him!'[31] She obviously took Andrew's health personally,
regarding herself as the guardian of it, but it is no clearer what caused
Andrew's depression/'breakdowns' than what had caused her brother
Harry's. She was unable to visit Harry herself, since 'I have to take
Andrew away. He is only over-tired, but that is bad enough. . . . I shrivel
up when I see anyone near me suffering.'

A few days later, it became clear that one of Harry's problems was
chronic, prolonged insomnia:

> What you say of Harry is terrible – I feel I have no right to
> sleep comfortably in my bed when he is suffering so,' she told
> May, on 13 January, adding, 'I have so many things to do and
> to think of that it is chiefly in bed at night and in the evening
> when I am alone, that I have any time for thinking – if one
> could think him in to being well!

Shortly afterwards, a long letter from May telling Janet 'the worst' about
Harry was so bad it had to be burnt (so we have no way of knowing
exactly what was in it), and Janet determined to start praying for a
miracle as 'miracles like that can and do happen – if only one can believe
hard enough'.[32]

Presumably Andrew, at least, recovered enough to carry on his
ministry at Hove after his winter holiday. By June 1929, Janet told May:
'Life has been a turmoil of late: so many things to do, and so little energy
to carry one through . . . our garden is flourishing – plenty to eat in it –
and I shall actually enjoy life here, with just a little more leisure'.[33]

---

29. From Pretoria, where he had been living and working.
30. Letter from Janet to May, 4 January 1929.
31. Letter from Janet to May, 17 January 1929.
32. Letter from Janet to May, 17 January 1929.
33. Letter from Janet to May, 11 June 1929.

* * *

Although there were six Presbyterian Churches in Scotland, which valued the principle of 'religious equality', a Plan of Union was adopted in 1929. Under the 'administrative readjustments', for the first time, 'the ordinand receives the imposition of hands by the Moderator', stressing the apostolic nature of ordination: both ruling elders and teaching elders were eligible to take part in these ordinations. In addition, a distant union with 'the Anglican and Eastern Churches' was seen as desirable.[34] It is not known exactly how Andrew viewed these developments, but, given his long-standing attraction to the Anglican Church, and the earlier influence of Alexander Whyte and his ecumenism, he must have been pleased by the prospect of such a 'distant union' which would also affect the Presbyterian Church in England.

Andrew had a capacity for literary friendships throughout his life. One of these was with the 'Georgian' poet John Freeman, who had known Edward Thomas, and through whom Andrew came to meet other poets. Andrew and Freeman corresponded and met in London or Hove, at intervals. Andrew was in the habit of asking Freeman's advice about his poems, e.g. what should or should not be included in *The Bird Cage* (1926). Freeman had won the Hawthornden Prize in 1920. He died suddenly and prematurely, aged forty-nine, in September 1929, which was a severe shock to Andrew, much as Cecil Simpson's had been in 1918: only this time Andrew was called upon to conduct the funeral. For a man not always sensitive to, or about, others, Andrew seems to have taken male friendships surprisingly seriously, much as Edward Thomas did with Robert Frost. However, it may be argued that Freeman's early demise helped to facilitate Andrew's movement away from his lingering traits of 'Georgianism' during the 1930s.

* * *

As there are no extant letters from Janet to her sisters between mid-1929 and the autumn of 1930, there are few family or domestic details covering this period, but life for the Youngs' must have gone on much as before, with Anthony away at Mill Hill, Alison at the local primary school, and Janet being wife, mother and pastor's wife in the parish. Andrew himself, now recovered, carried on his religious and poetic lives.

In October 1930, Janet finally went to see her brother Harry, still ill with depression in a London hospital. She told May: 'I am going to see Harry tomorrow (Saturday) afternoon – Andrew and I are going up

---

34. James Barr, *The United Free Church of Scotland*, Allenson, 1934.

today with some people (by car) and coming back with them tomorrow. *I shall go alone, of course, to see Harry. . . .* I will let you know what I think when I get back' (my italics).[35]

In Hove, Janet was nearer to Harry than her sisters: Margaret was in Cardiff, Alice in Birmingham and May in Middlesbrough.

Janet reported to May four days later:

> I saw Harry on Saturday afternoon. At first I was shocked to see him so . . . altered. He asked me what I had come for. He thought it was to talk about money. But later, when he spoke of his real troubles, he was tragically reasonable. . . . I think somehow he must be better than he was . . . and he tried so hard to . . . amuse me by tales of the people in the place. . . . I am going to write to Kate (his wife) and tell her . . . that she is retarding his recovery by sharing all her feelings with him. *I never tell my worries to my husband in common consideration. . . .* But . . . remember that what one says to Kate is said to Harry . . . about money . . . an infinite tact will be required [my italics].[36]

Several months later she admitted: 'I am afraid I did not write to Kate after I had seen him: I thought it wiser not – I have however just written for Christmas.'[37] Janet managed to keep her own family's problems away from Andrew, compartmentalising her life effectively.

In 1931, Bumpus published Andrew's eighth volume of poetry (and his sixth in eleven years), by which time both *The Bird Cage* and *The Cuckoo Clock* were out of print. The volume had no dedication and consisted of forty-one poems, but many, such as *Illic Jacet, Restalrig, The Signpost, The Green Woodpecker,* and so on, were not new, but tweaked versions of previous poems.

The Green Woodpecker, is seen as a 'popinjay' and 'that gaudy bird' in an effective eight lines, culminating in the unexpected:

> For earth I love enough
> To crave of her at least an angry word.

Andrew was to become very adept at puns, paradoxes and conceits in the final couplets of his poems. *The Old Flint-Breaker* has an unconscious echo of Wordsworth's *Lyrical Ballads* whereas the four-line *Autumn* introduces an unusually erotic note:

35. Letter from Janet to May, 24 October 1930.
36. Letter from Janet to May, 28 October 1930.
37. Letter from Janet to May, 24 December 1930.

Today I looked and saw the earth undress
With intimate and godlike carelessness.

The Chalk-Quarry, containing, 'A solitary yew' often found in churchyards, leads to an extended metaphor of death:

The strong sun darkening still
That yew's *memento mori*
Fills with a fiercer light out on the hill
The open sepulchre of the old chalk quarry.

In *At Grime's Graves*, Andrew acknowledges the relative 'mortality' of art:

Few poems keep as fresh as flints,
The green-eyed moonlight hints;
Yours will not last as long

A meditative tone is also evident in *At Formby*, a poem more personal than usual with Andrew:

But farther from the beach
The trees rose up beyond my reach,
And as I walked, they still grew taller
And I myself smaller and smaller,
Till gazing up at a high wood
I felt that I had found my lost childhood.

There is a dream-like quality here, focused on the changes of perception, a technique which Andrew was to refine later in the 'dream vision' poems of his poetic maturity.

The Hill-Wood, on the other hand, manages to convey a slightly nightmarish, almost paranoid quality: the walker feels he is being 'laughed at' by some unseen bird or creature, perhaps a:

wind-blown rook
That tosses like a black satanic book?

The landscape is 'bare and ruinous' and the poet admits:

_____ I turn my eye
At every sound . . .
Who is it that I fear . . . ?

Winter Morning has one good image:

the *fog's monochrome*
Painted by Constable, Cotman and Crome,

This was later and less effectively changed to:

> the fog's monochrome
> Painted by Cotman or Old Crome.

Paradox is also in evidence in this poem:

> The winter sun shows a round eye,
> That darkens and still brightens

Although, according to Alison, Andrew admired Eliot's *Ash Wednesday*, published the previous year, after his conversion to Anglo-Catholicism, there is no evidence of any 'experimental' influences on Andrew's own work. No doubt he appreciated its many biblical references and echoes, its many paradoxes ('Conclusion of all that / Is inconclusible') and its awareness of the inseparable nature of doubt and belief – but stylistically Andrew kept to his own path, particularly in terms of verse form, register and imagery. (Andrew's poetry from 1933 to 1947 will be included in the next chapter.)

* * *

On 1 March 1931, Janet wrote to May:

> I could have shouted for joy at the seeming good news of Harry. Of course on sober reflection
>   I realise that it cannot mean all it seems to mean, and yet what a blessed relief so far. . . when my own affairs worried me, the thought of Harry was the last straw.

Harry's mental health seems, for some years, to have been a series of recoveries and relapses, which perhaps accounts for Janet's scepticism, tinged with hope. In July, Harry and Kate spent a long weekend with the Youngs at Hove, which seems to have gone well and led to Janet telling May: 'I think Harry will go ahead now . . . he is really quite cheerful about his prospects, except that he says he is cut off for ever from a *permanent* Government appointment'.[38]

He worked in 'scientific abstracting' of reports on scientific, medical or agricultural matters, and had worked in various laboratories. Money was always a preoccupation, as he told Janet ('Jintie') in a letter dated 20 July 1931:

> On the whole I am beginning to be optimistic about the year 1932 – by this time next year I should be scraping together some sort of income – if only a revenue patched together

---

38. Letter from Janet to May, 3 July 1931.

from several sources – stray 'fees', journalistic cheques, 'ad hoc' grants, and so forth – I don't care much how the jobs are muddled so long as I can total up enough to live on.

Writing four months later,[39] Harry outlined his frenetic professional and family life: his weekend 'reviewing' of scientific papers, 'keeps the little cottage over our heads', and during the week he spent half of it working at Wye Agricultural College and half at Weybridge, barely seeing his wife, who worked in London, or their three sons, Murray, Kenneth and seven-year-old Nigel. His prospects were no more settled than they had been earlier: 'Andrews is pushing for me "whole time" at Weybridge and Wilson, of Wye, is trying to fix me up with a "Research Readership" in London University. But both are contingent on (a) the size of the block grant given in 1932 by the Government (b) *successful suppression of my medical history*' (my italics). And of course Wilson knows nothing of 'Northampton Mental' (Hospital) se London University would cold-shoulder me if it got wind of it (Damn Alice). . . although if I can get my foot well in *first* it might not matter so much if the facts leaked out *afterwards*' (his italics). The 'Damn Alice' comment refers to some indiscreet statement his sister had made about his hospitalisation, but to whom she made it is not clear. However, it *is* clear that his position was very difficult, as presumably was the case for all former mental patients at that time. It also explains more about why his family, especially Janet, were so concerned about him.

Some weeks later, Janet wrote to May: 'I enclose his (Harry's) last letter: it is obvious that he is doing too much, but I think if he could somehow get established and have some little certainty of the future, he would be all right' [40]

She added some thoughts of her own: 'I dread Christmas – there is so much to do, and so little really to show for it. Anthony will be home in a fortnight. Alison is a hefty schoolgirl and . . . has been remarkably well this term'.

* * *

During the 1930s, as well as writing two volumes of poetry and bringing out his first *Collected Poems* in 1936 (see Chapter 5), Andrew became increasingly interested in verse plays, including Gordon Bottomley's. It was an era which produced verse plays by John Masefield, Christopher

---

39. Letter from Harry Green to Janet Young, 1 November 1931.
40. Letter from Janet to May, 11 December 1931.

Fry and T.S. Eliot, which were actually encouraged by the Anglican hierarchy, especially Bishop Bell of Chichester, whom Andrew was shortly to meet.

Before this, however, there were several family crises. Alison described one of them as: 'the sudden discovery that Anthony, who had reached the age for confirmation, did not accept the Christian faith. After some painful discussion Anthony agreed, for his parents' sake, to be confirmed'. [41] There was obviously both genuine shock and dismay at this turn of events, but also, for a clergyman, the likelihood of deep embarrassment if it became known in the parish. It also marked a depth of division between father and son, which had been brewing for some years.

The second crisis, probably related to the first, was the recurrence of Andrew's depression: he was moody, and often withdrawn, at the best of times, but his outbursts became stronger and more frequent at this time, and, as usual, Janet bore the brunt of them: 'The gentle Janet suffered from these outbursts, from the deflection of his anger on to her, and from the failure of her repeated attempts to comfort him'. [42]

Andrew was also having some religious discontents, which he may have tried to assuage by writing a play for performance in a church/ cathedral. His earlier verse plays had not been written for performance as such, but rather to be read. He thought *Murder in the Cathedral* (1935) 'wonderful', but doubted that he had any 'dramatic instinct' himself. Nevertheless, he began work on *Nicodemus* in 1935-36, later inviting Imogen Holst (daughter of Gustav), then a music teacher at Roedean, to write the music for it.

Bishop George Bell (1883-1958), had got to know Andrew Young through Canon Colin Dunlop at St Thomas', Hove, then at Henfield. As a result of the 1920 Lambeth Conference, there were joint conferences between the Church of England and the Free Churches. Bell had been assistant secretary to this Conference and was a champion of Christian unity. He had set up diocesan religious drama when Dean of Canterbury, then later was Diocesan Director of Religious Drama. When Bishop of Chichester, in 1929, he set up Chichester Diocesan Players/The Pilgrim Players under the directorship of Martin Browne, and the Religious Drama Association (Diocese of Chichester) run by Miss Wyn Bruce Williams.

Bell told Browne that he liked *Nicodemus* and that Andrew Young was 'a true poet', when first asking him to read and consider it for production. Browne's response was positive: 'The verse is alive and the people are real characters, and it is all quite workable theatrically', as it proved.

---

41. Edward Lowbury and Alison Young, *To Shirk No Idleness* (Salzburg: University of Salzburg Press, 1997).
42. As 41.

Bell could be very persuasive and persistent, as when he asked T.S. Eliot to write a pageant play for Liverpool Cathedral, which the poet promptly declined, explaining that he had neither interest nor ability in pageant plays, and that he could not afford to take a year out from his own work as he felt that he had already wasted too much time. He then half-apologetically ended that he was aware that without Bell's support, he would not have written *The Rock* and *Murder in the Cathedral*.[43]

Bell clearly saw religious drama as a way of forwarding both original work and the Christian message.

Nicodemus: A Mystery was performed, after some revisions, in St Andrew's Church, Cheam, in the Easter of 1937, and was published by Cape that autumn. In some ways it is a new departure for Andrew: exploring the themes of guilt, betrayal and redemption; faith and doubt; cowardice and courage; sight and insight: The Blind Man regains his sight; Nicodemus, battling with all the major themes, gains ultimate insight. The council meeting of the Sanhedrin, with the Clerk reading the minutes, apologies for absence, and so on, is a humorous echo of *all* committees and parish meetings of the kind Andrew must frequently have sat through, or chaired. The language is therefore, for the most part, plain, everyday and non-poetic (unlike e.g. Eliot's *Murder in the Cathedral*); the hymns, sung by the angels, contain, by contrast, their usual archaic language. A deliberate use of anachronisms ('Constables') is effective and amusing. The whole is held together by the older John (The Beloved) penning his Gospel, with a 'flashback' to 50 years earlier, outside the tomb on the third day, with the Angel leading him there. The 'revelation' shown to John is that Nicodemus and the Blind Man arrived at the tomb *before* Mary, or the other disciples and witnessed the actual moment of Resurrection.

In Andrew's usual vein, paradox and irony come in to their own in so many places in the play:

'My silence was the witness that condemned you'. (Nicodemus)
'My weakness is my strength, my slowness speed'. (John)
'I must be blind again to see my way'. (Blind Man)
'Blasphemy as he blasphemes God.' (Annas)

It was to be Andrew's first and last performed play and showed his flexibility as a writer and thinker. It also helped to facilitate his friendship with George Bell, Bishop of Chichester; which in turn brought to a head a simmering religious conflict and its resolution.

---

43. All from the Bell archive, at Lambeth Palace Library.

CHAPTER 5
NEW DIRECTIONS
(1938-1959)

Comparing himself to John Clare, one of his favourite poets, who, 'preferred the Religion of the Fields to that of the Church,' Andrew said: 'I am thankful for a religion which is much deeper than the Religion of the Fields.'[1] In his own way, he was certainly devoted to the latter, being both a naturalist and a pantheist; but his two *passions* seem to have been religion and poetry, which for him must have combined in the Bible itself, of which he had an encyclopaedic knowledge.

In the early 1930s, a rare statement of his *poetic*, rather than religious 'Creed' is to be found in a letter to his friend Thomas Sturge Moore:

> *Words* (with their colour, rhythm, associated ideas and emotional content) are the real medium of the poet, as paint and sound are for the artist and the musician. A story or scene is only an occasion for a poem, almost an excuse; like a jumping-off board it can be left behind. . . . I think the *description* of a scene . . . can have a poetic value in two ways. It may satisfy our love of economy . . . (and) . . . our love of unity. As the scientist delights to combine two phenomena in a law, so the poet delights to combine two objects in an image.

The key words here seem to be *economy* and *unity*, along with the metaphysical concept of the *conceit*: all of which were to grace his mature poetry. More flippantly, he remarked nearly forty years later: 'I looked for poems as I looked for plants; I thought of a poem as written in the air; I had only to copy it down.'[2]

By the time Andrew's eighth volume of poetry *Winter Harvest* was published in 1933, by the Nonesuch Press, his first major publisher, he was calling himself 'Andrew' not 'A.J.' Young as before, and saw this as such a new departure from his past poetry, that he regarded

---

1. *My Life,* Chapter 3, Unpublished.
2. Ibid.

it as his *first* real book, trying hard to disown his earlier volumes. Of the forty-five poems in it, at least fifty per cent had appeared in earlier volumes, including: *The Green Woodpecker, The Spider, Illic Jacet, The Yellowhammers, The Pines, The Rat,* and so on. One, previously *Autumn* was renamed *Penelope* with a new verse added:

> A sad Telemachus
> I stand under the boughs;
> Patient Penelope,
> Her heart across the sea,
> Another year unweaves
> Her web of wasted leaves.

In *Burnt Leaves* there is another reference to 'O blue-eyed one,' (his mother) echoing *The Flood* of five years earlier:

> I thought of you, O blue-eyed one,
> Or thought about my thoughts of you . . .
> So I would think of you a little, yet
> So soon forget.

It is unclear whether this is a mature growing away from the mother-son bond, or a self-rebuke.

The Evening Star contains a mixture of conventional and startling imagery. It begins:

> I saw a star shine in bare trees
> That stood in their dark effigies

But it ends:

> For still I looked on that same star,
> That fitful, fiery Lucifer,
> Watching with mind as quiet as moss
> Its light nailed to a burning cross.

'Foul mortality' is a recurring theme seen in *The Farmer's Gun*, where 'The wood is full of rooks,' but they are all dead:

> How *ugly* is this work of man,
> Seen in the *bald* brain-pan,
> *Voracious* bill,
> *Torn* wing, *uprooted* quill
> And host of tiny glistening flies
> That lend false lustre to these *empty* eyes [my italics].

The phrasing is exact; the adjectives selected to suggest the poet's disgust at the inhumanity of man to wildlife; the tone, indignant. In *The Men*, the poet describes himself listening to a finch cracking a seed in a wood, and blue tits swinging on old-man's-beard when, suddenly, men and dogs came, 'crashing through the wood,' disturbing its peace: the poet knows, 'it meant small good' to '*us* who *owned* that wood' (my italics), including 'Badger, stoat, rabbit, rook and jay,' and like them, he says, 'I too crept off like any stealthy beast.' Clearly the poet identifies himself with the potentially hunted, not with the hunters; and Andrew, both as poet and naturalist, seems always to empathise with flora, fauna and miscellaneous creatures, but without sentimentalising them.

Reviewed in *The Observer* in December 1933, Humbert Wolfe commented: 'Mr Andrew Young is a . . . new nature poet . . . the last in our great line and the freshest.' Such reviews, though positive and initially pleasing, led to Andrew's being 'pigeon-holed' in a way which was also distorting. Andrew himself realised that some of his previous poems that he would like to have included in *Winter Harvest* needed 'radical revision' and 'seemed all right when I wrote them, but they were badly expressed and even unintelligible.'[3]

Andrew was a constant self-critic and reviser, and like certain painters, he went through definite 'periods' in his work; and although he was not too fond of Auden and his contemporaries in the 1930s, he was also outgrowing the Georgians. The Lowburys even suggested that this collection may have been intended 'as a sort of "thumbs down" to Drinkwater, whose collection *Summer Harvest* had appeared in the same year.'[4]

The White Blackbird was published (unusually, without any dedication) by Cape in 1935. As usual, of the forty-four poems, a number were recycled from previous collections, such as *Sea Wormwood, The Sunbeams, The Truck, The Cuckoo, To the River, Dove, The Loddon, Ploughing in Mist, The Fallen Tree*, amongst others. Some, such as *The Wood*, were later retitled (*The Dark Wood*). Amongst the new poems are some of Andrew's most outstanding and characteristic 'nature' poems: *The Swans* is a ten-line mini-masterpiece, concluding with a nice distinction, or paradox:

> How lovely are these swans,
> That float like high proud galleons
> Cool in the summer heat,
> And waving leaf-like feet

---

3. Part of a letter to Maurice Wellman, quoted by Lowbury and Young in Chapter 9 of *To Shirk No Idleness*, 1997.
4. Edward Lowbury and Alison Young, *To Shirk No Idleness* (Salzburg: University of Salzburg Press, 1997).

Divide with narrow breasts of snow
In a smooth surge
This water that is mostly sky;
So lovely that I know
Death cannot *kill* such birds,
It could but *wound them, mortally* [my italics].

The verse form of AABB CDECDE, along with the similes in lines two and four, and the repetition of 'lovely', add a certain simplicity to a poem both strongly visual, yet philosophic.

The Dead Crab, on a similar theme, is a sonnet in rhyming couplets, an unusual combination, suggesting a mixture of levity and seriousness: Andrew points out the combination of strength and weakness:

Beneath, the well-knit cote-armure
That gave to its weak belly power

Like *The Swans* it is visually descriptive:

The *clustered* legs with *plated* joints
That ended in *stiletto* points

This employs a masterly use of adjectives, with, once again, a paradoxical final couplet in the form of a wide-ranging, symbolic, rhetorical question:

Or does it make for death to be
Oneself a living armoury?

The albino *White Blackbird* of the title, a mere six lines, depicts the outsider or outcast, in a symbolic reversal:

You who are white as sin
To your black kith and kin.

The Eagle seems to echo Tennyson's poem of the same title in verse one but ends with a powerful Christian symbol in the second verse:

He hangs between his wings outspread
Level and still
And bends a narrow golden head
Scanning the ground to kill.

Yet as he sails and smoothly swings
Round the hillside,
He looks as though from his own wings
He hung down crucified.

The final word transforms the whole poem, giving it an unexpected dimension; a linking of strength and vulnerability reminiscent of Hopkins' *The Windhover*.

Gossip is an amusing piece of extended personification in which the poet-observer-eavesdropper 'hears':

> The wind shaking the gate
> Impatiently as though in haste and late
> Shook and shook it making it rattle,
> And all the other tittle-tattle
> It rushed to tell

of gamekeepers, chestnuts and pheasants, whilst, 'the flapping scarecrow stood' and, 'saluted with a broken arm'. The poet then:

> proudly thought
> That I, a man, whom most things hate,
> Shared country gossip with the wind and gate.

In *Mole Hills on the Downs* the poet plays with changing perspectives, where:

> every hill is overgrown
> With small hills of its own . . .
> where I can watch the earth
> Like a volcano at its birth
> *Still rise by falling down* . . .
> I swell with pride,
> Till the great hills to which I lift my eyes
> Restore my size.

The penultimate line echoes the psalmist and the italicised line is a typical Andrew paradox. Like Wordsworth, Andrew was interested in 'man in his circumambient universe', where, he tells us in *Wood and Hill*, 'Nowhere is one alone', but always in the 'small eye of bird or beast', whether squirrel, hare or lark, which makes 'of wood and hill a market square'. So many of these poems are meditations on mortality, and even in a poem which begins:

> Is this a lover's vow?
> Who else should tie it and for what,
> This olive-coloured sapling in a knot

death is never very far away:

But death itself can not untwist
This piteous tree-contortionist.
(*The Knotted Ash*)

This poem contains one of Andrew's most impressive uses of assonance
to date:

spring's sap must stoop
And bend back in a gouty loop
Rising from root to sooty-budded bough

Here the word 'contortionist' is as well chosen as 'ventriloquist' or
'popinjay' was in previous poems.

In *The Fear*, Andrew evokes almost archetypal anxieties, culminating
in a sense of awe, yet alienation:

How often I turn round
To face the beast that bound by bound
Leaps on me from behind,
Only to see a bough that heaves
With sudden gust of wind
Or blackbird raking withered leaves.

A dog may find me out
Or badger toss a white-lined snout;
And one day as I softly trod
Looking for nothing stranger than
A fox or stoat I met a man
And even that seemed not too odd.

And yet in any place I go
I watch and listen as all creatures do
For what I cannot see or hear,
For something warns me everywhere
That even in my land of birth
I trespass on the earth.

It is worth looking in detail at one example of Andrew's ongoing revision
and improvement process. The poem which began life as *In the Spinney*
in 1931 was transformed into *The Secret Wood* in 1935:

When I had stopped to mark
How scrub in winter sheds its bark
And how the privet's eyes of jet
With laughter in the sun were wet,

A hand touched me behind,
I turned and lo! A bough swung on the wind.

Why is it that I stand?
Half hoping that it was a hand
That struck the gentle blow?
One thing at least I know,
Beauty on earth I do not seek
More than I sought it on my mother's cheek.
(1931)

The middle of the first verse seems both graphic and amusing; yet verse two appears divided between a potentially erotic or aesthetic experience, until the reference to his mother seems to confuse the issue. Compared to the second version, this one lacks depth or resonance, and fails to clarify its purpose. Version two, with only an extra four lines, manages to say so much more:

Where there is nothing more to see
Than this old earthbound tree
That years ago dry sawdust bled
But sprouts each spring a leaf or two
As though it tried not to be dead,
Or that down-hanging broken bough
That keeps its withered leaves till now,
Like a dead man that cannot move
Or take his own clothes off,
What is it that I seek or who?
Fearing from passer-by
Intrusion of a foot or eye?
I only know
Though all men of earth's beauty speak
Beauty here I do not seek
More than I sought it on my mother's cheek.
(1935)

The imagery here is consistent and strong: 'earthbound tree', 'down-hanging broken bough', 'withered leaves', culminating in 'dead man', as though the poet himself is uncertain whether he is alive or dead, emotionally and aesthetically. 'Bled' at the end of line three is masterly. The simile of the 'dead man' who cannot remove his clothes, who asks, 'What is it that I seek or who' echoes Lear in his madness, asking, 'Who is it that can tell me who I am?' Keats' 'truth and beauty' mantra is subtly suggested too. The final mother image links perhaps to unattainable 'beauty', since she is both pure and dead. Two lines are also very revealing of Andrew's, at times, reclusive nature, even when out walking:

> Fearing from passer-by
> Intrusion of a foot or eye?

It was recorded by some who knew him that he would look down or away when meeting people outside, on roads or in woods, in order to avoid having to talk to them. *The Secret Wood* is, in a sense, part of Andrew's private world, with a private symbolism.

In this collection, more than any other to date, Andrew seems to be a poet who has *arrived*: come into his own, at last, with an assured idiolect which can only go from strength to strength.

His first *Collected Poems* appeared in 1936, published by Cape, and consisted of the complete reprints of *Winter Harvest* (1933), *The White Blackbird* (1935) and a section called *New Poems*, numbering seventeen, of which, as usual, most were either reprints or reworkings of previously published poems. Only eight were actually new and none of those particularly distinguished.

Geoffrey Grigson wrote a very mixed review of it in the *Morning Post* on 3 July 1936:

> Who knows Mr Young's name? Probably a small circle still, and yet he has been writing for years – writing poems, one would think, that many readers would be glad to know. Maybe a small poet, introspective, tragic. Mr Young sees in the natural world images for his grief. He is a 'nature poet'. He has not seen things witlessly, for their own sake, but significantly, purely and interestingly, to a degree that raises him far above the anthology class. . . . And he is a poet of humility.

Yet this *Collected Poems* rather mysteriously tries to conceal from readers just how good Mr Young's very best has been. *Collected Poems* it simply is not. It is *Selected Poems* and badly selected.

Grigson was one of Andrew's more perceptive reviewers over many years, although a number of his comments seem rather wide of the mark, especially the adjectives *small* and *tragic* in this particular review. However, his final comment is spot-on.

* * *

It appears that, after due consideration, Andrew wrote to Bishop George Bell to discuss the possibility of becoming an Anglican. He must, of course, have also discussed this with Janet, but there is no record of what was said. She presumably did not mind changing her own religious allegiance.

Andrew had tea with Bell at the Bishop's Palace and gave his old friend (by then, Professor) John Baillie as a reference. Baillie wrote, on 29 May 1939:

> My dear Bishop,
>
> It is very easy for me to write to you about Andrew Young, as I have known and admired him ever since student days. When at college I was privileged to be admitted into the friendship of a very remarkable group of young men, most of whom (or those of them who were not killed in the War), have now attained real eminence in different fields. Among these was nobody more influential or more respected than Andrew Young. His knowledge and understanding of French and English literature, and the fine arts, was then remarkable, and his judgment already very mature. I should say that what impressed us above all was the delicately intuitive quality of his mind.
>
> Ever since, I have been in more or less continuous touch with him, and have never ceased to learn from him. (During the War he came out to France at my invitation, and was my colleague in the work I was doing, for some six or eight months). . . He has proved himself a most faithful and conscientious pastor, well-liked by his people. . . . They have known that his habit of mind and life has always been deeply pious. . . .
>
> I am sure that Young is a most suitable candidate for ordination to the Ministry of your Church. Nor have I observed any serious defects in him, such as might offset his many fine qualities of mind and heart.

Andrew was told that before ordination he would have to attend a theological college for two years, presumably in order to digest some Anglican history, theology and church practices. Wells Theological College was suggested and Andrew readily agreed. Rooms were found in the nearby Vicars' Close, generously, and perhaps, ironically, paid for by his elderly father, now fully reconciled to Andrew's 'conversion', since his daughter Margaret had both married an Anglican and become one herself. Also, he had mellowed with age and Alexander Whyte's ecumenism had spread and become more acceptable.

For Andrew, this represented both a new direction and the fulfilment of a long-cherished desire: it was a more mainstream position and a more sacramental, ritualised worship, to which he had been secretly drawn since his days at New College. He may also have wanted a quieter life in a smaller, country parish, in order to have more time for writing.

Several versions of Andrew's departure from Hove Presbyterian Church emerge: one was that he simply told the parish he was going on a fortnight's holiday, then never returned; the other, that he resigned on health grounds, borne out by a reference in the *Brighton and Hove Herald* of 31 December 1938, that Andrew Young was 'retiring to take a complete rest for the sake of his health'. Either way, it was less than honest and shows a lack of moral courage in a minister of either church: it was the second 'skeleton' in the Young cupboard. Amongst the 'parting gifts' recorded by the *Herald* were 'a pair of handsome easy chairs, a third edition of Sowerby's *English Botany* and a cheque for a substantial amount'.

By the time the Youngs moved to Wells, Anthony was at Cambridge studying psychology and Alison was left with friends in Hove to finish her last two terms at school in Brighton. As Andrew commented later: 'Though I was a member of the theological college, I did not, of course, attend any lectures'. It appears that he was only required to read and study on his own, then give a written account of himself to Bishop Bell, although Alison maintains that he 'attended some lectures'.[5]

The bishop was keen to look after his protégé and enlisted the help of Canon Salmond, at the theological college, on 13 January 1939:

> My dear Canon,
>
> May I commend to your kindly interest the Reverend Andrew Young, Seamark, Lloyd Road, Hove? He is a Presbyterian minister whom I have accepted for ordination in this diocese. He is about fifty and is a delightful and scholarly man, who for nineteen years has been a Presbyterian minister in Hove. He is a poet of some distinction . . . a great friend of John Baillie of Edinburgh, and has many other friends, literary and theological. But he now seeks a home in the Church of England. It is his wish to steep himself in the atmosphere of the Church of England, and for this purpose he wishes to live in a cathedral city, and with my approval he has chosen Wells.
>
> His idea is . . . that he should . . . read on his own and attend the cathedral services and get the atmosphere of the Church

---

5.   Edward Lowbury and Alison Young, *To Shirk No Idleness* (Salzburg: University of Salzburg Press, 1997), Chapter 11.

of England . . . as well as reading and browsing and thinking. He would like from time to time to talk to a wise priest about religion and the Church of England. . . . I suggested that he might report himself to you when he goes.

Any kindness you would show to him would be very much appreciated, but at the same time I don't want in any way to presume, nor does he . . .

> Yours ever,
> George Cicester.

Within eighteen months, Andrew was ordained a deacon in Chichester Cathedral on Trinity Sunday 1939, then appointed to a curacy at a church in the village of Plaistow, in Sussex. Before this, however, Andrew was asked by Bishop Bell to write a letter, in answer to two questions (instead of a formal exam paper):

1. 'Why is the cross central to the Christian faith and its special significance today?'
2. 'Why do you wish to be ordained in the Church of England?'

It is worth quoting his answer in full, since it shows the development of his attitudes to ritual, episcopacy, church history, and the theology of the sacraments:

My dear Lord Bishop,

In trying to reply to your two questions, perhaps I may be allowed to deal with the second question first, as it leads naturally to the first.

The second question is, 'What are the special characteristics that you value in the Church of England?'
I was brought up (in Scotland) to believe that the English Reformation amounted to a compromise and the Church of England was a half-way house. My reading has shown me that the former was, as was intended, a correction of certain abuses and Roman assumptions, and that the latter was and is in historical continuity with the Apostolic Church. Such historical continuity is of great importance in a number of things, for example a Royal House or a tradition of art, but becomes of supreme importance in a Church, if one believes that that Church is the Body of Christ or, more simply, that it is guided and protected by the Providence of God. As to the means or method of this continuity, the Episcopate is so primitive and universal that one can safely believe that, apart

from anything else, it is the way that God happened to choose. A consideration that weighs much with me is this: we are taught to pray for a union of Christians and it must therefore be a possible ideal, but one cannot seriously contemplate it as possible except on the basis of the Episcopate.

Then again I was brought up to suppose that the freer worship is from ritual the more spiritual it is. This idea leads to bareness and crudity in worship, and its effect is also to concentrate attention on the 'officiating minister.' As a Congregationalist minister said to me once, 'The Free Churches have abolished all the arts except the art of elocution.' But I think this idea corresponds neither to the religion which our Lord Himself practised nor, still less, to the religion which has the Incarnation as its central doctrine. Human nature asks for certain helps. For example, while I always believed that God forgives our sins, I have found it a help to hear the Priest in the name and with the authority of the Catholic Church say so, in the words of the Absolution.

But what appeals to me most is the Holy Communion, which is more comprehensive and richer than what I have been accustomed to. The Offertory reminds us of God our Creator and Preserver, and is a kind of Harvest Thanksgiving, and is a suitable opportunity and symbol of our surrender to God. In regard to the nature of the Elements I had long held that they were the Body of our Lord in the sense that they were the medium through which He imparted to us His life-giving Spirit. I held this view on a metaphorical interpretation of the words, 'This is my body.' Now I take these words in a literal sense, believing that they are the Flesh and Blood of His glorified Body by which He imparts to us His own Life. Further, I see in this Sacrament a commemorative Sacrifice, commemorative of the one self-sufficient Sacrifice of the Cross.

Let me now try to answer your first question, 'Why is the Cross central to the Christian Faith, and what is its special significance today?'

'Salvation is like a mountain which can be sketched from many points of view' (H.R. Mackintosh). I shall look at it from only two.

It would seem very strange that God should not seek to communicate Himself to us. I believe He does do so, in a number of ways. Through Nature, which suggests Mind, and therefore Personality, but a Personality compared with which ours are scarcely personalities at all. Through Love, which being the highest quality we know must be an attribute of God Himself, unless we are morally His superiors. And so on. But considering the kind of world we live in and the kind of people we are, all these ways seem incomplete and insufficient. It could only be through the highest thing we know, personality. (I omit the steps that lead from this to the Doctrine of the Incarnation of God in Christ).

'He that hath seen me hath seen the Father.' These words must apply, surely, to the culminating point of our Lord's life, the Crucifixion. It is in the Crucified Son that we see the Father who suffers and waits for His prodigal children, who shows us all His love, and, our sight illuminated by the Holy Spirit, we believe in and commit ourselves to His mercy, His desire for us and His power and grace to forgive.

But another view is from our deep and instinctive need of atonement. I have sinned against God and I feel that something has to be done and there is nothing I can do. And because there is nowhere else I can look, I look to the Cross and believe that what had to be done God himself has done, in an Atoning Sacrifice for my sin.

I am not very concerned with theories of the Atonement, explanations of so great and divine a Mystery; I only believe and feel that there, on the Cross, God has Himself answered my greatest need.

I hope this is a partial answer to the question, 'Why is the Cross central to the Christian Faith?' I am not clear what is being asked in the question, 'What is its special significance today?' – for we are no better than our fathers. Perhaps it is that I should try to show that as only in the Cross God and men are reconciled, so only in the spirit of the Cross can nations be reconciled. But somehow I do not think you want me to do that.

I am afraid this letter will seem inadequate, but I wrote it immediately on receipt of your letter, as I understood that it needed haste.

I am, my Lord,
Yours obediently,
Andrew Young.
(22nd May, 1939)

The Youngs were to remain at Plaistow for two years, living in a small bungalow. In August 1939, Andrew was finally ordained a priest in the nearby parish of Kirkford. Earlier that same year, on 25 March, Andrew's father had died in Edinburgh, aged 94. Though not heartbroken, Andrew was sorry – perhaps sorry that he had not made more effort to get on with him latterly; perhaps sorry about the end of the old man's generosity.

Speak to the Earth, a collection of forty-three poems (published by Jonathan Cape in 1939) was Andrew's first 'post-Anglican conversion' volume, and he thought it his best to date. His close friend Christopher Hassall agreed with him. As usual, a number of the poems are reprints, notably: *A Dead Mole, The Gramophone, The Archaeologist, The House Martins, Climbing in Glencoe, The Cuillin Hills, Long Mab and her Daughters, Christmas Day*; whilst others are adaptations, such as *A Wet Day*, using the same ideas and imagery of the abandoned hat and coat swinging in the trees like a dead man in *The Sign* (1926), but not as accomplished. *Overtaken by Mist* contains a Miltonic oxymoron, 'bright darkness', presumably an unconscious echo of 'not light but darkness visible'.

Some of Andrew's imagery, as usual, can be startlingly apt and original:

The scarlet hips hung on the briar
Like coffins of the dead dog-rose
(*Autumn Mist*)

The darkness like a guillotine
Descends on the flat earth
(*Nightfall on Sedgemoor*)

It was the time of year
Pale lambs leap with thick leggings on
(*A Prehistoric Camp*)

At first the river Noe
Like a snake's belly gleamed below,
And then in mist was lost
(*Walking in Mist*)

From their long narrow beds
Asparagus raise reptilian heads . . .
And men who think that they are snakes
With shining knives
Walk to and fro, taking their scaly lives.
(*Fields of Asparagus*)

In *The Flesh-Scraper*, Andrew stresses human continuity and ingenuity:

> If I had sight enough
> Might I not find a fingerprint
> Left on this flint
> By Neolithic man or Kelt?
> So knapped to scrape a wild beast's pelt,
> The thumb below, fingers above,
> See, my hand fits it like a glove.

One almost feels there should be an exclamation mark after the last word.
  After the Gale begins with a humorous opening:

> I pity trees that all their life
> Have ivy for a wife

then develops into an extended metaphor, half-wondering, half-critical
of nature's promiscuity:

> So seeing oak twigs grow on thorn
> Where they were never born,
> And sprays of ash keys and pine cones
> Grow on a briar at once,
>
> I blamed the gale that through the night
> Had with perverse delight
> Quartered rich children on the poor
> Like foundlings at their door.

The Thunderstorm also has an uncharacteristically humorous beginning:

> When Coniston Old Man was younger
> And his deep-quarried sides were stronger,
> Goats may have leapt about Goat's Water

And has a visual simile ending:

> So quick the lightning came and went,
> The solid rock was like a lighted tent.

Passing the Graveyard, Walking on the Cliff and *A Prospect of Death* all contain
references to or aspects of mortality: one of Andrew's more constant themes.
  Passing the Graveyard uses a variation on the villanelle – only six three-
line verses, rhyming AAA, not the usual pattern. It is, however, a new
departure for Andrew. It is addressed *to* the dead person ('your grave'),
describing death as 'that most bitter abrupt brink'. This is followed by

some general observations on the idea that we change 'every seventh year' as though 'the bodies that we wear . . . in a new dress . . . appear'. The conceit is a neat one. The 'spongy brain and slogging heart' of age are less flattering, so that the poet is not surprised that the subject, presumably female, 'flung off the whole flesh at last'. Yet the final verse ends with a more poignantly romantic image:

> Let him who loves you think instead
> That like a woman who has wed
> You undressed first and went to bed.

Walking on the Cliff describes a near-miss with death as the poet, intently birdwatching, was, 'near. . . to stepping over / The brink' of the Birling Gap, but was saved by seeing that a gull 'dropped to soar beneath'. This gives the poet reassurance that he can now safely 'walk the cliff edge arm in arm with Death'.

A Prospect of Death is a much more serious and personal poem, clearly though not explicitly addressed to Janet:

> If it should come to this,
> You cannot wake me with a kiss,
> Think I but sleep too late
> Or once again keep *a cold angry state* [my italics].

Janet was the main recipient, or victim, of his 'cold angry state', yet the last verse seems to both acknowledge his faults and beg forgiveness:

> So do not dream of danger;
> Forgive my lateness or my anger;
> You have so much forgiven,
> Forgive me this or that, or Hell or Heaven.

Perhaps both of these states were present in their relationship?
Idleness starts almost like a child's prayer:

> God, you've so much to do,
> To think of, watch and listen to,
> That I will let all else go by
> And lending ear and eye
> Help you

Pathetic fallacy and paradox abound:

> rooks . . .
> Restore their villages,
> Nest by dark nest . . .

> hear that owl snore in a tree
> Till it grows dark enough for him to see

The poet then promises God that he:

> will learn to shirk
> No idleness that I may share your work.

Like all of Andrew's collections to date, it contains some gems, some new, some old; yet few as good as *The Swans, The Ventriloquists, The Dead Crab* and *A Dead Mole* from previous volumes. However, his imagery, phrasing and verse forms are often much tighter, and his poetic hallmarks of paradox, pathetic fallacy, irony and juxtaposition are well developed.

In September 1941, two years into his second world war, Andrew was inducted into the living of St Peter's, Stonegate, East Sussex, where he was to remain until his retirement in 1959 and where, arguably, he was to write his best poetry; and all his major prose. For the first time, Janet was to have a large vicarage, with six bedrooms and enough space for everybody and for visitors, next door to the church. She must have been delighted.

Andrew soon set about planting the large garden with vegetables: carrots, celery, beetroot, radish and cabbage, amongst other things. Utilitarian, Andrew remarked later: 'For a flower garden I may have an admiration, but no affection.'[6] This was not just wartime necessity speaking; Andrew's preference was always for wild rather than cultivated flowers. In addition to vegetable growing, the Youngs kept chickens and geese, as they had during World War I.

Just as T.S. Eliot sat in London during the Second World War writing humorous poems about cats (later published as *Old Possum's Book of Practical Cats*), so Andrew walked around Sussex making notes for his two deservedly famous flower books (see Chapter 9).

Shortly before Andrew's arrival at Stonegate, Bishop Bell, always keen to foster and maintain good ecumenical relations, arranged for a joint Anglican/Presbyterian meeting to be held in Hove Presbyterian Church Hall. Andrew glosses over the truth later when he remarks: 'Its purpose was to promote friendly feeling between the two parties; perhaps my conversion had suggested it.'[7] In fact, it was more of a 'peace and reconciliation' exercise, following the abrupt manner of Andrew's departure. Bishop Bell asked Andrew to speak and he had to agree but 'found it so difficult to know what to say'.[8] He was honest enough to

6. *My Life*, unpublished, Chapter 5.
7. Ibid.
8. Ibid.

admit though, that afterwards, when they were all supposed to 'mingle together' socially, the leader of his old Hove church choir gave him the 'cold shoulder' and that 'no one gave me a very warm welcome back to my old church'. They were not in a forgiving mood, perhaps understandably, despite Bishop Bell's intervention.

At Stonegate, 'As an Anglican I had more ritual and shorter sermons than I had before, and so more time to read'.[9] Andrew remarked later. It also gave him a lot of time for walking, ostensibly to visit outlying parishioners, such as the Clouts in Batswood, or Newbridge Wood across Witherington.

Jack and Mary Pennells, at Station House, Stonegate, remembered that he 'never made conversation on his visits' but would take tea, sherry or whisky. They thought his sermons 'over the head of ordinary people' and that he was known in the village for his love of sport and wild flowers, not for poetry. He had no small talk, or knowledge of current affairs, saying, 'I don't read newspapers.'

Johnny Brammall, of Cottenden Farm, remembered Andrew as 'a shy man, keen on athletics, cricket and wild flowers'. If he spoke, it was often about his holidays in Scotland. He was able to visit all sorts of people, and because 'the class structure was very strong in the village then, e.g. it was *tea* with the working class and *dinner* with the middle class, he was probably the only one who could'.

Mick Reid, at Maplesden, remembered Andrew visiting impromptu, then standing with his back to the fire, rocking gently whilst smoking a cigarette, then saying, 'Well, goodbye,' and off he'd go.

On one occasion, a lady he visited after a lengthy walk was so embarrassed by his silence that she offered him a book, which he proceeded to read before leaving some time later. On another occasion, Andrew went to see Miss Nelly Piper, who lived near Alan Atkins' village store, and was housebound with arthritis. They both sat so quietly that Andrew went to sleep and she had to wait until he woke up!

Janet was remembered by Mrs James as being 'tall and thin' and running the Women's Institute and Mothers' Union. 'She came to matins and sat at one end of a pew, behind a pillar.' Mrs Richards, the vicarage cleaner, told Mrs James that Janet had to 'wait on him (i.e. Andrew) hand and foot, and get the coal in, and no one was allowed to hoover while he was in the house!'

Mrs Johnson remembered that Andrew made 'teatime visits, ten minutes only, with a walking stick which he kept tapping when talking'.

---

9. Ibid.

Many remembered that he liked a drop of whisky and was less shy afterwards. Dr Dick Mowll, secretary of the PCC, went with Andrew to a Diocesan Conference at Brighton and remembered that he made sandwiches and would hand them out one by one. He always found it difficult to make a conversation with Andrew, as it seems most people did, but thought him 'a man's man', commenting that they 'saw little of his wife'.

As Andrew loved sport and athletics, he used to go and watch it on parishioners' televisions in Stonegate, as he had no television of his own. He also liked westerns, and other things such as dodgem cars, music hall and circuses that his wife thought rather vulgar.

Sundays at St Peter's, Stonegate, consisted of Holy Communion at 8.00am; on the second and fourth Sundays of the month it was morning prayer/matins at 10.30am, and on the third and fifth Sundays, Choral Communion at 10.30am, all from the 1662 Book of Common Prayer. Andrew preached during matins but not on Communion Sundays. His sermons seemed 'off the cuff', without notes, and were not usually related to the Collect or Gospel of the day. A dry, ironic humour was often present, but if he ever told a joke it was 'very dour'. During the week, he must have had a lot of time to himself, apart from sick visits, weddings and funerals, or deanery/diocesan meetings. In the early days at Stonegate he went often to the London Library, returning with a small suitcase full of books, having also visited various literary friends (see Chapter 8).

As there is a 'gap' in Janet's extant letters to her sisters between the late 1930s and 1946, it is impossible to know her feelings about and impressions of the move to Stonegate. It is also difficult to estimate whether she was kept busier in the parish than she had been in Hove; but in either case, she seems to have had precious little time to herself, ever. Anthony was by this time twenty-six and at Moray House Training College in Edinburgh, and Alison, then nineteen, had started at the Royal College of Music in London. Wartime brought rationing, blackouts, hardships and German bombers flying over Kent and Sussex towards London. Andrew, though a pacifist, followed events intently, listening to updates on the radio several times a day. Yet in his unpublished *Autobiography* covering this period, Andrew never mentioned the war and maintained that: 'We lived uneventful lives. When I was not engaged in church work, services and pastoral visits, I read in my study and occasionally worked in the vegetable garden. Janet had no domestic help.[10] So we were glad at times to make excursions with some interesting purpose', usually in search of

---

10. This was incorrect: she had Mrs Richards to clean.

rare wild flowers, although, 'While Janet took an interest in plants, she was more interested in prehistoric remains' such as the Cleveland round barrows, Stonehenge and Avebury, which they also visited.

By 1944, Andrew had finished the first draft of his first 'flower book' and began systematically rewriting it, much as he did with poems. He reread many of his favourite prose writers, such as Thomas Browne, W.H. Hudson, Burton, Walton, Gilbert White, and so on. He also branched out into Matthew Arnold and John Ruskin. He worked hard at his prose style, having so long written verse, and enjoyed its versatility. It can be argued that his prose is as distinctly his own idiolect as is his poetry: terse, witty, engaging.

Having more time for reading, as well as writing, at Stonegate, he soon set about a private programme of reading (often rereading) the Classics; poetry from Milton to Browning; novels from *Tristram Shandy* to Scott and Hardy; and Dante's *Divine Comedy*, an old favourite, from whom he must have partly taken the idea for *Into Hades*, which he began writing about this time. In the same year, 1944, he was elected a Fellow of the Royal Society of Literature, of which his friend Richard Church, a writer who lived at nearby Goudhurst, was vice president. Church was one of that (even then) dying breed, the all-round 'man of letters': poet, novelist, essayist, biographer and autobiographer, reviewer, journalist and editor. He knew everyone in the literary world of his day, from the Stracheys to T.S. Eliot. At Dent, he had first published Dylan Thomas. His tastes in literature were similar to Andrew's own: he loved clarity, euphony and directness, and disliked complexity, obscurity, fads and gimmickry. He had often positively reviewed Andrew's poetry and would later become a firm friend.

Andrew's working habits as a writer are never clearly outlined, but as he and Janet, sleeping in nearby separate bedrooms, rose at 6.00am each day, it is possible that he wrote then. Alison records that he worked in the 'basement' and concealed a sustaining bottle of whisky in the nearby shrubbery! But she does not specify *when* he wrote. He had by now a separate study in the house, where he often secluded himself, ringing a small bell for Janet whenever he wanted anything.

Strangely, given Andrew's innately unsociable tendencies, the Youngs agreed to give temporary shelter to Sir Edward Marsh (known as Eddy in the early years of the war, when he was bombed out of his London flat. He stayed for several months. He was an eccentric in both behaviour and dress, being known as 'The Last of the Dandies'. He recited poetry (usually Milton) aloud in his bedroom, and was heard in the lanes of Stonegate talking to himself. Andrew recalled mildly in his unpublished autobiography, 'He was an odd character'. He was a well-known and respected literary figure of the time, who had edited *Georgian Poetry* and corrected the texts of Churchill's speeches. A friend to many writers and painters, including D.H. Lawrence and Rupert Brooke, he was erudite, a perfectionist, and a social snob of the first order. Yet somehow he and Andrew managed to coexist quite happily in the vicarage, both being carefully looked after by Janet, whose cooking Marsh particularly enjoyed. Sometimes Andrew would ask Marsh's advice or opinion about a passage in the first flower book manuscript, and would accept Marsh's grammatical corrections – as he was still 'learning' to write prose!

Despite this apparent camaraderie, Andrew was relieved when Marsh left to live with his widowed sister in Cambridge. Alison was to remark generally – and revealingly – about Andrew's attitude to visitors:

His impatience with visitors sprang from irritation at being distracted from his own thoughts and activities, a dislike of being on his best behaviour, and a wish to have Janet's attention directed exclusively towards himself and his needs.[11]

In 1945, *A Prospect of Flowers* was published by Cape and eventually sold 10,000 copies and won the Heinemann Prize (see Chapter 9). Between 1946 and 1949 he wrote a second flower book during the summer months (published in 1950 as *A Retrospect of Flowers*) and continued writing his long poem *Into Hades* during the winters.

In early December 1946, Janet wrote to her sister Margaret, suffering from serious arthritis, with apologies for not writing as she had

> Grown very lazy: what I do not get done in the morning I am always tempted to put off till next day, and you can guess that no morning is ever long enough for me to find time to do all that I would do. . . . But it is worst of all in summer: for we have many visitors then, and there is all this fruit to bottle and make in to jam, and vegetables to dispose of. Winter is a very quiet time: we live like dormice during the week till Alison comes at the weekend to waken us up. . . . I am well enough – but have taken a dislike to sustained work. I get up early (to lengthen my morning) and go to bed as soon as I decently can.

This provides an interesting view of life behind the vicarage doors.

That Christmas they had John Arlott, the cricket commentator, and his family staying with them. John read the lesson at the Christmas Day service, which was broadcast. Janet commented that, 'The village is very amusing about it. They take it as a subtle tribute to their importance. In fact, the whole parish is patting itself on the back!'

---

11. Edward Lowbury and Alison Young, *To Shirk No Idleness* (Salzburg: University of Salzburg Press, 1997).

Andrew's last book of short poems, *The Green Man*, was published in 1947. After this, he would write long poems, prose, an unfinished *Autobiography* and the occasional shorter poem, either published or added to the various editions of his *Collected Poems* in 1950, 1960, 1974 or 1985. The Stonegate years were a seedbed of Young's genius.

The Green Man, published by Cape at 3/6d, consisted of thirty-eight poems, a number of which were, as usual, reprints. These included:

In Avebury Circle
Field Glasses
In Moonlight
The Blind Man
The Shepherd's Hut
At Formby
A Dead Bird
The Revenant
On the Hillside
The Dead Sheep
The Day Ends
By the Erme

Some of the new poems had clearly been written during the war years. *Hard Frost* is a case in point, where, although ostensibly a weather/season poem, the imagery is decidedly military:

Frost called to water, '*Halt!*' . . .

ferns on windows *shoot* their ghostly fronds . . .

ranks trees in an *armed host*. . . .

Hangs *daggers* from the house-eaves . . .

ferny *ambush* weaves. . . .

In the *long war* grown warmer. . . .

The sun will *strike him dead* and strip his *armour*.

It is a brilliantly descriptive poem:

tench in water-holes
Lurk under *gluey glass* like fish in bowls.

In 'every footstep breaks a brittle pane', the metaphor is visual, apt and precise. The whole poem is a graphic minor masterpiece.

Spring Flowers has an uncharacteristically soft, melodic tone:

And dandelions flood
The orchards as though apple trees
Dropped in the grass ripe oranges,
Boughs still in pink impatient bud.

This impression is aided by the enjambed lines, the ABBA rhyme pattern and the effective use of assonance in the last line. The death theme, as usual, is never far away, for example in the seven-line *A Shot Magpie*:

Though on your long-tailed flight
You wore half-mourning of staid black and white,
So little did the thought of death
Enter your thievish head,
You never knew what choked your breath
When in a day turned night
You fell with feathers heavier than lead.

'Thievish head' is neat; 'a day turned night' is aptly symbolic; 'heavier than lead' hardly seems a cliché as he has used it. The two decasyllabic lines (two and seven) add a ponderous, solemn quality.

May Frost is another short, death-centred poem:

It was the night May robbed September
Killing with frost the apple bloom

Later, the poet, confusing night and day, due to the sudden 'red sunrise' fears he is dying:

These are death's cobwebs on my eyes
That make the dawn so dim

Only to discover later that:

my sight was lying:
The frost had set on fire the full-faced moon.

This is a subtle, cerebral poem, using chiaroscuro, alliteration and assonance to good effect. In his phrase 'the earth's round rim', there is perhaps an unconscious echo of Donne's famous 'at the round earth's imagined corners'.

Another twelve-line poem, *Cornish Flower-Farm*, begins with an amusing visual image:

Here where the cliff rises so high
The sea below fills half the sky . . .
ships hang in mid-air

And after describing 'neat rows' of various flowers, notes that some others:

> from their quiet quillets pass
> To mix with wayside weeds and grass,
> Like nuns that from their strict retreats
> Go visiting the poor in their plain streets.

Whilst the final simile is apposite, the use of the archaic 'quillets' is curious, since it means a quibble or nice distinction and has some links to 'quiddity', the essence of a thing. Andrew is presumably suggesting that those who 'mix with' lesser things ('weeds') are diluting their own purity, or essence.

The Shower, about the seasonal cherry-pickers in the Medway area, contains one riveting image, reminiscent of Browning's description of red tulips as 'bubbles of blood':

> And cherries hung like gouts of blood
> Down the long aisles of whitewashed wood.

Andrew is so often at his best with death imagery.

The Beech-Wood is an accomplished short poem in rhyming couplets, with a more relaxed, assured description of the wood as, 'a haunted house' with 'long, varnished buds of beech . . . / tanned by summer suns' where 'Leaves of black bryony turn bronze'. The poet goes there in all seasons, yet admits:

> I never lose the feeling
> That someone close behind is stealing
> Or else in front has disappeared

The Swedes, a nine-line poem, amusingly introduces a new 'trinity': that of 'Horse, cart and man'. In the cart are swedes, 'heaped smooth and round / Like skulls that from the ground / The man has dug without the bones'. This leaves the poet in doubt:

> Whether the swedes with gold shoots sprout
> Or with fresh fancies bursts each old bald sconce.

Lady's Slipper Orchid, where he peers, 'in every place' for what he 'cannot find' (rare wild flowers), echoes A Prospect of Flowers, then recently completed.

In Twilight, the final poem in this collection, the mortality theme is again strong:

As daylight drains away
And darkness creeps out of the wood. . . .
I might imagine night was my last day

Yet he questions the need to 'rehearse' the part that one day he 'must play with my whole heart', even though 'Spectators may be moved to tears' as he acts 'these now-feigned fears'. Others 'summing up the part', however, might say 'His lines were terse'. These last four words could almost be his own poetic epitaph.

* * *

Having been an Anglican for less than ten years, Andrew was made a canon of Chichester Cathedral in 1947. That same year, his son Anthony met Kathleen Cleere, a psychiatric social worker, in Edinburgh, and announced his engagement and intention to marry that summer. At thirty-one, Anthony was just as agnostic as he had been at fifteen, when he initially refused to be confirmed, and shocked his parents by refusing a church wedding in favour of a London registry office. Finally, an uneasy compromise was reached and it was agreed that Andrew, in his capacity as a civil registrar, should marry the couple early one morning, without any religious ceremony, or guests. Andrew must have found this very difficult. Shortly afterwards, the couple moved to Manchester, where Anthony became 'educational psychologist to the city of Manchester, working mainly in child guidance'.[12] Later, the family moved to Leeds.

Earlier, in the spring of 1947, the Youngs met a newly demobbed young poet called Edward Lowbury, who was to become their future son-in-law.

Janet wrote to her sister Margaret towards the end of the year, hoping that she was holding her own against 'the enemy' (arthritis), but was soon talking about her own affairs:

> The outstanding event of the last year is, of course, Anthony's marriage. They are coming for Christmas, with Alison. Alison has been in a flat of her own in Hampstead for eight months: she is happy and very busy. She has private pupils for piano and specialises in harmony. She has an odd assortment of pupils – a great grandson of Liszt, a young Australian who won a sweepstake of £500 and is spending it here on music, a bus conductor, a society woman or two, a boy of fifteen who

---

12. Edward Lowbury and Alison Young, *To Shirk No Idleness* (Salzburg: University of Salzburg Press, 1997).

won an exhibition for Oxford and has to wait to be old enough to go up she does a lot of accompanying for Rosina Buckman. She comes for weekends, but not so frequently as formerly.

We are well – particularly when things go quietly and smoothly. The winter is our easy time. Summer is hectic and crowded: visitors come and there is all the work of bottling fruit. . . . I suppose you are in the same position – having practically no help. I dread to think of a time when I might not be able to do what I have to do now: perhaps it will not come.

These letters give insights into mid-twentieth century domestic life, before the prevalence of many labour-saving devices; but also show Janet's anxieties and her desire for perfection. Her letter-writing became less frequent and often seems to consist of annual pre-Christmas greetings to her sisters – May, Margaret or Alice. She comments on 'a sense of urgency and pressure that binds one to the things that really matter', adding of herself and Andrew: 'We are both well – in our separate ways – but much older and more easily tired.' Yet she is thrilled, in late 1949, about her first grandchild, due in May the following year: 'already I see myself rejuvenated, the old fairy tales I used to tell Anthony and Alison, again at my fingertips'.

Also due the following year were several books by Andrew:

> He is busy on a sequel to the *Prospect of Flowers* – of course it will be some time before it is ready – but . . . Cape is publishing his *Collected Poems* with illustrations by Joan Hassall . . . Trust them to miss the boat for Christmas – but anyway people don't make a rush for poetry these days, as they did a couple of years ago.

Whilst Andrew 'still finds his recreation in writing', Janet complained that 'my days seem to be too full and too long. . . . My ordinary routine absorbs all my energies.' She records that, one Sunday, she gave herself 'a black eye setting mousetraps in the loft (so) stayed at home (from church) – so I seize just a few leisure moments before Andrew comes in', that is, to write her letter. She complained that six hours help a week (presumably with cleaning) was not enough for 'a rambling old place' like the Stonegate vicarage.

In the summer they had family visitors: Anthony, his wife Kathleen and baby daughter Imogen, whom Janet refers to as 'an engaging little person'; followed by Janet's wayward brother Harry, on his way back from visiting his son Kenneth in St Leonards. Money is often much on Janet's mind, as she told Margaret at Christmas 1950, adding: 'There is no question of retirement for us: we shall go on as long as we can.' Andrew was already 65, and Janet herself 67. By the time they did retire, nine years later, they were 74 and 76 respectively.

Richard Church was one of a number of reviewers of *Collected Poems* (1950). He was a friend and admirer of Andrew's and shows perception, despite being referred to by Andrew as 'dim Church' (a rather cruel pun on the place):

> Andrew Young, like Mr de la Mare, has been at work for many decades, *without touching the fringes of literary fashion.* He has therefore received less attention from the critics than from the reading public. He carries no contemporary philosophy of life, and invents none of his own. He is a Christian of that kind who is content to relate faith to his love of the creatures of this world: the birds, beasts, flowers, clots of earth, trees, hills and streams, and an occasional human. Those manifests, moving or rooted, are his evidence of a paternal surveillance, and he is never tired of presenting them, intimately and individually, as demonstrators of a wisdom larger than the event in which he detects them.
>
> This is a simple way of interpreting life. It has the sanction of time, for mankind has been relating himself and the universe in this way since the beginning of human consciousness. It is the way of all poetic imagery: *the seeing of much in little*, as Blake saw a world in a grain of sand and eternity in the palm of his hand. . . . Again like Blake, Mr Young has kept the sharp vision of a child, seeing things always for the first time, by means of that *paradox* that we call wonder.
>
> This affects his thinking. It makes it immediate, confined, lucid. He does not build a cosmology, nor inflate his verse with abstract words. And although he is a priest in the Church of England, he does not dogmatise or dress his ideas in ritual. The reader has the sensation, rather than the certainty, that the theology is there, lurking beneath the wonder. . . . That is the second quality which makes his work *universal and timeless. . . .*
>
> The odd thing is that the general effect of this book of collected poems . . . is one of a gentle sadness, as it were a shaking of the head over the inscrutability of life. . . . The poems offer themselves almost nonchalantly. . . . Every poem has an idea that is axiomatic, original. Sometimes it is merely fanciful; often it is deeply imaginative. It is always simple. . . . But Mr

Young brings an additional faculty of scientific observation. Behind his simplicity are a method and a system . . . he is never content, in his verse, merely to catalogue what he has collected. Every observation is used for the purpose of a miniature drama, in which is established, firmly and authoritatively, one of those startling conclusions [my italics].

Schola Regia, the magazine of The Royal High School in Edinburgh, devoted a number of pages to old boy Andrew Young in the Easter 1951 edition,[13] in celebration of his *Collected Poems* and of Edinburgh University's decision to award him an honorary degree (Doctor of Laws). It printed a photograph, three poems (*Cornish Flower Farm, A Dead Bird* and *Nightfall on Sedgemoor*) and a lengthy biopic, including:

More than half a century ago, a young boy from the cathedral town of Elgin, on the way (though he did not know it) to the cathedral town of Chichester, stopped at Edinburgh to go to The Royal High School and the university.

In the recently published list of distinguished personages on whom, this summer, the university will confer the honorary degree LL.D., the boy appears as 'The Rev Andrew John Young, M.A. (Edin), Canon of Chichester, poet'. The citation is skilfully phrased: only the shrewd authority of a Senatus could hoist the word 'poet' in the context to a height at which its ancient stars and orders immediately catch the eye. . . .

If Walter Scott was the model for his truancy, at least Andrew Young has copied the great man no further. His *Collected Poems* . . . show that he has not only arrived at a clearer and more valid apprehension of real poetry than ever Sir Walter did, but also *he has done more than any twentieth-century writer to prevent the disappearance of genuine nature poetry* under green and sappy layers of sentimentality. The finest instruments of criticism could not isolate, in Andrew Young's poetry, a stanza or line that the poet had not personally experienced; this unimpeachable sincerity glows behind all the technical facets of his work. . . .

It would be interesting to compare Young's achievement . . . with that (of) . . . William Drummond of Hawthornden. For one thing, *each of them stands completely outside the Scottish literary tradition of his day, and Andrew Young . . . stands outside the contemporary English tradition as well.* . . .

13. *Schola Regia*, vol. 47, no.140, University of Edinburgh, 1951.

> For the present, the eminence to which Andrew Young
> has risen as a poet, and the pleasure his artistry has given
> to innumerable readers are ample justification for pride in
> a school that shared with Arthur's Seat and Carnoustie the
> privilege of educating him [my italics].

Quite an accolade! Andrew left an account of the actual event in his
unpublished autobiography (*My Life*), which shows a rather reticent
recipient:

> I received a letter from Edinburgh; The Senatus of the
> University were going to confer on me the honorary degree,
> LL.D. But that was absurd; I had been so irregular a student,
> how could I call myself a Doctor of Laws? But I went to
> Edinburgh and attended a ceremony in which various degrees
> were conferred, including my own. In the evening the Senatus
> gave us a banquet. I was the first to rise from my seat; I was
> in a staggering state, not because of any wine I had taken, but
> because of the burden on my shoulders: I had been appointed
> to give the company's thanks to the Senatus. I have no
> recollection of what I said, but I remember that sitting down
> I looked to the end of the table, where Professor John Baillie
> sat. His eyes fixed on mine, he nodded his head as though with
> approval.

Baillie had, of course, been a fellow student with Andrew at New College
many years before.

True to type, Andrew combined his visit with several days stay at
Kirkcudbright, of which he wrote more ecstatically than about the
degree ceremony: '"The Venice of Scotland" . . . is a place of charm and
dignity. . . . The beach is silver with blanched cockle shells. . . . You see a
long, low wall of surf, moaning to itself as it is pushed by a multitude of
impatient waves.'

Curiously though, on his return to Stonegate, according to his friend
and parishioner Dr Dick Mowll, Andrew always insisted on the title 'Dr
Young', not Canon, Reverend or Mr. Dr Mowll remembered his 'flowing
white hair, Highland brogue and good sermons'.

Into Hades (see Chapter 7) was published in the spring of 1952 by
Rupert Hart-Davis. After this and the *Collected Poems* of 1950, Andrew
was awarded the first Queen's Gold Medal for Poetry in November 1953.
He was aged 68 and it was probably assumed that he had reached the
pinnacle of his writing career. It was not presented by the Queen herself

but by the reigning Poet Laureate, John Masefield. Andrew and Janet
went to lunch with him in Abingdon, stopping at a hotel in Lacock on
the way, admiring its Abbey and surroundings: 'I am willing to declare
Lacock the most beautiful village in England.' On arrival at the Masefields'
house, Andrew recalled:

> His wife provided a splendid lunch, which he helped to serve,
> standing like a waiter behind our chairs. The lunch ended, he
> was faced with the office of presenting the first Queen's Gold
> Medal for poetry, the Queen's time too full of engagements.
> The office ended, I thanked him warmly. But I did not
> write to thank the Queen; I was too shy. Perhaps I deserved
> a year or so later to have the Medal stolen along with £30,
> burglars one night breaking into the house. Detectives rang up
> Buckingham Palace for a better description of it than I could
> give. The Palace expressed the earnest hope that it would be
> recovered, for it was of great value, having the first likeness of
> the Queen taken in metal after her coronation, earlier than
> a likeness on a gold or silver coin. The medal was recovered
> along with £25.[14]

A number of magazines wrote articles on Andrew at this time, including
The Church Times and *John O' London's Weekly*. In the latter, Joseph
Braddock states:

> CANON ANDREW YOUNG's literary fame rests upon three
> books, his *Collected Poems* and two prose works, *A Prospect
> of Flowers* and *A Retrospect of Flowers* (published by Jonathan
> Cape at 10s. 6d each). The award to him of the Queen's Gold
> Medal for Poetry has, I believe, been universally popular
> among traditionalists and experimentalists alike; for there
> seems to be a widely held opinion that his 200 or so nature
> lyrics, notable as much for their creative shocks of surprise as
> for their objective lucidity, are as likely as any contemporary
> verse to survive. . . .
>
> Canon Young's classical pastoral poetry stems from Hardy
> (he has told me himself that his favourite 'modern' poet
> is Hardy) and is perhaps related to an even older English
> tradition – that of Herrick, Barnes, Clare and Charles
> Tennyson-Turner – which is represented in the present
> century by Edward Thomas, W.H. Davies, Edmund Blunden

---

14. *My Life,* Chapter 3.

and Thomas Hennell. But it is the poetry of a devout scholar, whose life has been 'sufficiently close to the life of the rural community for the countryside to be a concrete, not merely a fanciful, reality. . . .

As well as being a fine poet, Canon Young's humane essays about flowers tell us clearly that he is also a scholar of deep erudition, a keen and persistent botanist, and an enthusiastic mountaineer.[15]

He then proceeds to give a potted biography of Andrew's education and professional life. What is curious about this article, in retrospect, is that it makes no mention whatsoever of *Into Hades,* published two years earlier, whilst extolling the virtues of *Collected Poems* (1950) and the two prose works. It is illustrative of the shifting sands of literary history and evaluation, that Barnes, Tennyson-Turner and Hennell are now totally obscure, and that Davies is a minor Georgian poet confined to ancient school anthologies. The only major poets referred to are, arguably, Hardy, Thomas and Young.

Predictably perhaps, *The Church Times* took a more religious view, declaring that 'of all the English nature poets, there is not one, neither Herrick, nor Clare, nor Edward Thomas, who has known more intensely, the joy of seeing God in "the meanest flower that blows"'. However, it *does* acknowledge the importance of *Into Hades*:

In his long poem *Into Hades* he imagines himself a spectator of his own funeral. After his excursion into dread, the poet takes on a new body and inherits a new heaven and a new earth. *Into Hades* is more revolutionary in form than any other of Andrew Young's work, but it is not difficult to read.

He also argues that Andrew's poetry is not 'objective' so much as 'subjective and intensely personal':

Andrew Young's poetry is certainly lucid; it is simple and delicate, suffused with a remarkable innocence. *He is a contemporary poet but hardly a modern one.* He writes in traditional forms and brings no grist to the mill of metrical disquisition. His vision is startlingly fresh. But, surely, it is not objective. For a poet of 70 years of age, his output has been remarkably small, but *all of it has been subjective and intensely personal.* His observation is always true. Even Clare's natural history was sometimes at fault; Andrew Young's never is [my italics].[16]

---

15. *John O'London's Weekly,* 8 January 1954.
16. *The Church Times,* 8 January 1954 (article signed 'S.E.').

In that his idiolect, or developed 'voice' was uniquely his own, this is true; but 'intensely personal' does not mean 'emotional' since most of his observations on nature are cerebral or philosophical.

A small insight into Andrew's writing life is also provided in this article:

> he took me into his garden, and near a large pond, showed me my first periwinkle. It was very near this spot that he does most of his work during the summer months. In the winter, he is confined more to his book-lined study, where works by Barth and Niebuhr and Berdyaev rest on the same shelves with those of Spenser, his favourite poet.

After *Into Hades*, Andrew started a sequel, *A Traveller in Time* (originally *Out of Hades*), which he worked on throughout the 1950s, along with another prose work, *A Prospect of Britain*, published in 1956 (see Chapter 9) which came out of his 'botanizing' travels around the UK.

On the domestic front, the Youngs' only grandson, Alastair, was born to Anthony and Kathleen in April 1952, a brother for Imogen. Alison was by this time seriously courting Dr Edward Lowbury. Janet complained about 'this unheatable house' and her inability to 'keep the hot water system going' in letters to her sisters. She joked to Alice that 'Andrew says he would like to live in a pre-fab – and he is really more than half in earnest. He loves small houses; I want space. When we retire he says too that he would like to go to the east coast of Scotland and live on fish . . . or to Loch Fyne and live on fresh herring. . . . The east coast would be far too cold for me.'

It is clear from Janet's letters that retirement was very much in the Youngs' thoughts from the early 1950s onwards. With this thought must have come a degree of anxiety about *where* they would be able to go, having lived all their married life in tithed houses/rectories. In this same letter to Alice, Janet confided that Lord Courthorpe, patron of the living, had asked Andrew to run an adjoining parish, along with Stonegate. 'It would have meant twice the work – also twice the salary – but also it would have meant living in the other parish, which is bigger'. However, despite the financial incentive, it would have made too big an inroad into Andrew's time, and in addition, Janet did not like the other vicarage: 'the ugliest of ugly houses – florid and pretentious, overlooked by council houses . . . It was like re-entering paradise to come back to our own gaunt, austere house'. So, despite being 'unheatable' it obviously had its points!

Christmases at the vicarage in the 1950s followed the same pattern: a brace of pheasants from Lord Courthorpe, cooked by Janet with all the trimmings; family and/or other visitors, including cricket commentator

John Arlott ('who makes a habit of coming for New Year'), Viola Meynell 'soon after', and sometimes Janet's siblings. Despite often complaining about her workload, Janet remarked to Alice, 'I do not entertain now, as I used to do, though I love having people in the house.' Andrew's views are not recorded, but would not have been as positive as hers!

In the spring of 1954, Janet was preoccupied by two main things: her brother Harry's health, as he was hospitalised once more; and Alison's approaching wedding to Edward Lowbury. Janet wrote to her sister Margaret's husband John (as Margaret was ill):

> We are very happy about it. He took a medical degree in Oxford (incidentally winning, as an undergraduate, the Newdigate Prize for English Verse – something (??) for a medical student) and is now working under the Medical Research Council in Birmingham. . . . He is a man of wide culture – interested in music and the arts – so that Alison's gifts will develop and (not) become stultified, *which does often happen with a woman after marriage* [my italics].

This comment does sound rather like the voice of experience.

The wedding took place at Hampstead registry office, on 12 June 1954, as Edward was Jewish and a Christian marriage was therefore out of the question. The Youngs went on from London by overnight train to Galloway, then on to the Western Isles for one of their many Scottish holidays. The Lowburys were to remain in Birmingham, where Edward was an eminent medical bacteriologist with an international reputation. He was to be awarded an OBE for his work in medical research. From 1949 he had been Head of Bacteriology at the MRC Industrial Injuries and Burns Research Laboratory at City Hospital. He later received many honours in both medicine and literature. They had three daughters, two of whom became musicians, whilst the eldest, who was also musical, studied languages, then social and political sciences, and worked in a series of roles in the health sector.

Anthony's family moved from Manchester and settled in Leeds, where he became a lecturer in clinical psychology at the university. Although Andrew did not approve of Anthony's field of study, he was pleased by this promotion.

On Christmas Day, 1955, the service from Andrew's church was broadcast on the Home Service, from 9.30am to 10.15am. This included Andrew's sermon, on the text: 'The dayspring from on high hath visited us, to give light to them that sit in darkness and in the shadow of death, to guide our feet into the way of peace.' After referring to Zacharias and his son John the Baptist, and childhood, Andrew continued:

We are still living in a world that is largely without Christ. . . .
We can be too much concerned as to how God is governing the
world and not enough concerned as to how He is governing
our own lives. Meanwhile the dawn has broken. Unto us a
child is born, unto us a son is given. Some people think they
are living in the sunset of Christ's religion; I believe it is only
the dawn. What the birth of Christ means is that God has
intervened in our human affairs; and with that faith we must
not . . . lose hope for a better world. . . .

For the Christian, the grave itself is a place of victory, and it
is through death that we shall see that kingdom's full and final
triumph. Thy kingdom, O Christ, is an everlasting kingdom.

This is perhaps the nearest we get to 'hearing' Andrew in the pulpit.

By 1956, the Youngs had four grandchildren and another due: 'We
are doing well, are we not, in the way of grandchildren. But they are the
best children!' Janet boasted to her sister Alice. There would eventually
be six. Alison was to recall later: 'To his grandchildren, Andrew made it
clear that he should be addressed as 'Grandfather' – not 'Grandpa' as his
own father had been addressed.'[17]

This insistence on formality is reminiscent of his preference for being
'*Dr* Young' in the parish, and was perhaps his way of establishing both
dignity and distance.

Andrew was often moody and irritable, though not apparently with
his grandchildren; whilst Janet, 'ageing, often felt tired and ill', Alison
remembered. At this time, Janet's sister Margaret died, but Janet was
unable to attend the funeral as 'Andrew was on duty at Chichester[18] and
his sister and her friend were staying here – both of them nearer 80 than
70 – . . . and quite incapable of doing everything for themselves.'[19] One
gets the impression she was rather glad of the excuse; yet she maintains,
in the same letter: 'We are very well: I myself am better than I have been
for some time' before returning to her old preoccupation: 'of course the
house remains something of a burden – but I should mind if I had to
leave it. That will come in due course – just when we have not decided –
for there is the problem of where to go and I shall hate not to be able to
entertain the children.' On a more intimate note, she added: 'I try not to
think of a time when I shall not be able to look after myself'.

17. Edward Lowbury and Alison Young, *To Shirk No Idleness* (Salzburg: University
of Salzburg Press, 1997), Chapter 15.
18. Where he was a canon of the cathedral and had to give an annual sermon
there.
19. Undated letter to Alice, 1956.

This thought had probably never occurred to Andrew, who was so well looked after by Janet.

Andrew continued to work on what he had described to Edward Lowbury in 1947 as his 'long escatological poem', *Into Hades*, originally published by Hart-Davis in 1952. Since then, it had been extensively revised during the mid-1950s, as he wrote its sequel *A Traveller in Time*. Both were published, again by Hart-Davis, under the combined title *Out of the World and Back*, in 1958, to considerable literary acclaim. Both poems showed the width and depth of Andrew's reading in the Classics, mythology, mysticism, history and philosophy. The 'Monitor'/guide of the first poem becomes his dead brother William in the second, being in a state of prelapsarian innocence, reminiscent of the child guides of the medieval dream vision poets. (For closer analysis and reviews, see Chapter 7.)

It seems that, during the writing, Andrew had had a recurrence of his depression, perhaps due to the intense concentration needed and the inevitable exhaustion. The use of the dead brother as a spirit guide may also have refocused his attention on family problems, including the unsolved mystery of his elder brother, David. In addition, worries about where and how they would live after his retirement must have been in his mind. His outbursts of bad temper had led to the resignation of their cleaner, Mrs Richards – a blow for Janet; and his behaviour was never too reliable when other people were in the house.

* * *

In commemoration of Andrew's work, Leonard Clark edited, and presumably organised, *Andrew Young: Prospect of a Poet*, published by Hart-Davis in October 1957. It consisted of twelve essays of appreciation by friends and admirers, including John Arlott, his old friend John Baillie, John Betjeman, Richard Church, Norman Nicholson the Lake District poet, Viola Meynell and the Bishop of Chichester, amongst others. It was introduced by Poet Laureate John Masefield (in turn much admired by Andrew) who commented on the 'high distinction' of Andrew's poetry.

Clark's longer introduction stated:

> The work of Andrew Young is still not as well known as it
> should be. It has never been taken up . . . by any clique. . . . He
> is certainly in no danger of becoming a literary fashion. . . .
> The truth is that Andrew Young's poems are timeless in their
> appeal. . . . He is master of his idiom . . . (which) bears all the

marks of his distinctive character. . . . He is of the company
of Herrick, Clare, Hardy, Edward Thomas, Frost and W.H.
Davies . . . *but is different from them all.* . . . He is a superb
miniaturist, of rare wit and fancy. . . . But his thinking is on
the grand scale.

Bishop George Bell, in this volume, praised *Nicodemus: A Mystery*, from
1937, and remarked of *Into Hades*:

It is an ambitious poem, in verse now easy, now exulted,
and relates to an imaginary period between death and the
last Judgment. . . . The poet's faith sparkles through it, and
there is humour and tenderness as well. . . . It is . . . significant
of the whole tone of Andrew Young's mind that both these
long poems, while clearly reflecting the love of Nature, are
concerned from different angles with the Mystery of the
Resurrection.'

Barely a year later, on 5 October 1958, Andrew himself wrote:

My dear Mrs Bell,
    It was with a sense of deep personal loss and sorrow that I
read the sad news in yesterday's paper.
Recognising in Dr Bell a really great man, with a wide and
courageous vision, it troubles me a little that, preoccupied
with so many affairs, he should have found time to show me
so much kindness.
    I shall always keep a fresh and inspiring memory of his
friendship . . .
        Yours sincerely,
            Andrew Young.[20]

In December 1957, Janet told her sister Alice:

the house remains bitterly cold. . . . Our winter regime is
simple, sometimes Spartan – but there always is a certain
amount of entertaining to do, which isn't quite the fun I used
to find it. My hands . . . have grown clumsy, and my wits are
not what they were. The years tell on us, and we grow more
and more like hermits: I am the guiltier of the two.

Talking, as so often, about the family, she confided: 'I couldn't have
believed, until I saw it with my own eyes, what a wonderful wife and

---

20. In Bishop Bell's archive in Lambeth Palace Library.

mother she (i.e. Alison) would become. Her interests in the past had been so remote from that kind of thing. As you can guess, it has made me very happy.'

* * *

At first sight, it may seem out of character that Andrew gave a poetry reading at Foyle's bookshop shortly after the publication of *Prospect of a Poet*, but he had given talks to literary societies in Hove and elsewhere, as well as addressing people from the pulpit for half a century. He was usually at his ease with literary people, and on this occasion met Christopher Fry, another writer of religious plays in verse, encouraged, as Andrew had been, by the late Bishop Bell. Shortly after this meeting, Andrew invited Fry, with Christopher Hassall, to visit Stonegate for the weekend. Janet commented sardonically to Alice, 'There will literally have to be a house-warming for the event'.

Hassall was one of a number of younger poets befriended by Andrew, including Norman Nicholson and Edward Lowbury. They discussed Hassall's new book *The Red Leaf*, then Andrew's revisions of *Into Hades*, which he had also discussed with a number of other people, including Basil Dowling (see Chapter 7). Andrew was probably happier in the company of other poets than of other clergymen: these were his peers, struggling as he was between the hammer and the anvil of creativity. They were not so much rivals as fellow travellers (see also Chapter 8, *A Literary Life*).

* * *

Before Christmas 1958, Janet was hospitalised for a week with a gastric problem and had a wart on the bladder removed. She 'thoroughly enjoyed' her stay, presumably for the rest! However, she knew that 'Andrew was worrying about the outcome. He had also to look after himself for that week (with what help my daily woman could give him), but he really was marvellous – especially as it was a worrying time in the parish – three funerals in that one week', she told her sister Alice, adding that: 'He is still treating me like an invalid, when I long to be up and doing things – I am, of course, not in bed – I simply rest a lot.'

Janet had never been ill before, and according to their daughter Alison, Andrew 'started to treat her with a new consideration, and to be much more attentive to her'. Not before time, perhaps. They were seriously thinking of retiring the following spring, and were remarkably lucky that these thoughts coincided with one of their close friends, Pauline Muirhead, receiving a substantial legacy. She not only gave the Youngs a generous annual annuity but also bought them a six-bedroomed house, Park Lodge, in Church Lane, Yapton, near Arundel. Andrew was keen to be nearer to Chichester Cathedral, whilst Janet was reluctant to leave Stonegate, although the new house was plenty big enough for children and grandchildren to visit.

Pauline Muirhead, who wanted to move herself, built a house next door, in expectation of socialising with the Youngs, in which she was to be rather disappointed.

The Youngs left Stonegate in April 1959 and were given a radio, a modern typewriter and a sum of money by the parishioners whom Andrew had served for eighteen years. In May of that year, their last grandchild, Miriam, was born to Alison and Edward in Birmingham. One consolation to Janet was that she would have more time to visit them; whilst Andrew, having reached his poetic peak in *Out of the World and Back*, entered his second major prose phase, uniting his naturalistic, topographical and poetic interests.

CHAPTER 6
RETIREMENT AND LAST YEARS
(1959-1971)

'Now that we are free',[1] Janet wrote to her sister Alice, she hoped to see more of her. She added:

> We are quite established here now, and comfortable and happy. Of course Andrew misses his pastoral work and his long tramps in the countryside to visit parishioners, but he does a great deal in helping here – the local vicar and also neighbouring ones. We miss too our old friends at Stonegate who were so very kind to us. . . . During the summer we had many visitors from Stonegate, and some from Hove,[2] but usually only for the afternoon. I have completely lost my zest for entertaining – I used to love it, but now the thought of having people even to lunch makes me weary. We have simplified life for ourselves, as far as possible – it seems to me I have forgotten how to cook.

The sudden contrast in lifestyles seems to have been difficult for Janet to adjust to, especially as she now had high blood pressure and a duodenal ulcer. Andrew seemed, by contrast, to settle in quite quickly, often going to Chichester with canonical duties, discovering the local walks, or sitting in his new study, described by Alison as: 'a large front room with a beautiful carved mantelpiece with books on white shelves up to the ceiling'.[3] He was busying himself with *The Poet and the Landscape* and the odd poem or sermon. He grew, if anything, more remote and eccentric. He manifested what Alison called 'obsessional routines' and would 'fly into a rage and shout' if anyone upset them. He had 'his own special cup and saucer' and 'his personal knife and fork' and at mealtimes

---

1. Janet, letter to Alice, 14 December 1959.
2. They had presumably forgiven the way he had left them twenty years earlier.
3. Edward Lowbury and Alison Young, *To Shirk No Idleness* (Salzburg: University of Salzburg Press, 1997).

with the family, developed the habit of sitting alone 'at a small table by the window'.[4] He was always served first, like an Old Testament patriarch. Yet despite these quirks, he continued to show acute awareness of Janet's increasing frailty due to health issues, and to help more in the house. Always having been possessive of her, he became even more so, causing her to refuse invitations from neighbours and friends such as Pauline Muirhead. Though hurt by these refusals, Pauline paid for the Youngs to have central heating installed, to combat Janet's continual coldness.

They had ceased having the grandchildren at Christmas, despite having six bedrooms, preferring them to visit in the summer. Their first Christmas at Yapton was to be on their own, a fact that Janet was glad of as it freed her from so much cooking. 'Andrew . . . is helping the vicar at two services here on Christmas Day, (so) it will be almost like old times,' Janet told her brother-in-law John, ten days before the event.

Soon after the move to Yapton, Andrew invested in a television: previously, at Stonegate, he would invite himself to watch football and other sports on his parishioners' sets. Now, able to watch at will, his preferences were often for lowbrow light comedy (especially *All Gas and Gaiters*, a skit on the Anglican hierarchy), westerns and sports, to Janet's dismay. He also liked the volume very loud, though his hearing was good. Janet entertained herself reading novels, despite eyesight problems, and dutifully wrote mainly pre-Christmas letters to family and friends. Over the years her letters became more repetitive and laboured, and often apologetic for her handwriting or delay in replying. Towards the end of 1960, she complained/explained to her sister May:

> I have never before had it (i.e. letter-writing) so bad at Christmas. Andrew, not long ago, was awarded the Duff Cooper Memorial Prize for his *Collected Poems* (definitive edition) published in the spring. People have written to congratulate him – most unexpectedly in some cases – and letters instead of cards had to be sent. However, that is all over, and I am drawing long breaths of relief.[5]

The prize had been presented to Andrew by Princess Alexandra of Kent, who seemed genuinely to admire his work. Curiously, Janet does not mention this in any of her extant letters. It seems that reviewers felt, as Janet did, that this was 'the definitive' edition of *Collected Poems*, although it did not include *Out of the World and Back,* and only those shorter poems that Andrew wished to preserve, edited by Leonard

4. Ibid.
5. Janet to May, 21 December 1960.

Clark.[6] Increasingly generous to his family with the years (not unlike his own father), he divided the prize money between Anthony and Alison. The friendship between Andrew and Princess Alexandra, of which he was rather proud, was cemented by her visit to Yapton in June 1961, where she met Janet for the first time, stayed for tea and walked round the garden with Andrew, discussing poetry. He dedicated *The Poet and the Landscape* to her the following year[7] and she invited the Youngs to attend her wedding in Westminster Abbey in 1963. Unfortunately Janet was in poor health and unable to accompany him, so he took his eldest granddaughter, Imogen, aged fourteen, with him instead.

As early as 1961, Janet's health gave cause for serious concern: as well as taking painkillers for her digestive problems, and sleeping pills, she told her sister May in October, 'my powers of concentration are not what they were, and my memory plays tricks – but I find the more I can ignore these things the better'.[8] Stoicism, like thrift, was always her hallmark. Later, in the same letter, commiserating with May's back trouble, she admitted: 'I do a lot of reading propped up on my bed'. Then she added,

> Don't think I am overworked in this house. I have a woman four mornings a week, for two hours. . . . And when she is not here, Andrew does the fires, carries in coal and sticks and logs – anticipates me at every turn – he even does the family shopping and washes up – I am very glad, however, that he does not tackle the cooking.

What a turnaround for a man used to being waited on hand and foot, and ringing a bell when he wanted anything! He had mellowed with age, knew that he needed Janet, and was prepared to put himself out to save her unnecessary exertions. A big blow to Janet was the death of her troubled brother Harry, late in 1961,[9] after a recurrence of serious mental illness. As she told May: 'I too have been sick with misery but I have had to take myself in hand for Andrew's sake. I keep thinking of Harry's tragic life and what might have been. He had so many outstanding gifts – combined with . . . an utter kindness of heart'. As on previous occasions with family funerals, Janet 'missed' Harry's at Golders

---

6. It was, in fact, the third *Collected Poems* (1936, 1950, 1960) and there were to be two posthumous editions in 1974 and 1985.
7. Inscribed, 'Dedicated, by kind permission, to Her Royal Highness Princess Alexandra of Kent'.
8. Janet to May, 23 November 1961.
9. It is suggested, though never explicitly stated, that it was suicide.

Green, as she explained: 'I nearly went myself but it just happened on
that Thursday we had a long-standing engagement to spend the day with
John Arlott in his new home near Winchester, and instead of getting
home at six o'clock as we planned, it was long after ten – just in time to
get Murray (Harry's son)'s message – and in the morning I couldn't face
it.'[10]

To her brother-in-law John, she remarked a few days later: 'I have
been utterly miserable since Harry's death – not that I would have it
otherwise: no one could have wished that his unhappy life should be
prolonged – but I think of earlier days'. She then added further details
of the funeral: 'Our reception on the telephone was very bad, with
the result that I mistook the time. Andrew went off next morning for
Golders Green, prepared to take part in any little service they might
care to have, only to find on his arrival that he was hours too late. I think
it was all greatly mismanaged.'[11]

* * *

Although Janet felt that 'I have no real friends here, except Pauline
Muirhead . . . but having Andrew I am never lonely'.[12] In fact, the
Youngs soon got to know a number of other writers, including Leslie
and Kitty Norris, Rosemary Sutcliff, who lived nearby; then later, in
1964, they met Ursula Vaughan Williams, widow of the composer, and
herself a poet. They also continued to see John Arlott and other old
friends.

Rosemary Sutcliff, the novelist, lived two and a half miles away at
Walberton, and told the present writer[13] that Andrew would walk over
on spec, every six to eight weeks or so, and they would discuss gardens,
birds and flowers, but *never* their writing! He would 'sit and chat about
all things under heaven, and have tea and then walk home again'. She
noticed that Andrew's Scottish accent would become broader when
anything excited him. She only met Janet once and thought her 'rather
shadowy, dry, tall, governessy'. When asked about his poetry, she said,
'I am one of those people who (despite my trade) find it impossible
to put my feelings about poetry into words. I know what I like, and
liked his work and found great pleasure and refreshment in it.' Pushed
a little further, her verdict was 'an Andrew Marvell with a touch of
Blake'.

---

10. i.e. Harry's cremation.
11. Janet to John Scott (Margaret's widower), undated December 1961.
12. Ibid (i.e. as 11 above).
13. At interview at her home, in the autumn of 1990.

A closer friend was the writer and poet Leslie Norris who, with his wife Kitty, lived at Eastergate, about five miles away. Leslie was one of a number of younger poets drawn to and encouraged by Andrew. Alison, who met him, described him as: 'a colourful personality, with ginger hair, a musical Welsh accent, a genial manner, a keen interest in soccer and a lively sense of humour'.[14]

Andrew often walked over to see the Norrises, whom he took to readily, or they would drive him to places of mutual interest, often leaving Janet behind as she lacked the stamina for such excursions. Andrew could be quite rude to friends, demanding or difficult, but they usually forgave him as, when on form, he was good company. Other nearby visitors included Christopher Fry and Robert Gittings, both living near East Dean.

In an unpublished manuscript, Andrew wrote, of this time:

> Living at Yapton I was not without clerical work. When Walberton became vacant I was (responsible?) for ten services and later I kept up a close acquaintance with its parochial offshoot, Binsted. Several times I took evensong in Arundel. And I frequently attended matins in the cathedral. I had given up my car but was driven to Chichester by a very kind Welshman, Leslie Norris.

When Alison was asked by the present writer[15] whether Andrew had been an affectionate father, she replied: 'Not really. He was moody and difficult. Sometimes we were in fear of him.' However, he was a warmer grandfather who 'delighted in his six grandchildren', arranging various activities, including poetry competitions and play-acting when they visited. Their parents, Alison and Edward, or Anthony and Kathleen, were asked to organise rather idiosyncratic 'parties' on these occasions, for adult friends. There was alcohol but no food, apart from peppermints, and guests sat in a circle and talked. They started promptly at 8.00pm, when the children would still be up, and sometimes encouraged by Andrew to perform plays of their own devising. Given that Andrew was far from being 'a party animal' in the usual sense, these occasions were certainly strange.

Early in 1962, Janet wrote one of her more revealingly personal letters. Harry's death, her own changed circumstances, poor health but more time, seemed to combine to make her analyse her life. I quote it more or less verbatim:

14. Edward Lowbury and Alison Young, *To Shirk No Idleness* (Salzburg: University of Salzburg Press, 1997).
15. During several visits to Birmingham in the mid-1980s.

My dear John,

Your letter made me *very* happy. Being happy is one of my habits. I am never unhappy unless my own shortcomings weigh too greatly on my mind, or I find myself having done something of which I strongly disapprove. I do not remember just what I said in my letter to you. But I do know I was utterly miserable at the time. Misery is not unhappiness: it can be palliated: unhappiness has deeper roots.

It was just after Harry's death. It was not that I mourned his loss: one could not have wished it otherwise. . . . But old memories of our life together came surging up – of our childhood in S.Africa, and of our youth in Scotland: and all I could feel was just the pity of it all.

I tried to drown misery in an orgy of letter-writing – letters which I had promised to write for Christmas. You know how yours turned out. The others were different. I *am* happy. All my life I have had so much that is denied to others, enjoyed little nameless things unappreciated by so many and the kindness shown to me has humbled me into a deep sense of my own unworthiness. . . .

And here at Yapton, a relative stranger, I found flowers coming to me at Christmas.

And my children and grandchildren are a great joy to me always.

So now you know!

Don't reply to this; I should be embarrassed.

With much love,

Jintie.[16]

Although this sounds rather a defensive, self-justifying letter, her fondness for and honesty to John Scott went back a long way – since she had been courting him, before she met Andrew, and he married her sister Margaret.

* * *

After *The Poet and the Landscape*, Andrew set to work on *The New Poly-Olbion*, a skit on Michael Drayton's original topographical poem of 1622. Drayton had aimed to give 'a chorographical description of all the tracts, rivers, mountains, forests and other parts of Great Britain. 'It was a poetic as well as topographical work – an idea ideally suited to Andrew.

---

16. Janet to John Scott, 16 January 1962.

However, it came about indirectly, having begun life as a possible rewrite of *A Prospect of Britain* (1956), without some of the topography. The result was a series of prose poems, sometimes heavily descriptive, at other times satirical, incorporating, as usual, paradox, pathetic fallacy and irony. It was to occupy him for several years, being finally published in 1967. It included, as introduction, his essay 'Early Days', his first directly autobiographical writing, and the basis for *My Life*, his unfinished and unpublished account, written between 1969 and 1971, at the suggestion of Leonard Clark, his first Literary Executor.

* * *

Whilst Andrew was busy writing, for Janet, 'The months pass . . . in a monotonous way: little variety and I don't like television,' she told May. [17] She continued to worry about money, the cost of the central heating, and her eyesight, which would often cause headaches and dizziness. She depended on reading for her primary relaxation, but procrastinated about going to the optician. Later she confessed: 'I have my new glasses – but I think it is new eyes I need!'

In the spring of 1962, Janet told May: 'We go on in our habitual way. Andrew, as usual, busy writing. He has been asked to do a few paragraphs by way of a Foreword in the Programme which is being officially prepared for Princess Alexandra's wedding. I suppose it is an honour to be asked!'

On 8 September 1964, the Youngs celebrated their golden wedding, an achievement by any standards, but in this case most of the giving and adjusting had been done by Janet, most of the time: she had subsumed her life totally to Andrew's wishes and needs, and only latterly had this really been appreciated by Andrew. In her last years, when *her* needs were uppermost, Andrew rose to the occasion: 'I find housekeeping quite a task, though Andrew has become domesticated *to an extent I should never have thought possible*' (my italics), she told John in the same year.[18]

As well as this transformation, Andrew now wrote affectionate, teasing letters to his grandchildren, especially to Ruth Lowbury, the eldest of Alison's three daughters, such as this one, dated 9 April 1963:

> Dear Ruth,
>   Here is something to buy Easter eggs for yourself and Pauline and Miriam.

---

17. Janet to May, 15 December 1962.
18. Janet to John Scott, 16 December 1964.

And here are three riddles:

1. Why do white sheep eat so much more than black sheep?

2. What can you fill a wooden barrow with to make it lighter?

3. Where can you build a square house with windows on its four sides all looking south?

I hope you are well

With love

Grandfather.

As a PTO, he put the answers:

1. Because there are more of them.

2. Holes.

3. At the N.P.

On another occasion he sent 10/- for Ruth, and '10/- for your sisters' to buy fireworks, with more riddles and answers on the back. They are charming, gentle and playful letters and show a softer side of Andrew.

In the spring of 1965, Janet suffered the first of a series of strokes, 'each leaving her weaker until the final one'.[19] For reasons of his own, Andrew kept the matter a secret and was angry when Pauline Muirhead, their neighbour and benefactress, told a bemused Alison about it, after she had detected something strange in her mother's voice over the phone. Andrew's 'sudden outbursts', after which he would behave as though nothing had happened, must have been more difficult for Janet than usual. Later that year, in December, she had another stroke, more serious than the first. Rather than calling an ambulance to take her to hospital, Andrew 'treated' her himself, with extra sleeping pills, before calling in a private nurse. Gradually, Janet began to recover and the nurse left four months later. Andrew had found her presence in the house irksome but did his best to control his temper.

Once she had gone, Janet's worst fears were realised: Andrew took over the cooking, as she was unable to do it. Alison recalls that it consisted mainly of tinned soups or vegetables, with fruit and biscuits. Andrew believed that Janet would make a full recovery and would not accept that her mental capacities were damaged. This caused conflicts within the family, when Anthony or Alison visited and tried to help, or made suggestions. Andrew became increasingly intolerant, even of close family and friends. Janet gave in to him, as she always had. Anxiety about her condition, e.g. her dizzy spells, curtailed his long walks locally, or visits to the London Library.

19. Leonard Clark, Introduction to *Collected Poems*, Secker & Warburg, 1974.

In early August 1967, Janet fell and broke her leg badly.[20] This resulted in many weeks in hospital in Chichester, but left her an invalid, needing a Zimmer frame for support. 'Andrew nursed her devotedly, not an easy task, and the strain of this gradually took the toll of his strength and, incidentally, left him less freedom for writing,' Clark recalled.[21]

Andrew himself had osteoarthritis in a knee and an inguinal hernia at this time, but did his best to ignore both conditions. Both Andrew and Janet missed their annual holidays in Scotland, where they used to walk and climb. During 1968, Andrew was preparing an anthology of religious poetry, with a commentary on each one, as Janet became increasingly dependent on him for basic tasks such as washing and dressing. In February 1969 she entered a nursing home in Victoria Drive, Bognor Regis, where she died on 12 March, aged 84, from 'cerebral thrombosis, sclerosis and senility'.

Understandably, Andrew 'was greatly affected by her death', Leonard Clark remarked, then added: 'His debt to her was enormous, for she scrutinised and criticised all his work from the earlier stages to its final form.' This was perhaps the one area where she came into her own, as a literature graduate and teacher; whereas in all other aspects of life, she seems to have been submissive. It is not recorded what her criticisms were or how he took them, but he did also take literary advice from other friends so was obviously amenable to it.

Janet was cremated in Brighton and her ashes scattered on the Downs. Life alone at Yapton must have seemed strange and lonely to Andrew after fifty-five years of marriage. He came to depend more on Pauline Muirhead for company than he probably wanted to; had a home help in twice a week; watched television, and worked sporadically on his anthology. Seven months after Janet's death he resigned his canonry of Chichester Cathedral, unable to fulfil its few duties.

As might be expected, Andrew's belief in the afterlife and eventual reunion with Janet was strong. It appeared at times that he was restless to get to the next world – having already *been* there in his poetic fantasies – and began to divest himself of earthly things. This took the form of giving away books and other items to family and friends; and throwing away letters, papers, sermons, poems and other items which would have had a value to his biographers.

He usually enjoyed *short* visits from Alison's and Anthony's families, and 'parties' with a few chosen friends, but his temper and behaviour were always uncertain: he could go from calm to rage in a matter of

20. This is what Andrew told Leonard Clark, but Clark said it was her hip, and so did her granddaughter, Ruth.
21. As 19 above.

seconds, usually about some trivial matter. Whisky was often an incendiary device with him! Leonard Clark remembered Andrew at this time:

> Although he was still capable of flashes of insight and wit, his memory and judgement were impaired. He turned to mysticism more than ever and maintained that he was in daily communication with his wife . . . he had *no real will to live* and scorned those who tried to cheer him up [my italics].[22]

He continued writing *My Life,* but Alison maintained that he never intended to finish it. (It ran to 64 pages, poorly typed, with *two* Chapters 5 and many wrong dates and facts). It was also very repetitive of his other writings, particularly the two flower books and his topographical writings. The well of his poetry had long dried up. At the same time, he was still working on *The Poetic Jesus.*

As always, a stickler for his independence, he refused offers of going to live with either of his children, and spent the first winter after Janet's death alone at Park Lodge, in Yapton. It was clear to his family by mid-1970 that he would be unable to cope on his own for much longer, and certainly not through another winter. In early December 1970, aged 85, he suffered a serious fall during the night when he got up and his arthritic knee gave way under him. Unable to get up again, he managed to summon help the next morning and was taken to St Richard's Hospital in Chichester, where he was diagnosed with a fractured femur. The surgical repair was not straightforward and left him with one leg shorter than the other, but he made a good recovery in the circumstances. As might be expected, he was quite a difficult patient, hating both hospitals and any dependency.

As it was obvious to everyone – as it must have been to Andrew himself – that he could not possibly return to Park Lodge, he went into a nursing home in Bognor, as Janet had done. He could walk with the aid of a Zimmer frame but was soon unhappy in the home, so his son-in-law, Edward Lowbury, managed to get him transferred to Moseley Hall Hospital for geriatrics. In Birmingham he could be visited daily by the Lowburys and their children, and often by the Youngs from Leeds.

Andrew found it all very irksome, despite drinking about a third of a bottle of whisky each evening, supplied by Alison. Eventually, with cerebral arteriosclerosis (reduced blood supply to the brain) diagnosed, Andrew was returned to Bognor, where he entered Ravenna House nursing home in April 1971. Barely seven months later, he died there,

22. Ibid (i.e. as 19, 21).

in his sleep, on 25 November. He would not have wished to live long as he was, having told his daughter Alison that he believed in voluntary euthanasia and that only his Christianity prevented him from carrying it out!

A post-mortem found that he had died from acute heart failure, due to myocardial ischaemia. He left £33,564, a tidy sum for even a literary clergyman. A codicil dated 1968 gave the Literary Executorship firstly to Leonard Clark; then it passed to Alison and Edward Lowbury, and on their deaths, to their eldest daughter, Ruth Lowbury.

Andrew's funeral service took place in Chichester Cathedral and was well attended by fellow poets, friends, family and parishioners from Hove and Stonegate. He was then cremated at Chichester Crematorium, and his ashes scattered in the grounds of the cathedral, presumably as he had wished.

There were, as was to be expected, a number of obituaries. The anonymous one in *The Times* smacks of Richard Church:

> Canon Andrew Young, who died on Thursday night, at the age of 86, was *a poet whose work was never in, nor out of, literary fashion.* . . . He was never a prodigal writer, so that when his first collected poems were published in 1936, there were just over 100 of them. Fourteen years later a second volume of collected poems had less than 200. . . . *Collected Poems* (1960) consists of 209 poems. . . . *Out of the World and Back* . . . published in 1958, is regarded as one of the finest religious poems of the day [my italics].

As well as giving details of Andrew's life, the writer attempts to assess his poetic qualities and his legacy:

> His unusual images have a quality which often hovers between serious wit and homely humour. . . . He will be remembered as a poet of the countryside with an individual voice and well-disciplined technique; although his range was not wide, there is much profundity in what he had to say. It is work that has its roots deep in the traditions of English pastoral poetry and which will always be enjoyed by those who find it refreshing in a world that is fast silencing the simpler pleasures of men.

The *University of Edinburgh Journal* (no. 25, 1971-72) also remembered Andrew, but made little attempt to assess the lasting relevance of 'this most distinguished graduate':

Canon Andrew John Young, M.A. 1907, LL.D., F.R.S.L.: at
Arundel, 25 November 1971. The Rev Canon Young had been
canon of Chichester Cathedral since 1947. He was a native of
Elgin and was educated at The Royal High School, Edinburgh,
Edinburgh University and New College. He was ordained as a
minister of the U.F. Church of Scotland at Temple, Midlothian,
but in 1939 entered the Church of England and in 1942 became
Vicar of Stonegate in the county of Sussex. His chief interests as
a student had been fine art and poetry, as a country parson he
added the study of British wild flowers. His prose writings . . .
brought him a considerable and appreciative public: they were
full of information and of the highest literary quality. But it is as
a poet that Canon Young achieved his greatest success. . . .

Canon Young was awarded a silver medal by the Royal
Society of Literature in 1940 and in 1944 was elected a Fellow
of the Society. In 1951 Edinburgh University conferred on
him the honorary degree of Doctor of Laws and the laureation
address paid a delightful tribute to this most distinguished
graduate.

On a more human level, Kitty Norris, wife of Leslie, who had known
Andrew (and his moods) well, remarked: 'He was a terrible man, but I
wept buckets when he died.'

Amongst Andrew's posthumous publications were:

1. *The Poetic Jesus,* SPCK, 1972.

2. *Complete Poems,* ed. by Leonard Clark, Secker & Warburg, 1974.

3. *The Poetical Works,* ed. by Lowbury and Young, Secker & Warburg,
1985.

4. *Parables,* The Keepsake Press, 1985.

5. *Crystal and Flint: Poems selected by David Burnett,* Snake River
Press, 1991.

6. *Selected Poems,* Carcanet Press, 1998.

Item 2, edited by Leonard Clark, belies its title by being *in*complete; only
item 3 has any claim to being the *complete* poems that Andrew wished to
preserve (and some he didn't!), including *Out of the World and Back* and
the verse plays. Clark was a conscientious if at times contradictory editor,
saying in one place, 'If he was *a minor poet* then he was also a superb
miniaturist, for he could compress vivid experience into a small space'
(my italics). Elsewhere he proclaimed that 'the signs of his *genius* were
already present in many of them (i.e. the earlier poems)' (my italics). He

cannot be both 'a minor poet' *and* a 'genius'. Clark maintains, rightly, that it 'would be inaccurate to consider him to be only a 'nature poet', then adds: 'But even if he is only to be considered as a nature poet . . . it is doubtful if any poet . . . has written more good poems about so many wild flowers, birds and creatures, the changing seasons, local scenery, the weather, hills, rivers, sea shores and archaeology'.

One problem with Clark's supposedly 'definitive' edition of Andrew's poems is its confusing, non-chronological organisation into two huge sections, with little explanation. However, Clark made many perceptive comments about Andrew, for example: 'He was a very fundamental poet, close to the earth, realistic, ironical, aware of the contradictions inherent in existence, as well as being a visionary.'

He also tried to 'place' him in literary history:

Although Andrew Young's poetry is peculiar to him, it has affinities. He belongs to the field company of John Clare, Robert Frost, Thomas Hardy, Edward Thomas and Edmund Blunden. Yet it is doubtful if he was ever consciously influenced by any of these. Tennyson and Housman may have been greater influences. The fact is that there is no other poetry in English quite like it. A poem by Andrew Young is instantly recognisable.

In other words, Andrew has a distinct and undeniable idiolect, as much as, say, Hopkins, Eliot, Auden or Hardy. Few would disagree with this.

The poet Roy Fuller, reviewing the 1974 volume, saluted Andrew as a 'latter-day Herrick', observing that 'the conceit is at the heart of Young's poetry, though triviality is absent because all is underpinned by a phenomenally accurate observation of nature'. It is strange that any critical thinker should associate 'the conceit' with 'triviality' to the point of having to explain why the latter is absent from the former! Fuller warns that, 'Exaggerated claims mustn't be made for Young. The Hardyesque stoicism . . . is the deepest part of his verse, though *Into Hades* and *A Traveller in Time* . . . rather improve on reacquaintance.'

Geoffrey Grigson, poet and literary critic, gave an altogether more personal response in *Country Life* in March 1974, describing how he first discovered Andrew Young's poems in the Bumpus bookshop many years earlier. He described Andrew as

> a poet who wrote with an uncommon directness. He had few readers, and no name until he was in his fifties . . . he is not a great poet, he is one who used language honestly and without vanity. His poems are love-and-life poems, about . . . places, rivers, monuments, flowers . . . himself, living, loving, dying.

Andrew's old friend Leslie Norris, reviewing *Complete Poems* in the London Magazine in mid-1974, noted that:

> He was accustomed to neglect but he was also sure of the value of his work. This splendid harvest edited by Leonard Clark convinces us he was right; it must surely establish Young as *a major poet.* . . . Throughout his long career he was very much his own man, apparently untouched by fashion . . . his own work . . . is brief, spare, hard as flint. . . . He was a metaphysical poet, exploring . . . layers of meaning [my italics].

Philip Toynbee, writing under the title *Rocks of Parnassus,* also perceives that 'Andrew Young is no more a minor poet than George Herbert was', although he was 'likely to slip through the coarse net of contemporary attention'. However, Toynbee rather undoes this critical enlightenment by these judgements:

> He made, I think, two major but easily forgivable blunders, the first in writing a religious verse play (*Nicodemus*) . . . the second, in devoting the last years of his poetical career to the composition of a long narrative metaphysical poem called *Into Hades.* This reads a little like Newman's *Dream of Gerontius*, a monstrosity, never quite redeemed, even by Elgar's music.

No critic worthy of the name could possibly think *Into Hades* a 'major blunder'. With its companion poem *A Traveller in Time*, it is arguably Andrew Young's *pièce de résistance.* It may be that Toynbee had a prejudice against religious writing.

* * *

Between 1974 and 1985 (the centenary of Andrew's birth), Alison and Edward Lowbury began two huge tasks: firstly to bring out a new, comprehensive and reorganised edition of Andrew's poems, and secondly the writing of a critical biography, relying very heavily on their (and particularly Alison's) intimate knowledge of Andrew in all facets of his life. This was to prove something of a double-edged sword: a warts-and-all life, showing the contradictions in his personality and behaviours (see Chapter 10), and insights into the poetry but without ultimate reassessment.

However, their splendidly edited and organised, though rather archaic-sounding, *Andrew Young, The Poetical Works*, remains the gold-standard edition. It was launched with readings (by Christopher Fry,

Robert Gittings and Ted Walker, introduced by Anthony Thwaite) and a celebration at The Poetry Society, then in Earl's Court Square, in January 1985. It was attended by many who had known Andrew, and others, like myself, who had never met him. There was also an exhibition of Andrew Young manuscripts and other material, such as letters and photographs.

Alan Bold, reviewing it in *The Scotsman* on 5 January 1985, made some attempt to reclaim Andrew as a Scotsman:

> In this New Year, Andrew Young deserves to be celebrated in his native Scotland and this book provides the perfect occasion for a reassessment of his many virtues. One of our more substantial poets, he survives as a marvellously readable writer who sustained the large body so lovingly presented in this fine edition.

Perceptively, Bold hailed *Out of the World and Back* as 'Young's masterpiece'.

P.J. Kavanagh, reviewing in *The Spectator* in March 1985, remarked that Andrew frequently made changes and revisions to his poems, yet: 'In his subject matter . . . he made no change at all in 50 years. This has caused him to be pushed aside as a "nature poet" and therefore, by definition, "minor".

This does 'him and poetry a disservice', he admits, yet never makes any claim of him being a 'major' poet, even suggesting that, 'in the neatness and lack of variety – you could say the lack of risk-taking – in the poetry of Andrew Young, there is a kind of stinginess . . . his vein was already exhausted, and he mined the last nuggets himself.'

Robert Nye, reviewing a number of poetry books in *The Times*[23] spoke patronisingly of Andrew: 'Young was a minor poet – but a splendid one, within his limits.'

Norman Nicholson, the younger Millom poet admired by Andrew, wrote a more thoughtful and insightful review in *The Church Times* of 31 May, saying that, although Andrew's poems were, 'not in the least modernist. . . . They were, nevertheless, obviously very good – concise, unforced, fresh, witty . . . (having) that terseness and precision which was characteristic of his maturity', he explained. He called the 1985 book 'admirably edited' and 'a great improvement on the (so-called) *Complete Poems* of 1974', principally because the poems were compiled in chronological order, included 'a generous selection from the earlier books' and 'a few hitherto unpublished poems', as well as *Out of the World and Back.*

---

23. Books Section, 28 March 1985.

Perceptive comments were made by George Szirtes, a poet himself, in *The Literary Review* in March 1985: Andrew had, he said, 'a Jacobean appreciation of the macabre [and] a dry metaphysical wit that verges on pedantic humour'. He seems to feel frustration that Andrew remains 'an enigma', someone hard to categorise: 'It is tempting to call Andrew Young a nature poet and have done with it', but he realises that he can't. He is correct in saying that, 'His earliest work is derivative and rather lame' yet finds in the later, longer poems, 'more vision' but 'less poetry'. He concluded, unexpectedly in the circumstances, 'we need a new, short *Selected Poems*, containing nothing but the best', in order to clarify Andrew to a new public.

As if to fulfil this requirement, the Lowburys edited *Andrew Young Selected Poems* in 1998, via Carcanet, a year after their biography of Andrew. A much slimmer volume, it does contain the best of his shorter poems, including some omitted from the 1985 edition, such as *The Dead Bird,* and *Landscape* (from *Songs of Night*, 1910). They omitted *The Bleeding Nun,* thirteen other short poems and the two long poems, and added two more 'prose poems' from *The New Poly-Olbion* (*In St Paul's Cathedral* and *Near Fowey*). It remains the last selection of Andrew's poems to date.

CHAPTER 7
OUT OF THE WORLD AND BACK
(1958)

By any standards, *Out of the World and Back* is a tour de force of its genre. By the standards of its own day, it is nothing short of a masterpiece: the denouement of Andrew Young's poetic achievement, on which, it may be argued, his reputation ultimately rests.

Indebted to his beloved Dante and linked to the English 'dream vision' poets (Langland and the anonymous poet of *Gawain, Pearl,* and so on) it is yet unique: a 'dream vision' of a journey from life through death and back, set unequivocally in the mid-twentieth century ('One midnight in the Paris Underground').

In it, Andrew extends his poetic repertoire, thematically and prosodically: his preoccupation with mortality, so evident in the 'nature' poems, takes a new twist, mixed with both fear and humour ('You cannot bury me; I am not dead;' / 'how false that coffin . . . It was my conjuror's box, with which I showed / The Vanishing Parson').

Like *The Pilgrim's Progress* it describes a 'journey from this world to the next', but without the Puritan symbolism and moral certainties, and it also brings the 'traveller' back again. *Into Hades* is written in blank verse, sometimes decasyllabic, and is frequently whimsical, paradoxical and ironic, using juxtapositions, rhetorical questions, biblical symbolism and classical references.

Bishop George Bell saw *Into Hades* as being primarily 'concerned . . . with the Mystery of the Resurrection',[1] and whilst this may be true, it is also an ontological poem about identity, time, the 'meaning of life', conflicting realities, consciousness and death. Bell also suggested that Andrew write a sequel, *Out of Hades*, a title Andrew considered, then thought better of, choosing the more descriptive, alliterative *A Traveller in Time*.

It is generally acknowledged, both by Andrew and others, that after *The Green Man* (1947), he made a deliberate decision to change poetic course: in a brief introductory note for *Out of the World and Back* (1958),

---

1.   *Andrew Young: Prospect of a Poet*, ed. by Leonard Clark, Hart-Davis, 1959.

Andrew explained: 'When the spring of short Nature poems ran dry, I was not sorry; for while my interest in nature was intense, it was not as deep as the underlying interest that prompted me to change my style and write *Into Hades*.'

Leonard Clark, his first literary executor, wrote: 'Both these poems, which are really one poem, crown his life's experience. He himself considers that all his previous work has been a preparation for this sustained escatological adventure.'[2] This is echoed by his friend Basil Dowling, a New Zealand poet living in Rye, whom Andrew first met in 1936:

He regarded his last work, the long poem *Out of the World and Back*, as his best and most important. He said he had outgrown the short nature poems, which he seemed to look on as a preparation rather than as a fulfilment.[3]

More interestingly, perhaps, Basil Dowling added: 'Dr Young told me the poem began when he was conducting a funeral in Stonegate churchyard and suddenly realised it was his own!'

From a series of notebooks in the National Library of Scotland archive, it is clear that Andrew conducted prolonged and in-depth research into the writings and life of John Bunyan;[4] he made notes on Spanish mystical writers and English poets,[5] including John of the Cross, Ignatius Loyola, St Teresa of Avila, Julian of Norwich, Langland, and lists of other source books, including C.S. Lewis' *Allegory of Love*. More importantly, perhaps, are his extensive and detailed notes on Dante, Virgil and others,[6] including *The Inferno*'s 'Dark Wood', 'Lion', 'She-Wolf', 'Greyhound', 'Lady in Heaven' and so on; and also on 'Paradiso', 'Purgatorio', 'Divine Grace' and very detailed notes on history, mysticism and philosophy.

Erudite and focused on his new project, Andrew seems to have begun it in the late 1940s. Both the 1952 and the cut/revised version of 1958, consisted of fourteen books/sections/or parts:

Books 1-9 and 14 are the same in both versions, but books 10-13 differ:

1952 and 1958:
1. The Funeral
2. The Prison

---

2.   As above.
3.   From correspondence with the present writer in 1990.
4.   MSS no. 19757.
5.   MSS no. 19761.
6.   MSS no. 19760.

3. The Body
4. The Prisoner
5. The Lover
6. The Ghost
7. Mattins
8. World's End
9. The Rainbow

1952:
10. The Void
11. The New Body
12. The New Earth
13. The New Heaven

1958:
10. The New Body
11. The New Earth
12. The New Heaven
13. The Three Hierarchies

1952 and 1958:
14. The Last Look

The spirit guide to the 'ghostly' traveller is The Monitor, unseen yet sensed, echoing perhaps The Interpreter in *The Pilgrim's Progress*.

Andrew plays on a universal fear with his comment: 'I was seized by my oldest fear, to be buried alive', a nightmarish scenario. After fear, comes curiosity about 'the strange novelty of being dead' (added in the 1958 version but absent in the 1952 version). After hearing snippets of the familiar Anglican burial service:

> Forasmuch – Almighty God – unto Himself
> The soul of our dear brother here departed,
> We therefore commit his body to the ground;
> Earth to earth, ashes to ashes

the 'ghost' shouts out that he is not dead, to 'those Three' ('the Three' in 1958), the rural dean, Fred the gravedigger and, presumably, his wife (or perhaps his wife and two children?) though echoing, of course, the Trinity . . . and is then, in a neat paradox, 'terrified by the silence' of his own voice, when they do not hear him.

Invisible to others but not to himself ('I could see my hand, my body') the 'ghost' wakes to a prison he later realises is of his own making:

> It was like waking
> In a strange room; I almost hoped to hear
> The opening of a door, a slippered step

Remembering the funeral, 'like the last scene of a play' (1952), he listens for 'night's stealthy noises', but hears nothing:

> No wind outside
> Drew its loose fingers through a bush; farm-cock
> Slept like weather-cock

The effect here is almost cinematic, reminiscent of a scene from Edgar Allan Poe; yet often the tone is witty, jocular, almost mocking in places:

> I stared in wonder
> at what had the appearance of a prison
> with thick-ribbed vault and iron-studded door
> in antique fashion. Yet it seemed hardly real,
> more like a prison in an opera,
> Faust or Fidelio

'Confused', he questions:

> Would someone come? The place must have its routine;
> a new arrival would cause no sensation.
> I should hear voices soon, friends at the door.
> Which would we be in heaven,
> our parents' children or our children's parents?
> We might be both. Time could be a clock
> with pendulum only and no foolish face,
> swinging us to and fro, backward and forward,
> from age to youth, from youth again to age,
> the psychological clock, our minds had lived by
> *in the interchange of memory and hope* [my italics].

The last line seems to have an unconsciously Eliotian echo.

In his state of 'waking dream', where 'nothing was changed, but all was visionary', he wonders:

> Was Death a monster,
> a cat that toyed with a mouse, caught but not killed?'
> Yet this,
> '... fear died in fascination,
> an amorous yielding to the softened paw

Despite these visions, the 'ghost' hovers around Stonegate and its old haunts:

> It had been piteous,
> the way the Three looked down on the lowered box,
> as though they left me there. My prison a smoke,
> could I not go to them as a ghost? From this side death
> ghost tales seemed credible. Would they be psychic?
> Or could I not be a determined ghost?
> I would be palpable, besiege the house,
> lay ambushes in the garden, look through a window
> [1952 version].

This passage becomes, in the revised 1958 version:

> From this side death
> Ghost tales seemed credible; could I not go back
> To the vicarage? Show myself to the Three,
> Who thought they left me in the lowered box?
> Would they be psychic? A determined ghost,
> I should be palpable, besiege the house,
> Lay ambushes in the garden, look through a window

From which we can see a streamlining and tightening up of phrasing, and a more logical reordering of thought. The paradox of being 'a dead man, live ghost', is played out as he remembers one such who:

> came and stood
> outside a lighted window of his house,
> face crushed against the glass, white as a mushroom,
> eyes burning like a moth's, and gazed within
> on wife and children, who were so unconscious
> a daughter rose and looked out on the darkness
> and seeing nothing, drew the blind

The 'fear' of a similar experience makes the ghost-dreamer hesitate, then realise that he could not 'force a passage back to those Three', but must continue forwards in his journey. In Part 3, 'The Body', although the dominant emotion, naturally enough, is fear, there is also a fascinated curiosity and a rational probing of the new reality:

> I had seen an elm trunk
> that hurt the ground with its dead-weight, sprout leaves,
> unconscious it was dead; I had caught fish,

flounders that flapped, eels tying and untying
slippery knots, not drowning in the air;
was I too living out my life's last remnant,
not living, only lasting? . . .
Or was I not myself yet,
recovered from my illness, cured by death,
but still convalescent? How was it I had died?
Had death come as a storm, tornado, razing
a tract of memory? There was a gap,
days, weeks and months torn from the almanac

Suddenly, an unexpectedly personal note is struck:

I remembered my father's death;
how I had watched the hard, humiliating struggle,
that made me half ashamed that I, his son,
spied on his weakness. I remembered too
thinking that some time I should go that way;
but had I then believed it?

In the 1958 version, several lines are added after 'weakness', before it resumes with 'I remembered too':

I remembered her,
Who held her son's last letter in her hand
Like a passport to heaven

This may be a reference to his mother holding his brother David's last letter, after which no more was ever heard of him, whether through death or disappearance. Thinking of this elder brother may have encouraged him to use his other brother, William, who had died in infancy before his own birth, as his spirit guide in *A Traveller in Time*.

The 1952 version continues:

Even now
seeing and touching my accustomed body
compromised the truth. Was it not out of place,
an obvious mistake? Raising a hand
I recognised a white scar on my wrist;
I felt my heart; that songless lark kept time,
shut in its cage of bones. Yet the funeral
had stared me in the face. I was confused;
there were two bodies, two scars, two bird cages?

Whereas in the 1958 version, the rhetorical question in lines 2-4 becomes an assured statement, two exclamations about the funeral are stronger, more amusing; and '*there were* two bodies' becomes a rhetorical question, '*Were there* two bodies...?' The 'songless lark' metaphor is strong in both versions:

> why, even now
> The sight and touch of my accustomed body
> Compromised the truth. Here it was out of place,
> An obvious mistake. Raising my hand
> I recognised a white scar on my wrist;
> I felt my heart; shut in its cage of bones,
> That songless lark kept time. But the funeral!
> The coffin with its cargo! I was confused;
> Were there two bodies, two scars, two bird cages?

As he looks at his own body,

> It stared back with a strange impertinence,
> Familiar, hostile, superfluous proof I was dead.

It was not like,

> that stiff, straight soldier
> Who kept good guard in his fallen sentry box.

The metaphor is apt, the word 'fallen' visually conjuring the coffin and the strangeness of out-of-the-body experience. It provokes the ghost-dreamer to realise that he must confront deep ontological issues:

> it was high time to answer
> The long-unanswered knocking at my mind's
> Back door.

Then he thinks of God, and, 'The thought was surgical.'
In Book 4, 'The Prisoner' asks pertinently:

> Which was this cell, convict's or anchorite's?

Just as the funeral seemed 'a hoax', so his surroundings seem 'stage property. . . . Like a church. . . . Turned outside in'. Yet, he feels 'it was dangerous to be dead'.
In Book 4, 'The Lover', he concludes paradoxically, 'There was no future in this future life,' since there was nothing to do:

> Dante set out to walk from hell to heaven
> For his soul's health, but mine had caught a cold.

'And Dante came back!' he reminds himself. Dante was also enamoured of Beatrice, his Muse, of whom he is supposed to have said: 'I did but see her passing by, and yet I love her 'til I die'. This 'chaste' love echoes the dreamer's own, when, with 'a ring of twisted silver' he 'married Chastity by proxy', placing the ring on his own finger. 'I found her (Chastity) most in Paris', where 'she cooled my blood' and 'I starved my body' like John the Baptist in the Latin Quarter, as Andrew was to write later, in his unpublished *Autobiography*.

There is much droll humour, as in Book 6, 'The Ghost':

> Morning was late that day,
> Delayed by thick fog. . . .
> How I came in the garden
> Was denser fog

Then he realised, 'it was my own garden I was haunting' as he 'saw the vicarage / Across the pond', yet felt 'warned away, a trespasser in my own garden'. Trying then to go to the Communion Service ('the Celebration'), since 'All mornings for a ghost were All Saints Night',[7] he walked down the road, seeing 'The boy with Sunday papers' cycling along, looking through him. He surmised sardonically, 'I had seen Death at last'. Reaching the lychgate, and seeing again the 'white chrysanthemums' on his grave seemed to weaken him:

> My ghostly hands had not strength enough to turn
> The door's iron handle

So he 'darted to a window', but not seeing the priest, 'Overflying the roof, I perched on an Irish yew' The dream-quality of speed and weightlessness, if not strength, are vividly conveyed, as is the feeling of ultimate exclusion, of being 'excommunicated', i.e. cut off not just from Man but from God. There is an 'awe-ful' resonance here, emphasised by the punning statement that he was:

> Locked out by St Peter's key!

that is, from his own church of St Peter's, Stonegate, but also from heaven, to which St Peter was given the keys. Still outside, the ghost sat 'through the Psalms / Like an invalid' (also, presumably, feeling in-valid). Gazing about the churchyard he saw:

> it was autumn; berries on the hedge
> Hung in bright bracelets

---

7. When the dead are said to rise from their graves on All Hallows E'en.

The metaphor reminds us that, escatological concerns aside, Andrew is still a poet, like Hardy, who 'noticed such things'. Looking through the window, the ghost-dreamer sees that:

> One of my friends stood at the lectern eagle;
> Jove's messenger, the brazen bird looked bored,
> It had so often listened to the Lessons.
> As I peered at the priest, the stranger in my stall,
> The congregation rose, filling the church,
> For the *Te Deum*. So they must have risen,
> When I was shouldered out, smothered with flowers
> To make my death the surer. The thought was bitter;
> It turned the *Te Deum* to the *Nunc Dimittis*.

There are a number of subtleties here, beginning with the humorous pathetic fallacy of the 'brazen' bird (it was made of brass) being 'bored'. The possessiveness of 'my stall' and the 'bitter' thought of how he had been 'shouldered out' (surely there's a pun here?) makes it clear that this 'ghost' is sinner rather than saint, providing a link to the reader's own experience. The *Te Deum* is a morning hymn of praise and trust, and a plea for mercy; but the ghost's own feelings turn it into something more like the *Nunc Dimittis*, the Song of Simeon just before his death, beginning, 'Lord, now lettest thou thy servant depart in peace, according to thy word'.

Yet Andrew is equally at home with classical references and implications. Standing by his own grave (of course, 'At the priest's end') the ghost describes how:

> I saw a wonder: the coffin-lid mere glass,
> I gazed down at the gaunt philosopher,
> I hardly knew myself; here was a change
> From Epicurean to the Stoic school.

Shocked by his own transition in death, he is even more shocked when the effigy, like some nightmarish jack-in-the-box, rises up to meet him:

> But the coffin was a trap; springing to life
> He rose, a towering wave of lust, and gripped me;
> I choked in his close embrace, cold awful kiss.

The last three words are perhaps reminiscent of Judas' betrayal of Christ.

The ghostly dreamer, at the beginning of Book 8, 'World's End', considers ironically that:

> Corpses so amorous, earth was not safe
> For wandering ghosts. The prison would be safer,
> No fear of being murdered by a dead man.

Disorientation, vulnerability and a sense almost of self-loathing are well conveyed:

> But was I back in prison?
> I gazed on nothing; even the floor had fled;
> The prison, not the prisoner, had escaped!
> All was so absent, I had the baffled sense
> That in looking I did not look. It was like a sea
> Without the water. Hung on a spacious point,
> I feared to stretch a hand; I might overbalance,
> Fall without end; it was dangerous as a dream.
> I viewed myself with distaste. Emphatic Ego,
> A speck of horrible conspicuousness,
> I felt exposed.

Very effective extended metaphors convey a series of contrasts, loosely based on naval and horological imagery:

> Flowing ectoplasm,
> This body would not last, not even as long
> As that other body lying in its sunk boat,
> Shipwrecked on land. This was a replica,
> That the original. I felt for its defeat,
> A self-pity: face that had hoisted the white flag
> To the invaders; veins, once fruitful rivers,
> Stagnant canals; the heart, that had kept good time,
> Stopped; inner works, that had gone of their own accord,
> While I, the engineer, had walked on deck,
> Run down

It ends with an angling metaphor, and the oxymoron 'solid wind':

> Trout in time's stream, nosing its solid wind,
> Helped by a heavenly hook, I had leapt out
> And landed on the bank.

Book 9, 'The Rainbow', echoes the Book of Revelation, itself a dream vision. Saints hear 'silent music' (of the spheres?) in 'the Godhead's mountain range'. At first, it puzzles the ghost-dreamer, as it was, 'a rainbow in a foreign language' whose colours he could not grasp. Whilst he 'gazed in frightened joy', the vision faded, and his 'makeshift body. . . . Melted away'. Being 'Too near to nothing', he craved for 'A limit to my false infinitude', yet 'All was so empty. I was not even defined by what I was not'; remembering that 'Saints were the world's adventure', the fearful dreamer's 'faith leaned hard on theirs'.

He concludes that:

> If others like myself were here
> Each had arrived with his own universe,

An extraordinary ontological idea.

It is rare that there is any hint of another poet's unconscious influence, apart from several Eliotian echoes, but 'the Dark Silence / Where all lovers lose themselves' is certainly reminiscent of Edward Thomas:

> The unfathomable deep
> Forest, where all must lose
> Their way[8]

Occasionally, Andrew's imagery takes unexpected turns, as in:

> Whatever it might be after the Judgement,
> Our universes now could no more mingle
> Than *the imaginations of a man and woman*
> *Lying in the same bed* [my italics].

He concludes 'The Rainbow' with the punning thought that:

> My sole support was God.
> The thought was electric

In 'The New Body', 'The New Earth', 'The New Heaven', the emphasis, being based on *Revelations*, is more overtly Christian, despite references to Greek mythology, Petrarch and Laura, and Plato's philosophy.

In 'The New Body', the 'old' body he had 'lived in, loved on earth', was superseded by a new one which was 'real in excess' not merely 'phantasmal':

> Fantastic coffin,
> The boat that bore it slowly sailed in sight,
> Lit by St Elmo's fire; it might have come
> From anchoring off the rainbow. Solomon's cargo,
> The gold and silver, ivory, apes and peacocks,
> Was not so precious as that solemn barge's.
> Its cargo was its captain, but not dead;

---

8. *Lights Out*, v.1.

> In sleep surmounting sleep he lay in state
> Distant, superior, unrecognising,
> My new authentic body!
> Holy, immortal, my eyes saw it so clearly
> They stung me like jellyfish, as I remembered
> How I had profaned its earthly prototype
> Though only a phantom.

The imagery is again naval but also reminiscent of Cleopatra's barge in *Antony and Cleopatra.*

After this, the ghost-dreamer sleeps and wakes, sleeps and wakes, floats, flies, fears being once more insubstantial. In 'The New Earth' he meets his Monitor:

> Yet I was not alone;
> I knew by the *different silence* there was an Other,
> Invisible, *hiding behind himself* [my italics].

This Monitor becomes his temporary guide, though invisible: 'Come, see the Bride,' an *unheard voice* says. 'The New Earth' 'now renewed / Reborn . . . was so transfigured, so unearthly / I felt I tarnished her by looking'. The word *transfigured* is laden with connotations of the Resurrection and is an example of Andrew's careful placing of individual words for maximum effect.

Miraculously, on this 'New Earth',

> All things were conscious, trees talking together,
> Streams their own Sirens, mountains might have moved
> Slow shoulders

Meanwhile his 'New Body' 'puts to shame' even,

> The miracle of loaves and fishes. It stirred,
> Sprouted with life, rose spreading, multiplying,
> Changed to a Jesse-tree. The sleeping Adam
> Had more ribs than a wreck: warm, fertile, breathing,
> They stretched as boughs, laden with all the bodies
> I had worn on earth, child, lover and man.

The root of Jesse harks back to the earthly genealogy of Christ, thus becoming Everyman.

Moving backwards and forwards in time, the 'ghost' sees 'Past following future, as future followed past', much as Penelope would 'unweave / Her historic web' at night to remake it in the morning. The 'ghost' imagines that:

cities would unbuild themselves,
Temples fly back to their quarries; fossils unfreezing
Would show toothed birds and five-toed horses; coal
Mining itself, would rise as ferny forests
Air feel again the weight of flying lizards

In this panorama of the past in 'Time's two-way traffic', the 'ghost' considers his own position:

And myself? I should wander to and fro in time,
Historian of all – its present ages.
I should taste Eternity. Why had I said,
There was no future in this future life?[9]

In 'The New Heaven', after the unexpected 'explosion' of 'a dead volcano', the 'ghost' finds himself, 'Dead and alive at once', yet aware of the presence of his Monitor, who 'proved a Mercury' and carried him off to 'see the saints in flight', though 'in a steadfast sleep'.

In 'The Three Hierarchies', Book 13, Mercury carries the sleeping 'ghost' off 'in flame-like flight' whilst 'Singing to music dumb as a music-score / A song inaudible as a bursting rosebud's'. The Holy Trinity, the sleeper is told, 'Is celebrated in three hierarchies' and he is invited to 'see the third'. Straining his sight, he glimpses the 'gold and purple feathers' of the phoenixes, which 'struck the Godhead' one moment, then the next were ashes, in their 'immortal deaths' yet 'Each was God's only phoenix'. The symbolism of both the Godhead and Man is clear.

In Book 14, 'The Last Look', the dreamer/ghost's Monitor leaves him, and a door with a staircase opens up, inviting his 'downward steps'. All that he had 'experienced' 'had been timeless' and the funeral at Stonegate was 'not finished' and 'Priest and people would stand by the open grave / Till I descended the stair'. He knew, 'by instinct', that he had returned to 'the old earth' which was still, paradoxically, in its 'ancient youth'. The Symbol he sees is Adam's tree:

Leafless, forlorn, clothed with a naked Man,
The Prodigal Son, who came to save the world.

The final verses, unchanged but for two lines, between the 1952 and 1958 versions, become less of a personal experience/vision, and more of a religious polemic/exercise in apologetics: the final vision is of 'the monster' of Original Sin (Adam's) spreading its 'ambitious arms' round the world, and of the Crucifixion (Christ's) in atonement; and, by

---

9.   In Book 5, line 2.

implication, human and personal resurrection and salvation. This gives credence to Bishop Bell's comment that *Into Hades* is primarily a poem 'about the Resurrection'.

* * *

Expatriate New Zealand poet, Basil Dowling, had first met Andrew in 1936 when they were introduced by J.G. Wilson (Andrew's publisher) at the Edward Thomas Centenary celebrations on Shoulder of Mutton Hill, in Steep. As well as both being poets they admired the same poets, especially Edward Thomas and Hardy. They became firm friends and Basil, who lived in London at that time, before moving to Rye, visited Andrew at both Stonegate and Yapton. Much as T.S. Eliot asked his friend John Hayward's critical advice about *The Four Quartets* before publication, so Andrew asked Basil Dowling about revising *Into Hades* between 1952 and 1958.

Dowling made 'about a dozen suggestions for revision' marking some passages as 'obscure' or suggesting Andrew should 'expand and clarify'. Of 'Martyrs . . . chariot of fire', Dowling remarked, 'Very fine and arresting poetry but too dogmatic perhaps?' Some things he found 'not clear'. At the beginning of Book 4, 'The Prisoner', Dowling commented: 'Not patriotic like Bernard de Morlaix' – query too cryptic? Who was B. de M. and how was he 'patriotic'?

These were quite searching comments, and Dowling was pleased to see that, after the publication of *Out of the World and Back* (1958), 'some of these suggested changes were in fact carried out'.[10]

The new style was given a mixed reception by reviewer/critic Richard Church (amongst others) in *John O'London's* on 18 April 1952:

> Andrew Young, usually so clear, so crystalline a spirit, as we have seen him through his quartz-splinter lyrics, has now written one of these strange, dreadful oracular poems, to which one must come again and again. . . . *Into Hades* (Hart-Davis, 5s.) is the story of a Dantesque pilgrimage into the underworld, and the emergence into a prospect of paradise, with hope and salvation for the desolate traveller. Like its great exemplar, it is told in the vernacular, for Young has deliberately chosen a prosody devoid of rhyme; and a rhythm, based on our conventional pentameter, tossed and broken so that at times the surface is scarcely recognisable. But still the music is there, with touches of slang and slogan to astonish the reader who knows the austerity of this poet. . . .

---

10. Notes sent to the present writer by Basil Dowling in the early 1990s.

> (At) the opening. . . . A funeral is in progress. . . . From there the pilgrimage begins, and . . . we travel with this disembodied priest and poet, through prison . . . metamorphoses of body, personality and very nature itself . . . finally to emerge to the last two sections of the poem . . . we are aware that somehow the pace quickens, the feet leave the ground . . . until we are in the midst of that power of rhetoric like a mighty wind, which sweeps through the verse with an immanence of wisdom, and carries us along, content to be in the power of such authority.

Later, when reviewing Andrew's posthumous *Complete Poems* (1974), Leslie Norris made some perceptive comments, including this one:

> The long poem, *Into Hades*, is where Young used his considerable learning and examined his beliefs. I think this work is *still underrated*. It has great strength, is eloquent and visionary, and reveals aspects of Young's poetry one would not suspect from reading the lyrics. After completing it he virtually gave up the writing of poetry [my italics].

These comments downplay the fact that *Into Hades* had a sequel, to which it was closely related. Knowing him as a friend, Norris acknowledged that Andrew was 'a complex man' whose work, 'almost from the first, is brief, spare and hard as flint'. He also remembered an occasion when:

> Walking into my room, he put a magazine on the table. 'It says here', he said, 'that Hugh MacDiarmid is the greatest living Scots poet.' And he smiled gently. He was accustomed to neglect but he was also sure of the value of his work. This splendid harvest edited by Leonard   Clark convinces us that he was right; it must surely establish Young as *a major poet* (my italics).

Some six months after the publication of the first version of *Into Hades*, Andrew met Basil Dowling in London and it is clear that they discussed a number of theories about time/time travel, history, philosophy and poetry:

> OFF-HAND ACCOUNTS OF MY MEETINGS
> WITH ANDREW YOUNG copied from my notebooks:

> October '52. Met Andrew Young at Charing Cross, had tea and walked about the pavements in wintry rain until 8p.m. (with pauses at pubs for a glass of ale). To Contemp. Arts Soc., Dover St. for reading of poems by A.Y. and Ronald Duncan – met him and Prof. Isaacs the chairman. Both said

it was the first time they had read their poems in public. A.Y. very modest and nervous, but excellent when the time came. When he read *Field Glasses* he remarked that having at one time got interested in birds (as well as plants) he bought some field glasses and was thought by some of his parishioners to be going to the races! He said that in his verse he always tried to use three words instead of five, and to introduce a touch of strangeness whenever he could.

Walking about Piccadilly in the rain, A.Y. and I talked about many things, but especially the problem of Time, which he said had always fascinated him more than any other. We discussed Dunne's theory, Bergson's and others, and then A.Y. gave me an outline of his own view which is a part of his belief in immortality – he thinks the difficulty is in the thought of there being too many people in the world; no room for them all, but that this is got over by a view of time which gives all these millions the freedom to move both forwards and backwards. He recommended to me a book of the twenties called *An Adventure in Paris* by two women who claimed to have stepped back into another century, and we exchanged various stories and ideas of a similar kind. Also we talked much of the idea of bodily resurrection, and agreed that a true immortality would mean the survival of those superficial characteristics, features, and even oddities by which we recognise our friends. A.Y. regards the N.T. account of the walk to Emmaus as the most significant of all, and I recommended him to read Stanley Morison's *Who Moved the Stone?*

When passing the gates of Buckingham Palace he casually remarked that he supposed he would be going inside before long, as he had just heard from Masefield that he had won the Queen's Medal for Poetry. But he warned me that publishing poetry had become too difficult and expensive, and said that to try to make some money (he is quite poor: though a Canon and a Doctor he gets only £350 a year!) he is writing a guide book to Britain — he urged me to do a popular book on New Zealand. Guide books, he declares, always pay well. But of course he is going on with poetry all the time, *reading systematically for the next part of his long religious poem.* I hope (as I told him) that he will put into it his wonderful ideas on Time and immortality [my italics]. [11]

---

11. Part of an account Basil Dowling sent to the present writer in the early 1990s.

This certainly shows that, even in 1952, Andrew was planning, thinking and talking about a sequel to *Into Hades*, but it was several years down the line before he decided to revise *Into Hades* as well. When he did, there were losses and gains, but more of the latter.

A *Traveller in Time* is divided into the following Books or Sections:

1. I Set Out
2. The Dale
3. The Tiltyard
4. The Abbey
5. I Travel Farther
6. The Nymph's Well
7. The Procession
8. At Eleusis
9. I Travel Still Farther (*very* long!)
10. At Nazareth
11. The Cave
12. Jerusalem
13. Back in the Dale

His 'guide' was his dead brother, William, whom he never knew.

His main themes were Time and Place.

In Book 1, the traveller emerges from the shadow, still asking about the Last Judgement, yet to be.

Referring, paradoxically, to 'Meeting that stranger, myself', his first question is:

> Was I free again to play
> My garden part, the ghost?

He realises he is 'in the world', which was 'familiar', yet asks:

> Escaping ghost, dead man on holiday,
> Where was I?

Frightened by 'a group of witchlike birches', he smiles to himself:

> for a ghost who should frighten others,
> I was too nervous.

Suddenly staggering in a strong gust of wind gave him the feeling that 'an invisible man' was 'walking through' his body. Soon he discovers:

> My eyes opened to a world I recognised
> No longer in a mode of separation,
> But intimate, reciprocal.

It was 'remote from time / Even outside space'. The 'incarnate beauty' seems to him, 'The Ecstatic landscape / Earth in love with heaven!' He then sees a man walking downstream, but oddly only 'a head and shoulders'.

In Book 2, The Dale, where he follows the vision of the partial man, he observes that,

> Herod was not so startled
> By the Baptist's head on a charger

He concludes that 'If I saw nothing / It was too real a nothing not to follow'. Walking along he notices that, 'autumn . . . had changed to spring':

> loose hazel catkins
> Dripped in a yellow rain, palm-willow wands
> Stretched out gold paws.

Time 'had moved with a jerk / Backward and forward' as it had in *Into Hades*.

In Book 3, The Tiltyard, the dreamer feels himself 'in an enchantment' since 'nothing looked real'. Eventually, he finds himself in the Middle Ages, at a tiltyard before a castle where 'people held a pageant'. At first he thinks it 'a phantasma', but soon realises that 'Those were real knights'. Andrew's description is vivid:

> A swollen sun hung over the purple hills,
> Its gold changing to blood

Then the joust began, the two knights charging, then falling, 'in a confused tumble'. Paradox is never far away:

> How strange to see these knights,
> Who died too long ago to be called dead,
> Now fighting for life . . .
> For the ancient castle was new,
> The spectacle extant

However,

> The fight stopping itself,
> They froze to figures in a stained glass window

a clever device to take the dreamer into Book 4, The Abbey, which he compares favourably to 'that cathedral, grey ghost of itself / Where I held my canon's stall' (i.e. Chichester):

Here clustered columns,
Sprouting gilt foliage from the capitals,
Blossomed like Aaron's rod, and in the choir screen
Dead timber, coming alive, renewed rich summer
With leaf, flower, berry

In the windows were 'Patriarchs, prophets, kings, apostles, martyrs', including St Sebastian who 'Bristled with arrows like a startled hedgehog'. Humour also, is never far away but is usually followed by seriousness:

But all were martyrs in those burning windows,
God's salamanders. Built more of flame than stone,
But most of spirit, reared on argument,
Of thrust and counterthrust, Thomistic[12] logic,
This adoring church wooed God.

In an instant the Abbey vanished, as the tiltyard had done, in cinematic fashion, and the mysterious head and shoulders reappear in Book 5:

His shoulders' shape,
Back of the head, woke in me a strange feeling,
Instinctive, warm

The identity of this guiding presence, appearing in Book 5, is only revealed in Book 10, At Nazareth, as:

I am that dead brother
You never knew

William, like the infant girl in *Pearl*, who died aged under two, yet grew to adulthood and spiritual wisdom in the afterlife to guide their respective 'dreamers' in their visions. The unknown author of *Pearl*, *Purity*, *Patience*, and *Sir Gawain and the Green Knight*, clearly influenced Andrew's thinking and his decision to write his own two dream vision poems. The 'dream' device itself gives the author a licence to invent, to link reality and fantasy, and to transcend the limits of time and space.

At The Nymph's Well, the dreamer has the 'profane' fancy that he sees himself in her arms, then is amazed that the picture of himself so seen is still a 'young man's face' and that 'travelling in time' had made him 'look no older'. This makes him wonder if things were,

All in reverse, sun rising in the west,
Spring following summer, old men born in graves
And growing younger?

---

12. A reference to the works of St Thomas Aquinas.

Finding himself then in Athens, in sight of the Acropolis and the Parthenon,

> I guessed it was late autumn; but what year,
> What century? Was Socrates alive?

Reciting to himself all the events and people he might see, including the Trojan War, Theodorus playing Antigone, Socrates discoursing, the dreamer concludes:

> Greece for a beginning,
> I should not find eternity itself
> Hang heavy on my hands.

In Book 8, At Eleusis, there is the Hall of Mysteries, celebrated with frenzied dancing, where the goddess Demeter gave mystical birth to 'her adopted children' helped by Bacchus. The dreamer says: 'I could not pluck the heart of the mystery' – and neither, alas, can the reader! The clue given is that 'All is the effort to accomplish death'.

The ninth Book is very long and in it the dreamer asks, 'did the Hall collapse / Because I read its secret? For all went' and he was 'in motion, travelling again'. Meeting the strange head and shoulders, now as 'Complete as Adam', the dreamer sees, but does not understand, 'The family likeness' of his companion, who proceeds to point out landmarks: Mount Gerizim, Mount Ebal and Shechem, all in Old Testament Palestine. A strange feast before a golden bull, with sacred slaves, ensues, while Hosea appears, shouting, 'A fierce "Yah-yah" . . . like a hyena's bark'. He had come to buy back a screaming woman: 'Gomer bath Diblaim, his children's mother'. As he led her away, 'hubbub rose in the hall', and the dreamer wonders if the 'ascent' from 'temple slave' to 'rigid wife' once again will be 'too sharp' for Gomer, as he watched them leave, hand in hand. The parallel is drawn between 'God's painful case with His adulterous people' and Hosea's with Gomer.

At Nazareth, in Book 10, 'Had the light gone out / As in a theatre when scenes are shifted?' the dreamer wonders, and what he should witness next. His companion/guide explains that, 'Here we take no account of time . . . / Nor . . . of space.' They witness Mary, staggering under the pangs of imminent childbirth, disappear into a house: 'how unlike God's chosen vessel / She made Christ's coming to the earth seem furtive'. If this seems strange, so does 'The paradox! that He who came as light / Should learn of the darkness'. As though trying to link together the disparate experiences so far related, for the reader's understanding, the poet-dreamer summarises at the end of this section:

The amorous earth had an unearthly beauty;
Love, too, though dark and native, bound the minnows,
That darted like a shadow from the stones,
In their mute brotherhood. When the two knights
Fought in the tiltyard, flags and hearts a-flutter
That summer evening, the sun of earthly love
Was at its meridian; and when I woke,
I saw a church, where pillars, arches, roof,
Had less been built than of themselves had risen,
Drawn up by heavenly love. It was by the Light
Illumined, the two Greek girls saw in the well
A divinity, a favourable Nymph,
And left their pious loaves; while at Eleusis,
Teaching the parable, the Seed of Corn,
It so inspired the mystics that in a symbol
They died to be reborn. If at Mount Ebal
Hosea, his shame so hot, laid a cold kiss
On Gomer's ill-starred brow, yet it prefigured
The kiss the father gave the prodigal son.
In Mary prophecy had reached its end;
The Light Itself was come.

In Book 11, as the dreamer and his guide 'climbed to Nazareth', they stopped, 'where a cave / Gaped with wide mouth' filled with 'warm light' and, 'we sat and talked together / That brother, dead before I was born, and I / Sharing news of our two worlds'. Later, finding himself suddenly alone, the dreamer feels 'alarm' then 'wonder' as he looks 'through the open door of a carpenter's shed', and sees, 'not Joseph, but / The carpenter's Son. I watched Him at His work / The eternal Worker, the Word within the word / "Let there be Light."'

Later, 'I almost saw the Darkness / With which He wrestled, clutching Himself in prayer'. Later still, the dreamer sees Him standing by a creek, where a boat runs aground and 'Two of the Twelve' who 'busied themselves with their nets' were then joined by a third, St Peter.

Jerusalem, Book 12, is the longest section, in which the dreamer, seemingly abandoned by his brother, sets off by himself on his 'maiden voyage': a 'flight / Across a Limbo', over a bridge, near a huddle of houses, where the people were 'strangely blurred' to him and he was invisible to them, a fact which 'alarmed' him, as it raises the old fear of physical disintegration:

My apparent body
Mere memory, old clothes, might I not vanish

> Like an image from a forgetful mirror, or slowly
> Dissolve . . . melting in tears?

This occasions the dreamer to recall what presumably was a real incident
in Andrew's own life:

> I once saw an apparition,
> A lady gliding across a lawn to vanish
> Through a wall of Ludlow Castle

As smoothly, he now glides upwards to a battlemented wall, and passed
through 'a guarded gate' feeling as 'Perplexed as a bat'. The sudden note
of humour almost breaks the spell of both imagined flight, and fear.
Soon, however, the dreamer, with the 'sure flight of migrating swallow'
approaches the Temple, then finds himself on 'the little hill, Golgotha'
at the Feast of the Passover too late for the Crucifixion, yet 'seeing' His
weeping mother, 'holy Mary' after 'The three crosses were gone'.

Travelling backwards and forwards in time, the dreamer had 'but to set
my heart' (like a compass) to take him where he wanted to go: yet 'night
falling at noon' warned him not to try to go back three hours to witness
the Crucifixion, since it was not for 'ghost-moths' like him, 'perhaps not
even for angels'. In a strange turnaround:

> I pitied Him who so transcended time
> His eternal eye could never escape the sight,
> His Son hanging on a cross.

In the final verse of this section, Andrew becomes overtly the Christian
theologian:

> All other loves,
> That in my trivial travels I had witnessed
> Were thin outcroppings of the primal love
> The creative Word imparted to the world
> On its six birthdays. They were geologic;
> This was Uranian; it fell vertical
> Faster than Lucifer, the very Word,
> God's Proper Name, creating a new earth,
> A kingdom, holy church, all, alas, more veiled
> Than the Word made flesh.

Book 13 concludes, Back in the Dale, where his journey began. The
old hermit he had seen in Book 2, he now realises, was 'Richard Rolle
/writing *The Fire of Love*', sitting on the same stone, 'though centuries

apart'. As night approaches, a cloud comes over the moon, identified by the dreamer as the anonymous *Cloud of Unknowing*. This introduces a catalogue of 'all God's mystic children' including Richard Rolle, St Catherine of Genoa, St John of the Cross and Meister Eckhart, a medieval German mystic. All these,

> escaped the shipwreck of the world and pierced
> The lightsome darkness, lost, annihilated –

Yet,

> Their nothing-at-all preserved in the All-in-all . . .
> of the Word . . . God in a point.

The dreamer concludes:

> The ghost must go; the *cocoon spun by the worm*[13]
> The butterfly would burst. New eyes would see
> The invisible world into which my brother vanished [my italics].

Thus, the end of the soul's/dreamer's journey is acceptance of the physical and spiritual paradoxes whereby the individual is absorbed into eternity: the 'death' of the self for a greater good.

* * *

It may be argued that this sequel lacks some of the power, impact and wit of *Into Hades*: it is more scenically descriptive and the 'destinations' of the ghost-dreamer more random. It is also more heavily impregnated with classical references and Christian dogma/polemic, both likely to alienate the contemporary reader. It is also 250 or so lines longer than *Into Hades*, with no particular benefit; and unlike the latter, was never revised or cut. How far these points weaken its effectiveness is debatable.

The Lowburys' assessment of *A Traveller in Time* was that it is 'a narrative that is so much slacker and more arbitrary than that of *Into Hades*,' which is generally true. Roger Sell, in a serious academic study,[14] suggests that '*Into Hades* is more metaphysical, *A Traveller in Time* more earthbound', in that the ghost leaves the world for most of *Into Hades*, only returning at the end; whereas in *A Traveller in Time* the ghost travels *in* the world, across historical eras and geographical places, so this assertion is true. In neither poem is Judgement Day ever reached, though fearfully sought. *Out of the World and Back* is an appropriate title for the pair of linked poems.

---

13. The reference to the cocoon echoes back to *Into Hades* Book 2, where the dreamer realises that 'like a silkworm' he had spun his 'own cocoon'.
14. Åbo Akademi, *Trespassing Ghost: A Critical Study of Andrew Young*, 1978.

Sell suggests that the dead brother is, 'a less satisfactory literary creation than The Monitor' and that this adds to 'a general unsatisfactoriness in *A Traveller in Time*'. The Monitor is certainly a stronger, more didactic figure; the brother more elusive, yet more emotionally charged.

'*Into Hades* is more finely wrought, more imaginatively unified, more moving and far more profoundly original than *A Traveller in Time*,' Sell rightly concludes. Of *The Traveller* he admits that it is 'never less than *interesting*, and is in *some points* very fine' (my italics).

It is arguable that a thorough revision such as *Into Hades* had would have much improved *The Traveller*, and rid it of what Sell termed 'a certain first-attempt sloppiness', along with 'a lack of artistic control reminiscent of the worst early work'. If this judgement seems a harsh one, it is because of the marked discrepancy in quality between the two poems. The present writer is in full agreement with Sell when he states: 'It is on the basis of *Into Hades*, together with the best of the shorter poems, that Young's stature as a poet must be judged' (see Chapter 11).

The 1952 edition of *Into Hades* had no dedication, whereas *Out of the World and Back,* in 1958, was dedicated 'To my Wife' as though a gesture of thanks for all her support and long-suffering.

Reviews were varied, some more thoughtful and perceptive than others. The anonymous reviewer in *The Times Literary Supplement* of 5 December 1958 devoted a full page to *Out of the World and Back*, and quoted extensively from Leonard Clark's edited *Andrew Young: Prospect of a Poet*, published the previous year. The review begins:

> In 1952 Canon Andrew Young published a very strange poem called *Into Hades*. Though Mr Richard Church greeted it very warmly, on the whole reviewers did not know what to say about it. . . . They reacted, on the whole, to Canon Young's poem with respectful embarrassment. . . .
>
> Canon Young has now very considerably revised *Into Hades* and has added a sequel . . . which makes the intention of the earlier poem much clearer. . . . It is impressive by its design; it is impressive also by the sustained dignity, the living unexpectedness and the occasional superb felicity of its writing.

The reviewer then quotes from the 1952 and 1958 versions of *Into Hades*, advising, 'people who care for his poetry to possess both versions of *Into Hades*'. Lengthy compared quotations then follow, with critical comment. The reviewer surmises that *A Traveller in Time* 'is a poem which, because more general, less personal or almost private in its matter, has obviously been easier to write'.

The reviewer concludes that *Out of the World and Back* goes 'deeper and wider, and taking more risks than any of the perfect, or as near-perfect-as-makes-little-matter short poems, these two long ones, late fruit of a lifetime's devotion to the Muse and to God, are also far more profoundly and subtly surprising. *They do not, yet, allow themselves to be "placed"'* (my italics).

Other reviews were not as full or as fulsome. In the *Sunday Times* of 28 December 1958, Richard Church selected it as 'Book of the Year': 'Andrew Young's long poem *Out of the World and Back* is a miniature *Divine Comedy*, as the title suggests. The verse is free, but austere, reined in by spiritual guardedness.'

Somewhat less lyrical than he had waxed in 1952!

In the *Spectator* of 21 December 1958, poet Robert Conquest wrote:

> in those two long and curious poems the poet drifts disembodied in space and time respectively, but without the vacuous immensities of ideological monologues that such a method implies

Apart from these, the poem was not widely reviewed. Andrew himself wrote to tell his publisher, Rupert Hart-Davis, that he thought the *TLS* review was, 'wonderful' because the writer knew what he was talking about! With comments like these, Andrew was right to be pleased:

Out of the World and Back is the only impressive long poem which has appeared in the English language since Mr Eliot's *Four Quartets*. (Mr David Jones' *The Anathemata*, impressive also, but moving on the debatable land between verse and prose, can be left out of account. Most critics think Mr Auden's *The Age of Anxiety* an interesting failure and the two long poems in *For the Time Being* much more impressive in incidental parts than as wholes. The other possible competitors are Mr Hugh MacDiarmid's *In Memoriam James Joyce*, a formidable anti-poem, a craggy height from which granitic landslides of poetry sometimes descend, and Mr George Barker's Villonesque *True Confession*. Mr W.S. Graham's *The Nightfishing* is not quite long enough to count for comparison).

Perhaps this also shows us what a high regard Andrew had for his own work, and his hopes for its ultimate placement in what was in his day known as 'the canon of English literature'.

CHAPTER 8
A LITERARY LIFE
(1910-1937 AND 1938-1971)

1910-1937

Despite being (according to his daughter Alison), a 'distant' father and family man; an often (according to his Stonegate parishioners) monosyllabic pastoral visitor; a retiring, reclusive figure on country walks; and an often reluctant social being, Andrew was yet a keen, companionable friend and raconteur with fellow writers, as he had been earlier with John Baillie, who became a lifelong friend.

Andrew seems to have had an innate empathy towards other poets, such as Gordon Bottomley and John Freeman. However, his tastes were limited and he could not abide 'modernists' such as Hopkins, Yeats, Pound and (for the most part) T.S. Eliot; and would have loathed poets like Larkin or e.e. cummings. He loved the Classics, particularly Dante, and deeply admired Bridges, Hardy, Clare and Edward Thomas, amongst others.

However, his dislike of 'obscurity' led him to overvalue the abundantly clear Georgian poets, such as W.H. Davies, de la Mare and J.C. Squire. Theirs was as much a rebellion against the 'high seriousness' of the Victorian age, as Wordsworth's and Coleridge's was against the preceding Augustans. Given that Andrew's own first two volumes were heavily 'Georgian' in character, it is perhaps not surprising that, at the time, he admired their work.

Though not himself a member of J.C. Squire's inner circle (known as 'the Squirearchy'), Andrew knew a number of people who were: principally John Freeman (1880-1929), who became a close friend. He was the director of the London Victoria Friendly Society, later becoming Chief Executive Officer in the Dept. of National Health and Insurance. As a poet he won the Hawthornden Prize in 1920 with *Poems New and Old*, and his *Collected Poems* were published by Macmillan the year before his death. His war poems were patriotic, in the vein of Rupert Brooke's:

Happy is England now, as never yet!
And though the sorrows of the slow days fret
Her faithfullest children, grief itself is proud.
Ev'n the warm beauty of this spring and summer
That turns to bitterness turns then to gladness
Since for this England the beloved ones died.
(From *Happy is England Now*, 1914)

Freeman wrote for the *London Mercury*, edited by J.C. Squire, had been a friend of Edward Thomas and was a member of a literary group which met at the Tibbald Restaurant in Theobald Street, London. It was a feature of London literary life, like the Poetry Bookshop, run by Harold Munro (who gave advice to Wilfred Owen when he was stationed in London, training with the Artists' Rifles). Andrew, on day trips to London, visited both places, where he met other poets and writers, including W.H. Davies, Conrad Aiken, Robin Flower (an Irish poet), de la Mare, Squire himself and John Freeman. Later, Andrew included visits to the London Library on these trips.

Andrew's correspondence with Freeman began in May 1926:

> My dear Freeman,
>
> You must have concluded I was dead – probably killed in the Strike – for how else could you explain my long delay in acknowledging and thanking you for your Herman Melville? But dry your tears – I am not dead – only I have been unconscionably rude. . . . But now that I have read your Herman Melville, let me proclaim, as loudly as pen, paper and my diminutive writing can mouth it, that this last book of yours is a great success. You communicate the fact of your enthusiasm for Melville and one respects it because you are able to give good reasons for it.

This was Freeman's second study of a writer, his first having been about George Moore, in 1922.

Their interchange of ideas was an ongoing but intermittent one, as is evident in a letter dated 30 November 1926, beginning 'My dear Freeman' and signed 'Yours ever, A.J. Young', not simply 'Andrew' as might be expected:

> I have owed you a letter for a long time – but I never had anything much to write about: and now I have *Solomon and Balkis*. . . . The poem is so beautiful and made so strong an impression on me that in sheer self-defence I must adopt a patronising attitude. Let me say now that you are beginning

to stretch your wings. . . . I care for nature more than I do for verse and I much prefer Wordsworth to Keats, and your nature poems will always make a peculiar appeal to me – I shall continue to think of you as the Poet of Trees, but I feel that *Solomon and Balkis* is bigger stuff. . . .

There is nothing – not a rhythm or an image – that I dislike in the book: I greatly admire the variety of the verse which completely saves it from any monotony. . . . My wife thinks your book should be popular and so do I.

In the mid-1920s, Freeman asked Andrew to read Grobo's novel *The Pleasure Lover.* An undated letter responds to it, showing Andrew's determined effort to be critically balanced: 'Some passages I found incomprehensible and others bad; I imagine too that a picaresque novel needs a little more humour to carry it off; but I do feel that the book is good, very good, and the characters are real. I am grateful for the loan of it'.

In the same letter, Andrew quickly reverts to talking about Freeman's own poems:

You tell me that your poems are never obscure, but my average intelligence, surely the best judge of a matter like that, tells me that sometimes they are. I am not sure that a certain amount of obscurity may not be a good quality in a poem . . . but certainly obscurity does not make for any kind of popular success. . . . I have wondered . . . why you are not more widely known and read. . . . Your poems have more *emotional thought* in them and more of *the fine spirit of abandonment that the truest poetry has* than the poems of any living writer. . . . In reading your poems again . . . I found that I had to give them my closest attention, and I can only think that the lazy 'general' reader finds them a little difficult [my italics].

This was an exercise in misplaced praise indeed! But it shows us what Andrew, at this time, valued in poetry, and perhaps what he was aiming for in his own? He was certainly keen to get his own poems into the magazines. It appears that Freeman sent some of Andrew's poems to the *Observer* and that they accepted one of them in the summer of 1926. The following year, Andrew asked Freeman's help in getting his poems in the *Spectator* and the *Saturday Review,* which had rejected them. He explained that he wanted to be able to say, 'My friend John Freeman suggested that I send a sheaf of poems, from which I hope you will make a selection'. He was clearly not above using his friends to aid his literary career. He *did* get one in the *Observer* in the first week of March 1928; and *Hard Frost* in March 1940. Andrew could often be wittily amusing in his letters to Freeman, as on 6 March 1928, when he wrote: 'I am glad your Muse is still on tap and has been running freely. Sometimes, if I stand long enough in a damp wood I get a trickle through, myself . . . a belated reconciliation of Science and Religion.'

Andrew remembered in Chapter 3 of *My Life*, many years later, that he had been introduced to Freeman by an old school friend, John Allan, at the Tibbald, and that: 'I came to know him well and called several times at his house'. Freeman also visited Andrew in Hove, where they would sit and talk and smoke together in Andrew's study. When he died in 1929, aged only forty-nine, 'his widow invited me to give the discourse at a memorial service which was to be held in a London church. Having consented, I was faced by a large audience; I had no idea his poetry was so popular'. However, 'the congregation . . . became almost restless' and Andrew discovered afterwards that they were mainly Freeman's insurance colleagues!

Just as Andrew had admired Freeman's work, so had he admired Gordon Bottomley's. On 20 December 1928, he sent Bottomley a copy of *The Cuckoo Clock*, as they had 'friends in common' and Andrew evinced 'profound admiration' for Bottomley's work. Later, Andrew found Bottomley's 'extremely kind letter . . . a little overwhelming'. In the late 1920s, Andrew was fulsome in his praise of Bottomley's verse plays; they also shared a love of Scotland.

W.H. Davies was also admired by Andrew, who recalled much later:

> I called on the Welsh poet, W.H. Davies, who lived in East Grinstead in Sussex. When I rang the doorbell one day, his new housekeeper opened the door and said, 'Mr Davies is composing.' I contrived, however, to enter and found that Mr Davies composed lying half asleep on a sofa. Perhaps he had had a tumbler of beer, for in one of his poems he addresses Bacchus,
>
> > only just to smell your hops
> > Can make me fat and laugh all day.

It was his regular midday custom to visit the local public house. But this suddenly ceased, and he told a friend, Richard Church, the reason why. He had been a tramp or, as he called himself, a supertramp. He was put on the Civil List and was due to receive a pension. He feared that if the Royal Family heard that he went regularly to a public house he would not receive the pension.[1]

---

1. *My Life*, unpublished.

Andrew enjoyed a widely based literary life in his Hove years, through the Sussex Poetry Society and the Brighton and Hove branch of The Poetry Society. Hilaire Belloc was president of the former and Andrew was on the committee. They had visiting speakers including 'Miss Sackville-West . . . (who gave) a deeply interesting talk on poetry' in 1927; Thomas Sturge Moore, who spoke on 'Are there any principles in Art?' in 1932; and in that same year Helen Thomas, Edward's widow, read from his poems, which must have delighted Andrew, who always regretted not having met Edward himself.

In 1930, Viola Meynell was invited to speak about her mother Alice's poetry. Andrew later recalled:

> after her lecture I invited her to a cup of tea. We became friends. Our daughter, now at a school for small girls, Janet, Rex and I – Rex was our small dog – used to visit the Meynells at Greatham near the Sussex border. Mrs Alice Meynell, the poet of the family, was dead, but Wilfred Meynell was still alive. An old man, he said to me a few minutes after I had been introduced to him, 'I am your oldest friend.' It was interesting to see the house to which Francis Thompson might by day or night come and, flinging himself on the floor, fall asleep. Drug-taking did not prevent him from writing *The Hound of Heaven*.[2]

According to Alison Young, Viola Meynell took over as Andrew's main poetic confidant after the death of John Freeman. She certainly became an enthusiastic reviewer of his books, and, Alison noted, Andrew had 'a high regard for her judgement and greatly valued her advice and encouragement'.[3] This would perhaps hint at some poetic insecurity, but certainly by the early 1930s Andrew had clearly distanced himself from the 'moderns', most of whom he disliked. This led to his being marginalised by most critics. Many of his admired contemporaries were more justifiably consigned to school anthologies: good, lightweight, competent versifiers such as de la Mare, Masefield, Harold Munro, Clifford Dyment, Robert Bridges, Richard Church, Frances Cornford, A.E. Housman, Hilaire Belloc, J.C. Squire and James Elroy Flecker, amongst others. They were still in the school anthologies of the 1960s. Some of Andrew's were too: *Hard Frost*, *Dead Mole*, and so on – but they were, and remain, in a different category.

---

2. *My Life*, unpublished, Chapter 3.
3. Edward Lowbury and Alison Young, *To Shirk No Idleness* (Salzburg: University of Salzburg Press, 1997), Chapter 8.

Andrew was a keen supporter of some younger poets, such as Laurence Whistler, Norman Nicholson, Edward Lowbury, amongst others. He always tried to make some positive comment about any books they sent him, as he had with John Freeman. In 1936 Andrew met Christopher Hassall, probably through Whistler, and quickly introduced him to the poetry of Robert Frost. Hassall had been an actor, then wrote lyrics for Ivor Novello, as well as writing his own poetry. He sent Andrew a copy of *Devil's Dyke*, to which Andrew responded that it had taken his breath away! He, in return, asked Hassall's opinion of his verse play *Nicodemus,* which he then rewrote, following Hassall's advice; as a thank you, Andrew invited Hassall to hear Imogen Holst play her incidental music for the play, before its public performance. This friendship, like many of Andrew's, was to last for thirty years. Hassall died in 1963 and Andrew wrote in his unpublished memoir *My Life* four years later:

> I had a . . . sympathetic audience when I gave a memorial address about Christopher Hassall in a crowded London hall, reading some of his poems. The audience was largely theatrical; Christopher, who had a wonderful voice himself, gave lessons on how to speak their parts to budding actors and actresses. He was my greatest friend, and his sister, Joan, made my books of verse worth buying by her wonderful drawings. I conducted the funeral service at Canterbury Cathedral.

Just before World War Two, Henry Simpson ran The Poets' Club in London, which existed just to have dinners with speakers. One of the guest speakers in 1938 was Richard Church, then a well-known, all-round 'man of letters' and publisher.[4] Edward Lowbury first met Church there: Edward was later to become Andrew's son-in-law, and Richard a near-neighbour at Curtisden Green, in Kent. Whether Andrew ever attended this club himself is unclear.

1938-1971

Before he left Hove, Andrew had been introduced to his bête noire, Yeats, by Thomas Sturge Moore. Andrew commented acidly in his memoirs later:

> Perhaps the Irish poet, W.B. Yates (sic) had not lost his popularity or his good and well-deserved opinion of himself, when I was introduced to him. He did not appear to desire my further acquaintance. Perhaps I should have told him I met his

---

4. He was an early publisher of Dylan Thomas whilst at Dent.

sister at the house of an Edinburgh lady, Mrs Whyte;[5] what
I said was that of all his poems, the one I liked best began
with the line 'When you are old and grey and full of sleep. . .'
He gave a startled look and showed no desire to continue our
acquaintance. I had forgotten, if I ever knew, that the poem is
a translation of a French poem.[6]

During his time at Wells, in 1938-39, Andrew had enough free time
to keep up a lively correspondence with a number of literary friends,
including Clifford Dyment, Laurence Whistler and Christopher Hassall.
He told the latter, in 1939: 'I read a good deal of Anglo-Catholic theology,
which is really quite exciting', although he had previously described the
Church to John Freeman, in 1927, as 'a house divided against itself, with
the antics of the Anglo-Catholics on the one hand and the groanings . . .
uttered by the Primitive Methodists on the other'.

On 2 May 1939, he wrote to Hassall:

> I am glad to read of your fruitful (i.e. literary) activities which
> contrast with my own dumb and static state – I went for a
> weekend to Dawlish hoping for a flower which doesn't exist
> except for an hour or so in the warm noonday sun – and it was
> cold and wet and windy. . . . So wet was it during the weekend
> that I was driven into a picture house. I saw *The Citadel* which
> I thought sheer claptrap. . . . (If the noble young doctor in *The
> Citadel* didn't make his fortune I suppose Dr Cronin did). I go a
> lot to the local picture house, which begins at eight o'clock with
> a gramophone record of "Under the Spreading Chestnut Tree".

All of which suggests as much boredom as engagement with his
theological studies at Wells!

In the same month, Andrew told Laurence Whistler: 'Getting old[7]
and lazy, and acquiescent in things, and *hating above all else the writing
of letters*, I am surprised that I should be starting to criticise your
introduction' (my italics).

This was to an anthology of poems by seven poets, of which Andrew
was one. He became quite cuttingly critical of particular sentences/
statements, then half-apologetic: 'it is very impudent of me to say
these things – I hope you will forgive me'. True to character, Andrew

---

5. Wife of Alexander Whyte (see Chapter 2).
6. This is by no means certain, as it is always regarded as an original, written to/
   about Maud Gonne.
7. He was 54 at this time!

proceeds to explain the nature of his grievances: 'I don't like to appear to be associated with your attitude of mild hostility to a number of . . . writers from some of whom I may have received a certain amount of consideration'. And finally: 'What I would have liked to see would be an introduction by a nameless editor (this would have obviated the slight awkwardness of including your own poems in good measure) – this introduction to state what on the whole the poems, not the poets . . . stand for'. Andrew then modifies these comments by stating: 'I admit that my judgement . . . is very unreliable.'

This nit-picking was part of Andrew's general attitude to life and literature; yet he seems to have maintained fairly amicable relations with most literary friends.

On 29 May 1940, Andrew was awarded the A.C. Benson Silver Medal by the Royal Society of Literature.

In 1941, the year he was inducted into the parish of Stonegate, in East Sussex, he told 'My dear Christopher' (Hassall) that he had read Burton's *Anatomy of Melancholy* – 'in parts heavy going', but 'a grand book to read'. He was, he said, now in the 'midst of Rabelais, Lucretius and Tacitus', all borrowed from the London Library. The letter is signed warmly 'Yours affectionately, Andrew'.

A year later, he confided to Christopher: 'I have not been cheered by a task I had always shirked – reading through the later Browning. He is such an intolerable windbag'. Presumably he meant poems such as *The Ring and the Book* (1864), rather than the more varied and engaging *Men and Women* of nine years earlier but he does not specify.

It is clear that, wherever he was, Andrew set himself programmes of reading and study which he not only discussed with literary friends in letters, but of which he kept meticulous hand and type-written notes, including quotes for future use, often crossed out, or underlined for emphasis (see Chapters 7 and 9).

In 1943, the cricket commentator John Arlott sent his poems to Andrew, who was, as usual, encouraging, and this began a long friendship of advantage to both. Arlott was also to produce a number of arts/poetry radio programmes for the BBC in which Andrew was involved. Many of these, for the BBC Eastern Service, were aimed at students at universities in India, where English writers were being studied.

Book of Verse 96, scripted by Andrew, produced by Arlott, was on Edward Thomas on 10 August 1946. Andrew showed himself to be very sympathetic to the predicaments of Thomas' life, not least his necessary hack-writing. Andrew also did *Book of Verse 90* that summer, on Robert Burns. It began:

When the one thing that can safely be said about *much modern verse* is that *more and more it is passing beyond the comprehension*, and even the interest, *of common people* . . . it is refreshing to return to this poet . . . who wrote the world's most popular song *Auld Lang Syne* [my italics].

It is clear that Andrew was not above using these programmes as a platform for airing his own poetic judgements; and after all, many people would find Burns incomprehensible.

In July 1946, the Eastern Service produced a series called *The Written Word* (English Essayists), and Andrew did no.18, about W.H. Hudson, one of his favourite prose writers. In October of the previous year, Andrew spoke about the Elizabethan dramatists, Beaumont and Fletcher. Both programmes were produced by John Arlott. On Wednesday 8 October 1947, the BBC's Third Programme (now Radio 3), broadcast a selection of Andrew's own poems, selected by John Arlott, produced by Christopher Hassall, and read by Anthony Quayle, John Arlott and Dorothy Smith. The programme defended Andrew as a pastoral poet of great technical accomplishment and sincerity, and as underrated. It was not until 12 March 1961 that Andrew introduced and read selections of his own poems on radio – rather ironically, perhaps, as he disliked hearing poetry read aloud.

Despite all this, Andrew claimed in a letter to Norman Nicholson[8] dated 22 December 1951: 'I never listen to the wireless.' He had first encountered Nicholson, poet of *Rockface*, who had lived in the same house in Millom all his life, in July 1942, after reading his *Five Rivers*, about which he said: 'it has given me a pleasure and excitement that I seldom get from new books of verse. . . . Allow me to offer you my warm congratulations and good wishes for your future work'.

Nicholson, in his turn, was to pay tribute to Andrew:

There is nothing sentimental about his poetry, no second-hand Wordsworthianism, no stock raptures, no ready-made responses. . . . Instead, his highly personal and sometimes eccentric imagery calls to our notice things we have seen, or ought to have seen, many times before. His wit acts rather like a snowfall, giving a strangeness to the familiar so as to make us look with a new interest.[9]

Andrew visited and/or corresponded with various writers at different times, including Leslie and Kitty Norris, Richard Church, Christopher

---

8. The Cumbrian poet, 1910-87.
9. *Andrew Young: Prospect of a Poet*, ed. by Leonard Clark, Hart-Davis, 1957.

Fry, Viola Meynell, Ursula Vaughan Williams and Basil Dowling, amongst others. It was almost inevitable that, sooner or later, someone would propose the idea of a literary magazine: it seems to have been Andrew himself and Laurence Whistler, in late 1946 or early 1947. It was decided that it should have a basically Christian background and should be called *Portico*, meaning not just a point of entry, or porchway, but also to counteract materialism and the cynicism of some literary magazines. Andrew said little of it later, except:

There was talk of a religious magazine being started, and some of those interested I invited for a weekend to Stonegate. Members of my congregation kindly provided hospitality, but Ruth Pitter[10] stayed at the vicarage. There was later a meeting in London, but nothing came of it.[11]

Those who attended the Stonegate meeting in May 1947 included Richard Church, John Arlott, George Rostrevor Hamilton, John Heath-Stubbs, Viola Meynell and Ruth Pitter. Others who were interested but unable to attend included: T.S. Eliot (who expected to be in America at the time), C.S. Lewis, Christopher Hassall, Norman Nicholson and John Betjeman.

Andrew had tried to canvas Betjeman's support in a letter dated 28 January 1947, with the idea for

a new periodical, mainly literary, with a more or less Christian background. We decided to have a house-party here, in Stonegate, during the second week of May, evening of 9th to morning of 12th. We should very much like you to be present, if that is at all possible. . . . So far, we expect Ruth Pitter, C.S. Lewis, Richard Church, George Rostrevor-Hamilton and Christopher Hassall, and there will be others.

Betjeman did not come. Those who did wanted Richard Church to edit it, but he refused – presumably on the grounds that he was too busy, both with writing and publishing (he worked, at different times, for both Hutchinson and Dent). For this reason, as well as a shortage of both money and paper in the immediate post-war period, the magazine never materialised. Andrew and Richard remained firm friends, however, over the following years. When Church's first volume of autobiography, *Over the Bridge*, appeared eight years later, in 1955, Andrew called it 'a minor masterpiece' and Church was one of Andrew's most consistently admiring, yet perceptive, critics.

---

10. This is curious, as Ruth Pitter maintained in 1990 that she had never met Andrew Young or discussed *Portico*, but she was then aged 93 and according to her solicitors, Parrott & Coales, rather 'confused'.
11. *My Life*, unpublished.

Leslie Norris told the present writer: 'That he (i.e. Richard Church) was a great friend may be guessed by something Andrew Young told me. Andrew changed his publisher so that he could continue to work with Richard,'[12] presumably at Hutchinson, who published Andrew's *A Prospect of Britain* in 1956.

Andrew's letters to Church began 'My dear Richard' and ended 'Yours ever, Andrew', a much warmer form of address than he used with many of his other correspondents. By February 1969, when Janet was very unwell, he explained that 'I have had to give up letter-writing except on very special occasions. . . . Yet in the evening after a glass of whisky, I am able to do some work that is not domestic. But I am not writing a long poem; the work is called *The Poetic Jesus*, because many of His sayings conform to Hebrew verse. The Sermon on the Mount is mainly a poem'.[13]

A month later, after Janet's death and Richard's condolences, Andrew wrote:

> My dear Richard,
>   Thank you for your very kind and beautiful letter. Janet and I had 55 happy years together, and latterly, when we parted at night, we said 'Omnia vincit amor'.
>   Affectionately,
>   Andrew.

Basil Dowling, who knew Andrew over many years, kept a detailed notebook of his meetings with other writers, including Andrew: 'We met from time to time, wrote letters, and he sent me all his books, kindly inscribed. For my small part I dedicated to him my second book of verse, published in New Zealand in 1944. In his reply he gave me the greatest encouragement I could ever have: that if he were making an anthology of modern verse he would include "several" of mine, and he always meant what he said.'

Andrew sent Basil Dowling the first draft of *Into Hades* (probably in early 1952) for comments and Dowling duly made a dozen or so suggestions, some of which Andrew followed (see Chapter 7). This was no mean honour and shows the depth of their friendship and Andrew's regard for Dowling's critical ability. In 1957, Dowling wrote an account of his visit to Stonegate the previous year:

> Before I forget the details I must jot down something of my visit to Andrew Young last September.

---

12. Letter from Leslie Norris to Richard Ormrod, dated 9 July 1984.
13. Letter from Andrew to Richard Church, dated 12 February 1969.

I set out from Hastings about half past four of a perfect late summer day. The countryside was pleasant and peaceful all the way to Stonegate. . . . My memory is of nothing but woods and valleys and cornfields, with here and there . . . some fine old parish churches. Stonegate station is a mile or so from the village and made me think of Edward Thomas' *Adlestrop*, 'only the name': it was as quiet and deserted too. I got out and strolled up the hill, with the quietness deepening as the sound of the train died away. . . . Then I saw a man coming towards me and recognised A.Y. by his manner of walking: leaning forward a little, with a bold swinging stride. He was full of apologies for not having met me at the station: he had had some unexpected duty to perform, and the station master had forgotten his promise to look out for me.

The vicarage is a large old house hidden from the road by trees and bushes, with its front and rambling garden overlooking a beautiful prospect of woods and farmland without a building in sight. After greeting Mrs Young (who had aged little since I first met her in 1938), A.Y. took me into the garden and showed me his favourite haunts. On the lawn outside the French windows he suddenly stopped and looked down. 'Do you know what those are?' he said, pointing to a cluster of tiny, delicate flowers in the grass. 'Lady's tresses orchids! But there aren't many wild plants in these parts,' he added. He then showed me a little pond shut in with greenery where he did much of his reading and writing.

When we went in to tea I persuaded him to show me his favourite books, and also the Queen's Medal for Poetry, which he had lately won: a heavy gold medal of simple design. Though as usual reserved and modest he soon warmed up, and we talked for an hour or so about books and writers. Darting here and there among his shelves, he pulled out volume after volume of his treasures, and talked in lively fashion about some of them. He had been reading, he said, through all English fiction except that of the present day, and remarked how poor, as a whole, he thought it. One of the finest books, he said, was *Cranford*. He still liked Scott as much as ever, but couldn't read Dickens or George Eliot; wanted to like Peacock as much as he did once, but found he couldn't. . . .

He then picked up a notebook in which he'd made a list of the poets he most admired after reading them all through again during the winter. This was his choice (as nearly as I can remember): Keats, Shelley . . . Byron's *Don Juan*, Wordsworth (parts of *The Prelude* and some others), Coleridge selected, Ben Jonson, Cowley (much underrated, he thought), Giles Fletcher, Milton's *Paradise Lost* and *Samson Agonistes*, James Thomson's *The City of Dreadful Night*, Young's *Night Thought*, Herrick, Marvell, Francis Thompson, Vaughan, Hardy selected, A.E. Housman, Swinburne selected . . . Meredith's *Modern Love*, Bridges, Frost (middle period), Emily Dickinson, Arnold and Tennyson.

He showed me a fine edition of Izaak Walton, and a recently printed volume of poems by Siegfried Sassoon, inscribed to Andrew Young, with a couple of letters which he allowed me to read. The poems he described laconically as 'good, but not good enough'. His most constant reading, he said, was among the Greek and Roman Classics, the medieval romances, the Elizabethan dramatists. . . . He reads much theology too. He also praised Mandeville and Bunyan, and had what he described as a very personal liking for Doughty.[14]

Then Mrs Young called us to supper. 'Are you hungry?' said A.Y. 'There'll be nothing to eat!' But there was. The dining room, like the rest of the house, was simple and charming, and Mrs Young a delightful hostess, quiet and cultured.

A.Y. declined to show me the church next door, which he said was not old and had no architectural interest. The darkness and silence were intense as we walked down the long, unlighted hill to the station, talking on the way of the problems and hidden sorrows of a small rural community. Pointing in the direction of a large house which we had earlier stopped at to talk to a fashionable lady, A.Y. told me of a series of domestic tragedies which had happened there, and remarked, 'Who would have guessed such things were going on?'

When the train drew up at the station, I felt I was saying goodbye to one who was what a poet should be: quiet, straightforward, likeable and human, a scholar with great reserves of energy, intellect, humour and kindness.

---

14. Charles Doughty (1843-1926), author of *Travels in Arabia Deserta* (1888), regarded as a prose classic.

The last recollection Dowling commended to paper was of Andrew visiting him in London, after the move to Yapton:

> Tues. 29 Dec.'59: A.Y. dropped in this afternoon to our surprise and pleasure. He had come to London to sign copies of the new selection of his poems, *Quiet as Moss*. He said he had nothing at all to do with it. I said there seemed no reason to make a selection of his poems since there were so few of them, and every one was perfect. A.Y.'s characteristic stance: feet apart, body swaying or rocking sideways, cigarette in mouth. He talked about his favourite counties: Shropshire and Wiltshire. He does not care for Cornwall and Devon — doesn't like the red earth. He also talked about his own village of Yapton near Arundel, about his new TV set (bought with part of the £300 given him by the parishioners in Stonegate, and about 'thrillers' — he likes Erle Stanley Gardner and other American writers in this class for their economy and slickness. He gets much pleasure from some of the TV programmes, especially plays and sport. Tony Hancock he greatly admires, but thinks there is a sad deficiency of humour in the other programmes. I asked what he was writing: two prose books, he said, but did not tell me what they were about.

These books were probably *The Poet and the Landscape* (1962) and early work on *The New Poly-Olbion* (1967). Shortly after Andrew's death on 25 November 1971, Basil Dowling wrote a poem, *In Memory of Andrew Young*:

The sudden news of your death
Dashed me, dear Andrew, but soon
Routine, that brisk heart-healer,
Bluff curtailer of grief,
Banished you for a while.
Now in bad times I'm reminded
That you were a good man,
And as a student of nature
None more shrewd and devoted.
You talked little, but always
Wisely, wittily, kindly,
Standing often in mid-floor,
Feet apart, swaying sideways,
Your speech terse, pleasantly Scottish,
Your vast learning worn lightly

With the modesty of true greatness.
Being with you in the country
Was a liberal education
Rigorous but delightful
As when, crossing a meadow,
You stopped abruptly to look down
At a tiny column of petals
And named a rather rare orchid.
Another memento I cherish
Is you with a suitcase of books
Leaving the London Library
For your vicarage in Sussex.
Most of all I remember
Your spidery handwriting
And short, exquisite poems
Like boxwood beautifully turned
Or a bronze leaf fallen in autumn.

It is hardly great verse, but what is significant is the affection and respect which inspired it.

To commemorate Andrew's seventieth birthday, Rupert Hart-Davis commissioned Leonard Clark to collect together a series of 'essays and tributes' from fellow writers and other notables, including the Bishop of Chichester and theologian John Baillie. This was published as *Andrew Young: Prospect of a Poet*, in 1957.

Clark wrote a lengthy introduction to the volume, mainly biographical, but also containing some still true, pertinent facts 60 years on: 'The work of Andrew Young is still not as well known as it should be. . . . He is certainly in no danger of ever becoming a literary fashion. . . . The truth is that Andrew Young's poems are timeless in their appeal.'

He went on to list those who had 'wished to be associated with the book . . . but were unable, for various reasons, to write anything for it': including Edwin Muir, Cecil Day-Lewis, Stephen Spender and Laurie Lee.

Andrew's friend John Arlott made some perceptive comments in his essay, the first in the book: 'Andrew Young is not an unsociable man; but he is not, from choice, a 'social' person. He makes friends – cautiously – and both cherishes and relishes them; but he is not concerned to make acquaintances'.

However, he was wrong on one point, when he said: 'I am convinced that it would never occur to Andrew Young to write his autobiography.'

John Baillie recalled meeting Andrew at New College, Edinburgh, in October 1908 and being struck by 'the ascetic Dantesque profile and . . . the spare figure of Andrew Young'. He also noticed a Swinburnean influence on Andrew's poetry of the time.

Richard Church, always one of Andrew's most consistent admirers and reviewers, was both generous and insightful: 'What . . . then, does it contain, to make it outstanding?' he asks of Andrew's body of poetry. Then he answers his own question: 'It contains the personality of its author; something wry, witty, epigrammatic, shrewd, and finally, elusive. It is that last quality, the elusiveness, which may give the poetry its staying power. Our curiosity is whetted to a nice edge.'

Viola Meynell spoke of the 'excitement' in discovering Andrew's poetry, in which 'there is throughout an unsentimental understatement of feeling'. She also notes his 'considerable art of compression' and 'the rightness of the chosen word'.

For George Bell, Andrew was 'a student of nature who is also a poet . . ., a poet who is also a priest'.

For George Rostrevor Hamilton, Andrew was, 'Essentially . . . a reflective poet, in delight no less than in melancholy. . . . He knows the fascination of words, but uses them above all to illuminate and clarify.

PART 3
THE NATURALIST AND TOPOGRAPHER
(1945-1967)

CHAPTER 9
THE NATURALIST AND TOPOGRAPHER
(1945-1967)

Andrew's almost lifelong obsession with wild flowers – *never* cultivated ones – was to culminate in the two whimsical, colourful, anecdotal, amusing 'flower' books: *A Prospect of Flowers* (1945) and *A Retrospect of Flowers* (1950).

He called himself a 'botanophil' rather than a botanist, as he was an inspired – but very well-informed – amateur. In the *Retrospect* he said that he was too lazy to study botany,[1] but that 'so great is my respect, I should always want to take off my hat to a botanist'. In typical Andrew fashion, he added: 'Unfortunately I do not often wear a hat.'

In his unpublished autobiography *My Life*, Andrew remarked: 'wild plants were my own main interest; even in the New College days they shared my mind with dogmatics and apologetics'. Even before that, he noted in 'Early Days'[2] that when playing truant from The Royal High School in Edinburgh, he 'developed an interest in wild plants' by trespassing, 'on a fine estate owned by the Earl of Rosebery, Dalmeny'.

His old school magazine *Schola Regia*,[3] under the heading *A Note on Andrew Young*, noted that:

> Andrew Young's most passionate interest, apart from his professional duties, has been the study of British wild flowers, of which he modestly confesses that he has a 'pretty fair knowledge'. For that reason . . . it is improbable that he ever arrived on time at a particular milestone, or passed it without a close investigation of its site in search of the minute Spring Speedwell or some other rarity. And it would be a task for Scotland Yard to plot his journeys and quests, and striking behaviour, on *un*classified roads, on recondite paths, across

1. This was untrue, as his son-in-law, Edward Lowbury, recorded that Andrew had read Strasburger's *Textbook of Botany*.
2. An extended autobiographical essay in *The New Poly-Olbion*, 1967.
3. In 'Memorial No.1951'.

quagmires and over precipices, all the way from the Sussex
Downs to the Sutherland hills. The evidence in his beautiful
book, *A Prospect of Flowers* – written in a prose style so vivid
and feather-weighted that it kills the gloom even of Rannoch
Moor – is that Andrew Young, making for Bannockburn,
would probably choose to go round by Brighton Pier –
though for reasons different from Chesterton's. One or two
autobiographical 'disclosures' in *A Prospect of Flowers* suggest
that in his early youth, heading for the high school, he
sometimes felt not disinclined to go round by Bannockburn.

Andrew had made extensive notes about wild flowers and his adventures
searching for them over the years; he also reread his favourite English prose
writers: W.H. Hudson, Thomas Browne, Izaak Walton, Gilbert White,
Kilvert and Milton, amongst others. He obviously intended to write a 'classic'
of its kind. Of White's *Natural History of Selborne*, Andrew commented:

A remarkable thing about Gilbert White's *Natural History of Selborne* is
that it has not gone out of date. . . . [4] Another remarkable thing is that the
book is read, and even loved, by people who have little or no interest in natural
history. They find in it, of course, a few things curious and memorable.

This applies equally to Andrew's own two 'flower' books.

A Prospect of Flowers was subtitled 'A Book About Wild Flowers', but it
is so much more than that. The title was taken from Marvell's poem *The
Picture of Little T.C. in a Prospect of Flowers*. Divided into 24 short, pithy
chapters, beginning with *The Year's First Flower* (Winter Heliotrope) and
ending with *The Year's Last Flower* (Ground Pine), it includes chapters on
Spring Herbs, Buttercups and Lilies, June Orchids, and more unexpectedly,
on *The Morals of Plants, Poets' Botany, Types of Botanist,* and so on.

In a chapter entitled *A Confession*, Andrew notes that 'worst of all of
course is the habit of picking wild flowers, maiming or destroying plants',
hoping that the poets would speak out against it, and that he himself
would never do it. However, he proceeds to quote Wordsworth's lines
from *The Excursion*:

Rapaciously we gathered flowery spoils
From land and water

He then admits that:

so far as water lilies are concerned, perhaps I am the least person
who should cast a stone. One day I went to Loch Lubnaig to
look for that rare plant, least water lily. I thought I saw it, but

4. It was published in 1789.

could not be sure that what I saw was not the common yellow
water lily. As it grew 'in dangerous deeps', I started to undress.
A road runs by the lochside, and on that summer afternoon
cars kept passing up and down; but as I could not see the people
in the cars, I imagined they could not see me. 'In any case it's
their lookout,' I said, perhaps more truthfully than I knew. I
waded towards the plant and was standing waist deep in water
when I saw an open charabanc, full of holidaymakers, sailing
down the road. I felt that was a different matter, and tearing off
a flower I hurried back to the shore. My struggles to pull over
wet shoulders a shirt that offered determined resistance were
watched with interest from the approaching charabanc, and
when just in time I succeeded, the hearty holidaymakers rose
from their seats and, so to speak, 'greeted the unseen with a
cheer'. Some people, I know, despise my methods of botanising;
yet few botanists have had their efforts publicly applauded.

This passage is typical of the slightly self-deprecatory, humorous,
informative and absolutely un-dated style in which Andrew tells many
of his adventures in his 'chases after plants'. Others include how he
was nearly 'beheaded' by a low bridge when rowing in the dark with a
white Amaryllis he had just picked on the bank; or the embarrassment
of tripping over pairs of lovers in a dark Surrey wood on a Sunday
afternoon, whilst searching for the rare Martagon lily with his host's wife;
and the art of trespassing quietly and eluding gamekeepers.

The book includes snippets of mythology, history, herbal medicine,
folklore and poetry, which, as well as being entertaining to the reader,
show the breadth of Andrew's own reading and knowledge. Like all good
teachers/preachers, he brings it to life: of the Cuckoo-pint he tells us: 'It
prepared for spring by storing its rootstock with so much food, that people
used it to starch their ruffs and make a pudding called Portland Sago.'

He wears his learning lightly, as the following extracts show:

few poets have been botanists, though Simonides says, 'The
poet dwells among flowers, like a bee busy with golden honey.'
Gray kept two books on his table, Shakespeare and the *Systema
Naturae* of Linnaeus, the latter so interleaved for notes as to
double its size. Beattie must have had some perception of
flowers to be the first to identify the small two-leaved Linnaea.
Crabbe wrote a flora of the Aldeburgh district, but was so
browbeaten by a Cambridge don for writing in English instead
of Latin – an insult to science – that he flung it into the fire. His

botanical studies were unprofitable in another way, for when
he practised as a doctor, his patients, seeing him come home
with handfuls of weeds, argued that as he got his medicines in
the ditches, he could have little claim for payment. . . .

But perhaps we should say that poets have a botany of their own, which
differs in some respects from the textbooks. When Herrick explains *How
Lillies Came White or How Violets Came Blew*, we accept his statement
without further investigation. Only when he says that Primroses came
green because they were Virgins troubled with Green-sickness, we raise
a query, Are they green? But Spenser also speaks of 'primroses greene'.

There is no difficulty, however, about accepting Emily Dickinson's
that bees from clover, 'their hock and sherry draw'; botanists themselves
speak of a flower's nectar rather than its honey, and the nectar the gods
drank may have included both these wines.

Of the difference between *botanists* and *botanophils*, he observes
wryly:

> While a botanophil searches for plants, a botanist may not
> have time to do so, or even the interest. . . . Usually a botanist's
> place is by the microscope, his field of vision a slide, his flowers
> iodine stains. It is pleasantly said that some botanists would
> not know a daisy if they met it in a field; only when they had
> taken it to their laboratory, pressed and dried it, and spread it
> on paper, would they exclaim, 'Ah, *Bellis perennis*.' We like to
> think that the specialist overreaches himself and is in some
> way stupider than ourselves. We should remember that idiot
> means literally one who is not a specialist, but an amateur or
> layman.
>
> The botanophil is so much a plant-seeker that in winter,
> when there are few plants to find, he usually hibernates.
> Indeed it is by this habit of hibernating that he may be
> best distinguished. While the botanist is like an evergreen,
> working throughout the year, the botanophil is like one of
> those perennials that die down to a rootstock in autumn and
> lie more or less dormant till the spring.

The *Prospect* refers to many meetings or encounters with many different
people, in many different places; which would suggest that Andrew's
normally retiring, introverted personality became more animated and
extrovert on his flower-hunting trips, much as it did with fellow poets or
in the pulpit. He admits, however, in the unpublished *My Life*, that:

When I had a wild plant in view, I usually went alone. That was as well, for I sometimes had the unpleasant experience of not finding it. Or I might have a worse experience even though I found it.

Andrew's friend Richard Church reviewed *A Prospect of Flowers* in the *New Statesman and Nation* on 12 May 1945, showing his usual perceptive grasp of Andrew's personality:

Under this charming, late-seventeenth-century title, Andrew Young, the skilfully simple poet, offers his first book of prose. It consists of that old-fashioned device of pressing flowers in books; but Mr Young reverses the process: he presses the book in the flowers. Gardens and their fat inhabitants fill him with disgust. He calls them concentration camps. And in his enjoyment of the flowers of field, hedgerow, bog and mountain, he confesses to an almost mad, inhuman infatuation (comparable to Hudson's anti-human and anti-dog devotion to birds). A fellow minister, observing him in the throes of his passion, observed: 'What a disgusting habit!' No doubt this orthodox priest shied at the element of mysticism which the author must have betrayed – as he betrays it in this book. It makes of him a hermit of the emotions. 'The presence of a friend on a country walk makes me uncomfortable; I even try to avoid strangers.'

Out of these 'disgusting habits', Mr Young, like his fellow morose solitary, Hudson, has produced something uncommonly beautiful and original. It is a timeless book, neither modern nor old-fashioned. If I had to catalogue it I should put it amongst the books of information – but the information of pleasure rather than of facts. Yet it is full of facts, but each one of them is lighted up by imagination, or sometimes fancy, and a constant play of pensive humour. The method, with its ample ingredient of scholarship and exquisitely apt quotation, is comparable to that of Burton and Sir Thomas Browne – and that, of course, begins to give a date to this poet's personality. Is he not, then, of this current world? Is he escaping to some paradise of his own among ancient poets, quaint herbalists, odd divines? I think not, for he wears his learning with an innocence, just as W.H. Davies wore his ignorance. What he does, says, thinks, is so natural that it becomes as acceptable to the reader as the very habits of the wild flowers described. Indeed, Mr Young is in danger of being confused with them, and treated as an odd, prickly bloom obstinately hiding itself away in some high and rocky place. But it is worth a climb to find him. Such is the author.

Church concludes humorously, before turning to the book itself:

His book is as shapely as his poetry, and its method of drama in miniature is like that which makes his poems so memorable. The artistry is cunning (outcome of the solitariness), both in its choice of epithet and its use of fact. Thus, speaking of the water crowfoot, a degenerate member of the buttercup family, he says: 'This buttercup has completely taken to water, losing its hairs and bitter juice, no longer needed to protect it from land animals, and also its yellow colour, though it still keeps at its heart a speck of the ancestral gold'. Note how he keeps that 'ancestral' until the end of the sentence. And with what a charm of surprise he keeps the reader informed, as in 'a hawthorn hedge is called a quick to distinguish it from a fence of dead wood, but its blossom has a warm, heavy scent that reminds some people of a death chamber'. For long it was a common belief that it kept the smell of the Great Plague of London. Botanists say it contains a substance, trimethylamine, which is also found in decaying fish.

Throughout the book there is this sort of clear, bell-like quality of phrase; a most fitting vehicle for the flowers which the poet is observing. . . . One can, for example, almost *hear* the chime in such a phrase as 'bees visit the snowdrop, eating honey in its white parlour'. The combination of theme, obsession, scholarship, and rare poetic gift gives this book distinction. It is one to look into again and again with delight.

Andrew, seeing this review and being pleased with it, wrote to Church on 20 May 1945:

My dear Richard,
    I have just seen your review in the *New Statesman*. Don't think I am reflecting on your critical judgement when I say, 'How very kind! Too kind!'

This was clearly false modesty, as Andrew wrote to Church seven years later, on 21 March 1952, when the latter was about to embark on a lecturing and broadcasting tour of Denmark, that he had 'the greatest faith in your literary judgement'.

As a spin-off from the book, Andrew was invited by the West of England Home Service to give a talk on 'Some Rare Flowers of the West Country' on Friday, 12 October 1945. He spoke about the Hispid Marsh Mallow, Pale Blue Toadflax, Greater Spearwort, Marsh Helleborine and his searches for them. The book, not surprisingly, went on to win the prestigious Heinemann Award. It sold 9,737 of the first edition of 12,120 copies, and was posthumously reprinted in hardback in 1985, on the centenary of his birth. A paperback edition was published by Penguin in 1986, on the back of which the *Country Life* reviewer was quoted as saying, 'A lively, humorous potpourri . . . forty years on, this delightful book has already proved itself a hardy perennial.'[5]

After this success, it is hardly surprising that Jonathan Cape commissioned a follow-up, *A Retrospect of Flowers*, published five years later, in 1950. This time, however, only 2,978 copies were printed, of which 2,720 were sold. For some reason it has never been reprinted, though it is easily as good, witty and amusing as the *Prospect*. As usual, he uses conceits, pathetic fallacy and graphic imagery: contrasting north and south in spring he remarks, 'The Gorse in Sussex was coining its gold into seeds, shutting it in black furry purses; on the sea cliffs of the Pentland Firth it was all bullion, as though Midas had touched the bushes'.

Elsewhere he speaks of 'meeting' plants as though they were people, for example: 'Behind my house was a wooden glen, where I often walked, and there I first met Toothwort.' Sometimes the references are biblical: 'An excuse for picking violets might be that in any case they seldom set seed, so that in picking them you would not be out-heroding Herod, slaughtering innocents even before they were born.' But mostly they are poetic: he quotes Keats, Euripides, Crabbe, Wordsworth, Hardy, Milton, and so on, effortlessly blending them into his text. His lexical interests are also never far away: 'Dog' prefixing any plant, e.g. Dog Violet, Dog Rose, Dog Mercury, was, he tells us, 'a name given in an age less dog-loving than ours and meaning with no sweet scent'.

As in the *Prospect*, Andrew once again appears to take the readers into his confidence, especially when relating his various mishaps and mistakes, which endears him to them, even when he compares himself to a deluded, pompous character: 'The finding of a rare and beautiful plant causes me great excitement. . . . I go through the rest of the day smiling to myself like Malvolio'.

Returning to the thorny subject of 'to pick or not to pick' wild flowers, he observes, with particular, pithy humour in the last two sentences:

5. Richard Ormrod, *Country Life*, 16 May 1985.

If . . . you collect plants only in memory, you do not rob other people. Of course with nothing to show for it, it may seem a foolish occupation; yet you pick up with the plants you do not pick, great masses of scenery, sand dunes and bogs, streams, forests and mountains. I carry more scenery about with me than a touring opera company. It is so far from being a profitless occupation that I hope to die one of the richest men in England.

An article in the *Church Times* of 8 January 1954, signed simply 'S.E.', commemorates Andrew Young as a religious poet, mentioning his nature poetry and *Into Hades*, which was published two years earlier. The article also refers to the *Prospect* and *Retrospect of Flowers*, commenting that: 'It is in his prose books . . . that Young most lucidly *reveals his own personality*' (my italics). This links with something Andrew said himself of Gilbert White: 'The great virtue of White's writing is that it is so *communicative of himself*' (my italics).

These comments raise the issue of the dichotomy between *personality* and *persona*, and how far, if at all, they are linked. The revealed (or is it reconstructed?) *persona* in Andrew's prose writings is that of a genial, companionable, amusing, light-hearted, self-deprecatory individual, with whom it would be pleasant and entertaining to spend an evening. However, this was often at variance with the *personality* manifested to those closest to him: family, neighbours and parishioners. Which was the 'real' Andrew, or were they just different sides of the same coin? His wife and children were certainly *not* on the receiving end of this geniality: at home he was autocratic and austere. However, it is only fair to say that his grandchildren did find him both 'fun and funny'. Perhaps the *persona* was the person he wanted to be, like the ego and the id, or the dark and light sides of the moon? Whilst it is not the job of the biographer to psychoanalyse his subject, it is relevant to ask leading questions about conflicting evidence, even if no definitive answers can be given.

* * *

Andrew was a keen archivist who kept small, lined, closely written notebooks in small, spidery writing, each one detailing sources of information for whatever he was working on, or thinking of working on, at the time. One of these notebooks[6] contains notes for *A Prospect of Britain* and other prose works, covering Thames, Hardy Country, Cotswolds, South Coast, Western Isles, Melrose, Wiltshire, and so on. He

6.   MSS no. 19750, National Library of Scotland, Edinburgh.

comments on inns, bridges, arches, almshouses, with the pages carefully numbered for cross-referral: all very methodical. Of Maidenhead, he noted: 'good brick almshouses of 1659 in main road near bridge – town – nothing much else'; or, 'Magnificent Quarry Wood. S.E. of Marlow'.

He was a keen traveller and topographer who had a special love of mountains, prehistoric monuments and cathedrals/churches. With a painter's eye for detail and a poet's power of description, a commission from Hutchinson, on the back of the 'flower' books, was a good commercial 'prospect' for both sides. It reflects the scope of Andrew's own travels/holidays, especially the six chapters on different parts of Scotland; his literary interests (Haworth, Hardy's Wessex, the Lake District); and, of course, flowers (Spiderwort, Lizard Orchid); churches and cathedrals; English inns, and chalk-hill figures.

Strongly echoing the two flower books, *Lizard Orchid* begins:

> Not many people have been left a legacy by a complete stranger, but such was my misfortune. First news of it came in a letter from Kent. The writer, an old man, had in his younger days found a strange plant, which on being taken to Maidstone museum was identified as a lizard orchid. For over thirty years he had treasured it, a dried specimen, and now his concern was to leave it to someone by whom it would be appreciated. Would I accept it? In thanking him, I did not say that at a place on the Kent coast I could have picked 200 lizard orchids.

Once again he wears his knowledge lightly, inviting the readers to share it, in appropriate imagery:

> But the lizard is not our rarest orchid, not as rare as the *monkey*, whose only *menagerie* is the corner of a small field overlooking the Thames. Nor as rare as epipogium, whose choice is to spend most of its existence buried alive, so seldom lifting a flower from the earth, that the number of times it has been seen you could count on your fingers. *The Lady's Slipper* may have gone entirely, *Our Lady no longer walking* the Cleveland Hills or a Yorkshire wood. Of course one cannot tell; for many years *the soldier* orchid was thought to have *deserted* us, but it reappeared [my italics].

The first chapter, 'English Inns', gives a flavour of what is to come: a mixture of personal reminiscence, anecdote, history, linguistic changes and varied quotations from poets, diarists, historians, and so on:

At one time I shared rooms with a young man who earned
a small salary as a civil servant; a quiet, retiring fellow, he
appeared to have no ambition in life. Yet he had a curious
custom: travelling to and from his parents' house at weekends,
he went first class in the train! For half an hour it gave him
a feeling of distinction, adding a cubit to his stature. Such a
feeling we may get by staying in certain inns, not, however,
because they are more expensive than others, but because they
are in some way distinguished, ancient or beautiful or historic.
They are usually called hotels, but it seems unnecessary to give
a French name to a kind of building in which England excels
other countries. And inn is a more intimate word, meaning
originally a dwelling place and still used in that simple sense
by London lawyers, as in Inns of Court. But it may be not
improperly applied in the same sense to a house where we
lodge for a night or more. It is our inn, in fact, and it may also
be ours in feeling. The words 'This is your room, sir' work
magic, making something our own which was not our own.
And it is not just the room; we are as free to walk in and out
of the building as the proprietor himself. If it is ancient or
beautiful or historic, our appreciation makes us more than a
mere proprietor. It gives us a feeling of distinction, and for
once that is no vanity.

This chapter is something of a quick survey, but also provides a potted
history of inns:

An obvious inn of the kind is the Star Castle on St Mary's in
the Isles of Scilly. Set on its rock, this imposing Elizabethan
fortress lifts you above yourself; walking round its ramparts
in the evening, you are not sure you do not own the island.
It must lend lustre to the many honeymoons, of which it is
the scene. Or there is the Lygon Arms at Broadway in the
Cotswolds; a dignified Jacobean building full of old furniture,
it gives the impression you are staying in a great and wealthy
mansion. Or there is the Lion at Shrewsbury, which has
a ballroom with minstrels' gallery designed by the Adam
brothers. Recalling it was given to him in his youth as a
bedroom, 'I entered upon my kingdom,' De Quincey wrote,
(i.e. in *Confessions of an English Opium-Eater*). At some inns
you are staying in an old manor house . . . or an inn may have
been someone's town house. To town houses Shrewsbury

owes much of its charm, though it was in Chester the Earl of
Shrewsbury had his town house, now the Bear and Billet. But
an inn may have been one of many things. At the Dolphin
near Norwich, you can call for as much beer as you like in
what was once the Bishop's Palace.

Humour is never far away:

> Some inns have a distinction which they owe to former
> occupants. They are not haunted by their ghosts, yet you have
> a thin feeling of their presence. If ghosts had their own ghosts,
> it might be of these you were aware. Such a duplicate, derived
> from Charles I, seems to be in the room of the Saracen's Head
> at Southwell, where that king last slept before surrendering
> to the Scots. But nothing is palpable, and you need not be
> alarmed to think, if you are given the room, the king is sharing
> your bed.

Nor is Andrew's strong sense of the links between landscape and history:

> Though some inns are ancient, there were of course still earlier
> inns; the oldest inn in Gloucester, almost in England, is called
> the New. Inn signs point back to a time when few people could
> read, perhaps to the time when the Romans built the roads.
> The Chequers may even be derived from the Romans, for it
> was found as an inn sign in Pompeii; but a more likely link is
> the Bush. In Rome it would be an ivy bush, symbol of Bacchus,
> in England a bunch of any evergreen foliage, suspended on a
> pole.

The chapter on 'Edinburgh' is inevitably partly autobiographical,
outlining his circuitous walk to school, truanting expeditions, and return
there many years later:

> Thomas Hardy tells in a poem of the mistake he made in
> revisiting his old school; he should have waited and gone as a
> ghost. I was not conscious of such a mistake in revisiting the
> Edinburgh High School; I felt I was a ghost! Much water had
> flowed under the Dean Bridge since Queen Victoria sat on
> the throne and I sat on a school bench; I was in another life.
> And the situation was unreal; how could I, who had been so
> poor and unruly a pupil, have been invited to make a speech
> to the boys? The rector of my time would have turned in his
> grave.

The conversational tone is engaging, almost confessional, so that the reader can sympathise with the writer. These observations lead, seemingly effortlessly, into:

> But Edinburgh itself is conducive to a belief in ghosts. Other cities may remind you of the past; in Edinburgh you feel it is still present. You feel it more in the Old Town, where the buildings have an intensity of character such as you get nowhere else; in walking down the high street you have a strange sense of the livingness of the past. . . . It draws the dead out of their graves, queer people like Deacon Brodie and Major Weir. But you feel it in what was once the New Town. Its Georgian architecture is conservative; it has a somewhat heavy air, as though frowning at the thought of change. . . . And of course there is always the chance of the city itself becoming a ghost; that happens when the chill mist, the haar, blows up from the North Sea. Everyone has seen what Allan Ramsey describes in the line:
> 'The sun was wading through the mist'
> But at all times Edinburgh is a ghostly place, never able to shake off its past, haunted by itself.

'Haworth' gets under two pages, with a bare mention of 'those celebrated sisters, Charlotte and Emily Bronte'. What about Anne, one asks? It is clear where Andrew's interest lies, however:

> The new church, which keeps the old tower, is poor, but it has an astonishing graveyard, full of smoke-blackened flat tombstones, looking like tables spread with crepe for a feast of ghosts.

'Haworth', like 'The Tweed', was repeated verbatim in *The Poet and the Landscape* six years later. The habit of 'quarrying' past work was not confined to Andrew's poetry.

Mixing anthropomorphism with pathetic fallacy, Andrew writes of *English Parish Churches* that a typical church 'seldom troubles the landscape, as it would if a tower lapsed into sentimentality or other bathos. If it asserts itself in Lincolnshire by a tall spire, we commend it as suitable in a flat, fen country. A church knows its place; among hills there would be no such spire, only a low tower like Crosthwaite's in the Lake District. In mountainous Wales there is likely to be a bellcote instead of a tower. French churches are different . . . they would look restless in the placid English landscape'.

He can, however, be descriptively critical:

> Saxon churches . . . hardly seem at home in the cultured
> English countryside. . . . Escomb in Durham is very crude;
> small chancel and large nave, it looks like a monk's cell with
> a people's shelter attached, which indeed is the likely origin
> of an English church. A Saxon church may give you a queer
> feeling, as . . . though clearly Christian, it seems unable to
> shake off heathen fears.

The chapter on 'English Cathedrals' is a potpourri of history, anecdote,
asides, and brief, apt quotation:

> For one reason or another, English cathedrals continually
> ask for something to be done, a rebuilding or addition; at
> Chichester work went on for four centuries almost without a
> break. It was common for spire or tower to fall; Norwich's spire
> was blown down, and Lincoln's central tower collapsed killing
> some people who were listening to a sermon. Ripon had three
> spires; when one of them was struck by lightning, the others
> were removed, giving it a somewhat squat appearance. Fires
> were frequent; at Gloucester there were five great fires in little
> over 100 years. It was the fear of fire that compelled men to
> vault their naves with stone and not to be content with such a
> wooden ceiling as you see at Peterborough.
>
> Then again, a major reason, men craved for more light; what
> appealed to Milton, 'a dim religious light', seemed unsuited
> to God's temple. So they kept on building larger windows,
> till in Gloucester's Perpendicular choir you feel yourself in a
> glasshouse.

There is also an amusing, faintly ironic levity of touch underlying what were,
for Andrew, serious issues. Talking of 'a love of pilgrimages', he comments:

> it is not by chance that the first great English poem is *The
> Canterbury Tales*. Pilgrims flocked to a shrine, their numbers
> creating a need of new building, and their offerings the means.
> The Rochester monks found so popular a saint in a certain
> William that they began to enlarge the cathedral itself; but the
> work was not completed, as his popularity fell away. That was
> not surprising, for he was only a baker from Perth, given to
> good works, who had been murdered for his money in the
> neighbourhood. So great was the faith in relics that when
> Edward I's falcons fell sick, he sent them to be cured at the
> shrine of St Thomas of Hereford.

Like Sir Thomas Browne, Andrew 'loved a rarity' and, like Hopkins, 'All things counter, original, spare, strange', even the oddities and incongruities of English cathedrals:

> All this rebuilding and adding to at different times, also the development of a style of our own, the Perpendicular, have given English cathedrals their strange heterogeneous appearance. . . . Yet something can be said for buildings so rich with the sense of time, each a kind of visible history. Also it might be argued that one style offsets another, as massive Norman the graceful Early English. Certainly they do not lack variety. If Salisbury is the most unified, it is also the most monotonous. How different is Lincoln, or even Chichester, full of surprises. And unity, which implies more or less contemporaneous parts, allows less for the outbreak of individual genius, which can happen only once in a while. Perhaps that is why you remember more things about English cathedrals than about French, the Five Sisters of York, Wells' chapter house, the Angel Choir of Lincoln, Ely's lantern tower, the fan vaulting of Gloucester's cloister. They have parts which are unrivalled elsewhere, as Salisbury's spire and Exeter's vault.

In *Hardy's Wessex*, Andrew takes him to task for his use of pseudonyms, complaining that:

> The pseudonyms are not always improvements; in the name Salisbury we see as in a crystal a tall tapering spire, but in Manchester it is somewhat stunted; Weymouth presents us with a wide beautiful bay, which in Budmouth is cramped to a cove. The village names of Dorset he could hardly have improved; it is claimed they are the prettiest in England. Though the disguise is only thin, the effect is curious. . . . As this Wessex is mainly Dorset, Hampshire could find cause to complain of the name. After all, Winchester was the capital of King Alfred's Wessex, and there is nothing in Dorset comparable. . . . And Hampshire makes great claims for itself as a county.

As well as showing his knowledge of Hardy's novels, Andrew quotes from Izaak Walton, Nancy Mitford, Jane Austen, Coleridge and Pope; yet his erudition is never heavily oppressive, just introduced to illustrate a point. 'The Lake District' similarly.

'The Thames' has a charming use of extended pathetic fallacy:

> Broad and sedate, not breaking into occasional runs like other
> rivers, the Thames has a middle-aged look. That is natural
> enough; it is not the young river that, born on hills higher
> than the present Cotswolds, once came down in dashing style;
> with its feeders, as hungry as itself, it has eaten away so much
> of those hills that it now has an easy descent of less than 400
> feet. . . .
>
> The upper river, however, Matthew Arnold's 'stripling
> Thames', can hardly be said to have this middle-aged look; it
> keeps young like the Scholar-Gipsy, who after 200 years still
> haunts it with the black-winged swallows. You would hardly
> know the stripling was one with 'Old Father Thames'; it looks
> like a poor student of old times making his way to Oxford.
> It does not grow excited in the manner of young rivers, as,
> for example, the Wye among its Welsh mountains; for the
> most part it is content to wind its quiet way between grassy
> meadows, very lonely except for those watchers with their
> large thoughtful heads, the pollard willows. It winds about as
> if unwilling to leave a scene so typically English, tranquil and
> benign rather than beautiful. . . .
>
> Yet this stripling can suddenly put on weight, flooding
> heavily and overflowing its bounds. It is because the youthful
> Thames is more prone to such trespasses than the middle-
> aged, that it has the somewhat deserted look of a canal; below
> Oxford there are towns and villages on the gravelly parts of the
> banks, usually in pairs, as Goring and Streatley, Pangbourne
> and Whitchurch, but between Godstow and Lechlade there
> are none. From the adjacent fields, which are more or less
> floodland, the villages keep at a safe distance.

Not surprisingly, *A Prospect of Britain* has dated in the 60 years since
it was written , as a topographical work; but it was hardly intended as
a guide book of the UK even then, and can still be read and enjoyed as
a series of observations and descriptive anecdotes, in an English prose
style both clever and amusing.

The Poet and the Landscape follows on quite logically from its
predecessor seven years earlier: as the blurb says, 'Andrew Young has
found a subject peculiarly suited to his genius, for it consists of a series
of chapters about English pastoral poets as seen in their own rural
settings by one who is himself a distinguished English pastoral poet.'

In a mixed review, Geoffrey Grigson wrote in the *New Statesman* of 14 September 1962, as much about Andrew as a poet as about *The Poet in the Landscape*:

> He is not a 'nature' poet . . . he is not loco-descriptive, though places attract him. . . . Inside a descriptive technique, and between many pleasant trivia, he is . . . most uncomfortably aware of negation, farce, blankness, pain, end and hopelessness . . . (he is) – the sad, fatalistic, fortitudinous pupil of Thomas Hardy. . . . If a bird or animal makes him write a poem, it is more often dead than living.

As though suddenly realising that he is *not* reviewing the *Collected Poems* of two years earlier, Grigson continues:

> The same qualities exist inside the easy . . . essays in his new book, which are mostly about the environments of one poet or another, formative or incidental. . . . Sift the book through, by way of . . . Donne and the primroses of Montgomery Castle, Vaughan and the Usk . . . Marvell and Nun Appleton . . . Crabbe and Aldeburgh, and facts begin to accumulate about Andrew Young.

They begin to accumulate about the reviewer too: his dismissive attitudes and determination to score points off the author, who cannot answer back:

> He finds the hydrographical mythology of *Poly-Olbion* rather silly. Milton was blind before blindness. Daffodils in *Lycidas* fill their cups with tears. But how could that be? Sorrow for Lycidas would not cause them to hold up their down-hanging heads. . . . He rather dislikes Crabbe for disliking nature. . . . He writes a curious note . . . on a poem few people will have heard of, Disraeli's *Revolutionary Epick* of 1834. . . . He remarks that Tennyson escaped problems by way of the outer charm of nature.

Shakespeare's Flowers explores the many references to, and uses of, flowers in the plays, including cowslips, purple orchids, mandragora, camomile, rosemary, heart's-ease, and so on, as love potions, poisons or cures.

Andrew writes in warm praise of Gilbert White's *Natural History of Selborne*, which he cites as being, in its time and after, largely responsible for natural history becoming so popular: 'Here was a book on natural history that people could read.' Through minute observation and 'autopsias', White explained, for example, that peacocks' 'brightly coloured tails' were actually 'stiff quills' and that 'their gorgeous trains grew from their backs'. Much of White's book is about 'the life and conversation' of birds; yet, Andrew remarks, 'in writing about birds, beetles and grasshoppers, he is all the time writing about himself. The book is an autobiography, all the better for not being one.' White would seem an odd inclusion in this book, since he was not a poet, as such; yet he wrote, at times, quite poetically: 'Owls move in a buoyant manner, as if lighter than the air . . . crows and daws swagger in their walk . . . herons seem encumbered with too much sail for their light bodies . . . the kingfisher darts along like an arrow'.

Andrew observes that 'these simple words have a visual quality; in reading them, it is the birds we see, not the pages of a book'.

The chapter on 'The Reverend George Crabbe', comparing his poems *The Village* and *The Borough* (set in his native Aldeburgh) to Goldsmith's *Deserted Village*, is rather stilted by comparison to some of the others, and it is hard to imagine many contemporary readers warming to it, despite Andrew's conclusion that even when Crabbe 'shows no love for nature, he shows what is better, a love for people he disliked'.

John Clare, one of Andrew's favourite poets, was clearly a man much like himself, whose 'chief pleasure was in the society of plants' and who went alone on the heath 'to botanise/and hunt the orchis tribes'. Andrew says, in admiration: 'About 120 different plants have been counted in his poems.' Andrew's own 'count' was probably similar! Even more praiseworthy than that, 'With insects he is even more familiar. A strange Gulliver, he enters "The Insect World" where totter-grasses are mighty oaks, rushy burnets as tall as castles, and every leaf a town.'

Clare seems to have shared Andrew's 'religion of the fields', a pantheism where 'solitude and God are one', and the poet 'found (his) poems in the fields / And only wrote them down'.

When Clare was in the asylum (where he died, aged 71) Andrew remarks: 'It is pleasant to think . . . Clare never lost his love of earth's wild creatures, and even wrote of them in a new and more lyrical way. A love of that kind may lead to a religious experience.' Comments like this make one wonder about Andrew's own mystical/religious experiences, but whatever they were, they are unrecorded.

What he calls 'a sense of the numinous' pervades a number of these essays, Clare and *Young Wordsworth* included. The latter opens with an unexpected description: 'He was of a stiff, moody and violent temper, the one child out of five about whose future his mother felt anxious'.

The essay becomes a biopic of Wordsworth's experiences as man and boy, in Hawkshead, Cambridge and Dorset, France. Andrew expounds on Wordsworth's 'philosophy' that 'we are all one life', contrasting this with Spinoza's: 'his philosophy had an advantage over Spinoza's in not needing thought or study. The "meddling intellect" was out of place in a "breathing world"; indeed, "we murder to dissect". All that was needed was a "wise passiveness".' This sounds very like Keats' 'negative capability'. Andrew was able, in this essay, to showcase his knowledge of poetry, philosophy and topography.

At what stage Andrew decided to write *The New Poly-Olbion: Topographical Excursions* (published in 1967) is uncertain – but he had long been familiar with Michael Drayton's 1613 *The Poly-Olbion, A Chorographical Description of All The Tracts, Rivers, Mountains, Forests and other Parts of this Renowned Isle of Great Britain, with Intermixture of the most Remarkable Stories, Antiquities, Wonders, Rarities, Pleasures and Commodities of the Same, Digested into a Poem,* an encyclopaedic tome written in rhyming couplets, incorporating description, maps, history, myths and legends, historical tables, illustrations and more, but he had written a chapter on it in *The Poet and the Landscape,* five years earlier.

In this essay, Andrew explained, '*Poly-Olbion* is little less, though a great deal more, than a gazetteer of Britain. Wales for its size occupies a large place in the poem, while Scotland is nowhere'. One senses Andrew's annoyance at the latter, yet he praises Drayton for his love of mountains, of which Scotland is well endowed. Andrew continues: '*Poly-Olbion* is less than a gazetteer for being a poem,' adding caustically, 'that it is in verse does not matter greatly, as for long stretches the verse falls little short of prose'. However, '(It) is more than a gazetteer by including with other things natural history. Drayton gives a list of birds in his native Warwickshire', which clearly pleases Andrew; as does the fact that, 'it follows winding rivers and even streams. . . . And there is not a gazetteer's emphasis on big towns'.

Andrew sees Drayton's main interest,

> being mythology. . . . The mythology is of the poet's own making, natural objects personified. Sometimes it is connected with classical mythology; Albion, who according to Milton ruled the land for forty-four years, was Neptune's son. . . . Rivers with their movement and sound are readily turned to live beings. Drayton personifies them. . . . A large part of *Poly-Olbion* is taken up with their love affairs, the most notable being that of the Thames.

Andrew's *New Poly-Olbion* has been called a skit on Drayton's, being a series of mini-essays, or prose poems about places, people and flowers, written in whimsical, poetic prose, often incorporating bits of his own and other people's poetry. Andrew explains in his brief foreword that '*Poly-Olbion* means "very happy", the reference being to Albion'. Albion was also a poetic name for Britain, as used by Blake and others. Andrew acknowledges his 'quarrying' of parts of 'a book now safely out of print, *A Prospect of Britain*'.

Eric Gillett, reviewing *The New Poly-Olbion* in the *Times Literary Supplement* on 8 June 1967, remarked:

> This is a very happy book, delightful to read.... The descriptions of places in Great Britain that the author loves could only have been written by Andrew Young ... praising with fine economy ... in a few hundred words, people and things that have enriched his life.

Andrew was 82 at the time. He sets the scene, as it were, with a lengthy opening autobiographical essay entitled 'Early Days', describing his background, schooldays, student days, early travels, entry into the Church and marriage. Much of it was to be expanded or repeated in his later unfinished and unpublished autobiography, *My Life*.

The 'excursions' cover a range of hills, dales, rivers, mountains, buildings, and so on. 'The Thames' echoes *A Prospect of Britain*:

> The stripling Thames is like a poor student of the old days on his way to Oxford. ... It goes down from Oxford with an air of importance. ... It approaches London with a portly dignity, the poor Oxford student become an alderman.

'In St Paul's Cathedral' extemporises about John Donne, never named, just referred to as 'the Dean', and Andrew imagines that 'in heaven he was not a dean, but a well-behaved choirboy . . . now he beheld real angels. Did he delight them with his wit? . . . Did they call him Jack? . . . His desire had been to die in the pulpit; he had done better, become himself a sermon'.

Of 'Bath and Wells', Andrew jests: 'both towns have watery names – the Bishop of Bath and Wells must be an amphibian'.

Other humorous asides include:

> There was goutweed, a singularly virtuous plant, for it cures gout and also by its other name, bishop's weed, warns certain persons of their bibulous habits. (*Chelsea Physic Garden*)

On a Rockland Broad, remote and lonely. . . . Watched by a ghostly heron perched on a pole, I followed Wordsworth's example at Ullswater and stole a boat . . . I knew . . . water, churning it with my oars. . . . I hung between earth and heaven; if at Heigham Broad and Horsey Mere I was subhuman, on Rockland Broad I was an elevated saint. (*On the Broads*)

Orchids look odd, the flowers being upside down. Bog orchid is an exception, but hardly to be congratulated on having its head screwed on the right way. (*Lizard Orchid*)

Andrew writes affectionately of Scotland:

If like Sancho Panza you would own an island, nothing prevents your having one of the Western Isles; Wordsworth is said to have owned the Lake District as though the title deeds were in his pocket. Your only difficulty might be in the choice. . . . Perhaps your best choice would be Arran. Though it lies south of the English town, Berwick-on-Tweed, it is a pocket version of the Western Highlands, and with the title deeds in your pocket you would be proud. . . . The view from the ridge is almost frightening; their calm air of majesty thrown off, the mountains appear naked and savage. But the ridge offers you a safe and easy track. . . . One stride will take you across the gap, but if you lose your head, you will also lose your life, falling hundreds of feet below. That would be a pity, if you had already lost your heart to Arran and, the title deeds in your pocket, you were as rich as that poor man, Wordsworth. (*The Bad Step*)

In keeping with Drayton's original, Andrew often referred to mythological stories, and wrote a potted summary of the King Mark, Tristan and Iseult story based on 'the Tristan monument' in *Near Fowey*. However, he is also keen to debunk aspects of it:

But the Tristan monument is telltale. Mark was not king of the two countries, Cornwall and England; he was a Celtic chieftain. He did not live at Tintagel in a castle . . . he lived in an earthen camp with a long wooden building, Castle Dor. On the monument . . . he is not Tristan's uncle; he is his father! Perhaps the famous romance rose out of nothing more than the sad sound of the name, Tristan. But it would be none the worse for being moonshine like the lunar mountains, waste heaps of exciting beauty.

'Cold Cotswolds', with its mixture of metaphor, pathetic fallacy and oblique references to both *Into Hades* and to Janet, is worth quoting almost in full:

> Crocuses in gardens were awake, stretching themselves and yawning; if daffodils are the spring's trumpets, as poets tell us, every garden had its brass band; the flowers even trespassed on public roads. But it was still winter on the wolds; the long lines of beeches were shamelessly naked, shivering in a wind you could see; even violets shivered in their purple hoods. There were no primroses, for those sweet Infantas of the year keep off the cold wolds. I felt coldly towards them myself. But I warmed myself with old memories, of chambered barrows . . . of buildings in the Tudor tradition, from manor houses with an ambiguity as to what they are, domestic or ecclesiastical, to small houses that have a dignity . . . the Royal Family could live in Chipping Campden's almshouses.
>
> But the cold Cotswolds added a new memory. Driving over the edge in twilight, I saw what was apocalyptic. Dark cloud shadowed the sky and the Severn Valley lay in deep shade, but between cloud and shadow burned a sunset, a long sea of fire. There, if anywhere, were 'the flaming ramparts of the world'. Or was I seeing farther, not a sunset, but a sunrise on another world? No, it was too lurid; it was a reflection from some infernal region. And I was hastening down to it, leaving not only the Cotswolds, but the earth itself. Drawing closer to my companion, the sharer of old memories, I said silently:
>
>> You have so much forgiven,
>> Forgive me this or that, or Hell or Heaven.

It was included by Alison, with another, in the 1985 *Poetical Works*, under the heading 'Prose Poems'.

The strangely named *The Poetic Jesus*, Andrew's last prose work, was published posthumously in 1972 by SPCK. The blurb states that:

> The poetic quality of Jesus' teaching and of the Gospel narratives has often been remarked upon, but it is a theme that needs a poet to do it full justice . . . who . . . gives us a portrait of Jesus which is in itself an extended prose poem: simple, crystalline, eloquent and scholarly.

Andrew himself explains at the outset that:

> *The Poetic Jesus* is based on the Synoptic Gospels, but borrows
> from the Fourth Gospel the correct date for the institution of
> the Last Supper. Some modern scholars regard certain sayings
> in the Synoptics as too poetical not to have been the invention
> of the early Church; the title *The Poetic Jesus* suggests that the
> opposite of that is the case.

It is, in fact, a very readable, immensely interesting book. Andrew brings
what must have been Jesus' everyday life, as a child and youth, into focus
for what came later, relating it to his teachings, so that they become living
metaphors, e.g. the leaven in the bread, the salt that lost its savour, and so on:

The small one-roomed house gave him a close view of Mary's domestic
work. He remembered her throwing salt out into the street. Severely
taxed, salt was not cheap, but coming mostly from the Dead Sea, called
also the Salt Sea, it was apt to lose its savour. That lost, he was to say to
his disciples, 'It is fit for nothing but to be cast out and trodden under
foot of men.' He watched Mary baking bread in the mud oven; she mixed
leaven with the meal and worked it with her fingers till the lump was in
commotion with rising bubbles. He remembered it when he began his
ministry; his proclamation of the coming Kingdom worked like leaven
in the listening crowds, stirring them with a like commotion.

Andrew is careful to give textual references for his quotations, which
any diligent reader could check for himself, ranging across both Old and
New Testaments. These comments give us a flavour of what his sermons
must have been like: linking the practical with the spiritual in a way that
people could visualise:

> At six o'clock on Friday evening, the double blast of a horn
> sounded from the flat roof of the synagogue master's house;
> the Sabbath had begun. As a new year began in autumn, a
> new day began in the evening; 'the evening and morning were
> the first day', says the Book of Genesis. . . . As the synagogue
> was the prototype of the Christian Church, their services were
> similar, two lessons, psalms, prayers and a sermon. The lessons
> were from the Law and the Prophets, written on separate
> scrolls; they were read in Hebrew and then translated into
> Aramaic. This would be the beginning of the Boy's knowledge
> of Hebrew.

Some of Andrew's comments are clearly speculations, yet have the ring
of truth about them:

'Probably they (i.e. Jesus' family) could afford meat only for the Sabbath supper, cooked of course on Friday, the day before.'

'Galilee abounded more in stone than in wood, and 'carpenter' meant less a worker in wood than a stonemason. He was to show an unusual interest in that hard element. He himself was a stone, the stone which the builders rejected, though it was to become the head of the corner; his teaching was a rock on which a wise man would build his house so that it would not be swept away by a winter flood like a house built on sand.'

Andrew's deep Presbyterian knowledge of the Bible and his love of language came into their own in this last fitting book: 'He found John not far from where the Jordan buries itself without resurrection in its deep grave, the Dead Sea.'

Jesus was said to be particularly interested in the books of Jonah and Hosea, 'Jesus' and 'Hosea' both being forms of Joshua. Some of the vocabulary is certainly challenging, such as 'thaumaturge' (worker of miracles). As the book goes through Jesus' life, it inevitably ends with the Crucifixion, Resurrection and the Trinity. This is almost a distillation of a lifetime's thought on the subject:

Perhaps the six hours, three before noon and three after, were drawing to an end, when with a loud voice he uttered the cry, 'My God, my God, why hast thou forsaken me?' That the words are in Hebrew, not in the spoken Aramaic, shows they are a quotation, the opening of the *Twenty-Second Psalm*. It was the only occasion he said, 'My God'; even in the Garden of Gethsemane it was 'My Father'. And when he quoted another psalm, 'Into thy hands I commend my spirit,' he added 'the Father'. How he, 'meek and lowly in heart', came to know he was God's son, it would be pointless to ask, for, if he was, he could not have been ignorant of it. That it was with a loud voice he cried, 'It is finished,' suggests a sense of triumph. Perhaps it was less of his Crucifixion he was thinking than of his incarnate career. It was so finished that of the dead and derelict figure on the cross, St Paul could say, 'Christ crucified . . . the power of God and the wisdom of God', the strange seal of God's omnipotence and answer to all men's questions.

* * *

It may be argued that Andrew would be remembered for the two flower books, even if he had never written poetry: for their innate charm, whimsicality and knowledge are distinctive, their persona amusing and engaging. Certainly they have *dated* far less than *A Prospect of Britain*, and to a lesser extent *The New Poly-Olbion*; and *The Poetic Jesus* was always going to be a minority interest book. Andrew *learned*, he said, to write prose partly by studying Izaak Walton, Thomas Browne, Kilvert, Gilbert White, Hudson, and so on, after a lifetime of writing poetry and sermons. He is arguably amongst their number, as a distinctive prose stylist in his own right, giving the lie to those who think that a poet writing in prose is rather like a concert pianist playing the violin; or, put another way, this concert pianist plays an excellent violin!

Andrew Young, portrait by Howard Coster, 1937

PART 4
REASSESSMENT

CHAPTER 10
OLD AND NEW ASSESSMENTS

OTHER STUDIES

There have been two other critical studies of Andrew Young to date, both of which, ironically, came out of foreign rather than British universities. The most comprehensive of the two was chronologically the last, written by Andrew's daughter, Alison Young, and her husband, the poet-scientist, Edward Lowbury (both now deceased).

To Shirk No Idleness, subtitled 'A Critical Biography of the Poet Andrew Young', was published by the University of Salzburg in 1997, and on which the present writer has drawn for domestic and family details. The Lowburys also edited the centenary edition of Andrew's *Poetical Works* in 1985, which remains the definitive selection.

It is a revealing and intimate portrait of an erudite, creative man, who was also a distant yet dictatorial father, and a difficult, demanding husband. The insights it gives are therefore unique, since those who knew him well are now long dead. Yet this very intimacy is a double-edged sword: almost by definition such closeness cannot be unbiased or objective; and there is an argument in favour of biographers *not* knowing their subjects personally, but taking 'primary testimony' from those who did.

Alison was very frank and forthright about her father, life at home, and what she saw of her parents' marriage, when the present writer met her in the 1980s, and this frankness was very evident in the biography that was eventually published over ten years later. Andrew's strengths as a poet seem to contrast with his limitations as a man, but perhaps this is true of many creative artists.

Alison maintained that the lack of 'much variety or complexity in his verse forms' was due to the fact that 'visual elements and ideas were more important to him than original sound effects'. It is certainly true that his poetry is very visual, even poems like *The Ventriloquists,* and that he disliked hearing poetry read aloud, despite having made a number of recorded readings himself.

Andrew's poetry is almost a landscape without figures, and Alison maintained that 'his lack of interest in . . . other people . . . is reflected in his writings, which are rarely successful in depicting human beings' – but are very empathetic in their descriptions of animals and birds, living or dead.

The Lowburys concluded that Andrew's 'strength lay in the ability to experience and describe visionary and mystical states', aided by 'a passion for collecting oddities, paradoxes and recondite knowledge'. They rightly detected some 'echoes of Wordsworth, and . . . of the metaphysical poets', some similarities with Hardy's 'subject matter' and an 'obvious influence of Robert Frost and Edward Thomas in their use of a conversational tone'. Dante's and biblical influences are also seen as being undeniably strong.

Significantly, they fall short of confirming Roger Sell's assessment of Andrew as 'a major poet' twenty years earlier; instead, they say, 'Andrew must be given full credit for having evolved his own highly individual style,' and that, despite changes of taste, he 'stands a good chance of survival'. The appeal of Andrew's poetry, they conclude, is that it is 'intelligible without being unsubtle, individual without being pretentious'.

Faint praise from his nearest and dearest, but the reason is not far to find. Thinking perhaps of poets like Byron, 'There is a better chance that a poet's name will survive if his personality was known to be colourful and eccentric than if it was blameless and respectable,' they suggested. But:

> Andrew's eccentricities and contradictions were *not* well known, because of the sharp distinction that he cultivated between his public and private personae; he was conscientious in performing his public duties, a highly respected clergyman, a benign lover of wild flowers, Gothic churches and mountain scenery, but there were a few – *perhaps only his wife and children* – with whom he had a personal relationship close enough to reveal *his intensely self-centred character; it was they who bore the brunt of it, Janet devoting her gifts and energies totally to the fulfilment of Andrew's wishes and aspirations.* Those who knew only his public image think of him as an uncomplicated, genial, comprehensible person [my italics].

This seems a strange argument, in which personal angst is also very clear; and after all, poets like Byron are not remembered because they were 'mad, bad and dangerous to know', but because the content and quality of their poems has appealed to succeeding generations of poetry readers. And so it will be for Andrew.

> *Trespassing Ghost: A Critical Study of Andrew Young* by Roger Sell
> was issued as a supplement to a Finnish academic journal by Åbo
> Akademi in 1978. As Alison remarked (in Chapter 8 of *To Shirk
> No Idleness)* it therefore 'reached few readers in the general public'.

In his Preface, Sell says: 'He is now respected as a fine poet, by other
poets, critics and the poetry-reading public alike, and there have even
been gestures towards a comparison with T.S. Eliot.' This may have
been true thirty-seven years ago, but is hardly true today, when, outside
universities, Andrew seems largely forgotten. It is sadly *not* the case that 'a
basic appreciation of his work is now secured', but it certainly should be.

Sell goes systematically through the 'canon' of Andrew's writing
from 1910 to 1972, quoting, commenting, interpreting, criticising. In
summarising that: 'Young has been described as: a conservative Georgian;
a new-classical poet of Eliotian 'objectivity'; a tough and tormented
exponent of neo-Romantic Modernism; a Metaphysical born out of time;
a neo-Aesthete master of the crystalline miniature, and a mystic.'

Sell sets out to 'offer some less confusing suggestion as to *where Young
really belongs on the literary map*' (my italics). 'It is impossible to classify
Young as either old-fashioned or modern in any straightforward way,'
he asserts in Chapter 5, 'Towards a Placing'. Much of this is, however, a
summary of Young's critics and reviewers' views over the years, mixed
with vague generalisations, such as: 'Indeed, the least one can say of
Young's best work is that it is very fine and of very considerable interest.'

In his final chapter, *The Best of Young*, Sell remarks that: 'Young
himself may *feel* like a ghost, but this makes him *see* like a naturalist-
cum-painter-cum-man-of-wit'. He also praises his

> intense awareness of the sheer non-human otherness of the
> natural world, its completely separate autonomy, and . . . (his)
> wit . . . can suggest nature's self-sufficiency in several ways:
> through . . . Marvellian . . . constructions; through . . . conceits,
> whereby the life of man is aligned with the life of animals only
> to the sharpening of the difference experienced between them.

Referring obliquely to Plato's theory of anamnesis (that heaven/paradise
lies behind, not in front of, the soul), Sell suggests that

> there are certain other authors whose image of life does
> resemble Young's . . . Wordsworth, Vaughan and Traherne,
> in well-known passages, share a sense of man's life as
> a continuous and unsatisfying retreat from some early
> condition of simplicity and beauty. Their attempts to recover

> the 'auroral vision' are similar to his own, entailing a similar effort to transfigure the physical. . . . Young's beloved Clare . . . experiences similar existential uncertainties *vis a vis* nature, and draws an equally shadowy distinction between his muse of nature and a more aetherial inspiration. Again, Clare, Hardy, and Edward Thomas share with Young a sense of marriage as a kind of second best, where the greatest hope lies in mere affection, tolerance, understanding and honesty. With varying degrees of intensity and clarity, they all conceive of some kind of body-and-soul rapture, which a human lover is incapable of giving or receiving, and their searching desire for 'home' and love, all unattached to anything or anybody here and now, can render strangely indeterminate the boundaries between physical and metaphysical, bodily and ghostly, past and present . . . true reality is somehow Platonic or ghost-like.

Certainly the comments on marriage would help to explain those particular poets' attitudes to their wives! Sell tries to see Andrew's work in the context in which it was written, though how far it 'harmonises' is debatable:

> in a very general way, *Into Hades*, no less than Young's early-middle and late-middle work, harmonises with the literary period during which it was gestating. It represents Young's equivalent of Eliot's Anglo-Catholicism and mysticism, Graves' *The White Goddess*, and Yeats' *A Vision*, showing a similar move towards a personal system or mythology which will enable life to proceed with less sense of absurdity, and with some confidence.

Sell rightly acknowledges the formative influences of Hardy and Edward Thomas on Andrew's poetic development, and, as importantly, stresses that 'Young can achieve that alliance of intellect and emotion which Eliot and other modernists made their goal'. Sell maintains that 'Young's (poetic) growth . . . is little less than prodigious', since it occurred 'in spite of the unsatisfactoriness of the earliest work', but that 'even if he had written nothing after *Winter Harvest* (1933), his achievement would have been considerable'. *How* considerable, without the superb poems in *The White Blackbird* (1935), and the prose works, especially the two flower books? And what of *Into Hades*?

He places Andrew in the 'contemplative' tradition of English nature poetry, exemplified by Wordsworth, Vaughan, Hardy, Edward Thomas and Edwin Muir. For some reason he excludes Clare from this list. He also sees some 'similarities of one kind or another' between Andrew and twentieth-century poets such as Auden, Empson, Graves, Yeats, Frost and Eliot. Frost is perhaps the clearest to see.

Sell also speculates that 'In the long perspective of history, Young may well turn out to be central in certain ways that, say, Eliot, Pound and Auden were not.' Thirty-seven years on, this remains to be seen, but may yet happen.

In the change from short pastoral to long epic poems, seen as 'a profoundly original feat of creative self-renewal', Sell sees Andrew as forging 'a new genre, the ghost parable, which has in every respect an inevitable rightness'. Certainly there is nothing in English poetry quite like it. Sell's final accolade speaks for itself: 'From 1926 to 1958, Young, at best, is always and only his ever-renewed self. He evidences not only . . . the growth . . . the centrality, but also, and very powerfully, the sheer unimitating and inimitable individuality which we look for in *a major poet* (my italics)'.

Certainly, by his maturity (arguably in and beyond *The White Blackbird*, 1935) Andrew's was a singular voice, or idiolect, as much as, say, Hopkins', Thomas' or Eliot's was; but unlike them, Andrew has had no obvious imitators. The phoenix image Sell employs is most apt, as Andrew revises and recreates, or 'quarries' as he goes along; outgrowing one mode and going into another, e.g. from lyric to epic, poetry to prose, from *Into Hades* to its very different sequel *A Traveller in Time*.

The latter is seen by Sell as vastly inferior to the former, which he describes thus: '*Into Hades* is a work of *the very highest order of significance* . . . a uniquely complete instance of all that is finest in Young (my italics)'.

It is hard to disagree.

TRADITION AND YOUNG'S INDIVIDUAL TALENT

Andrew Young was said, in his own time, to be 'in no danger of becoming popular' (Leonard Clark) and 'in no danger of being forgotten' (Philip Larkin). Like most poets, he had his detractors and his defenders: those who dismissed him as a minor 'nature' poet; others who accorded him 'major' status.

Leonard Clark admitted in 1959 that 'the work of Andrew Young is still not as well known as it should be';[1] and this was echoed in an article by Rachel Trickett in 1983: 'during all this time he was consistently writing poetry which was read by few people but admired by an increasing circle of poets and critics.'[2]

---

1.   Introduction to Prospect *of a Poet,* Hart-Davis, 1959.
2.   'World of Books' page, *Daily Telegraph*, 28 May 1983.

Since his death in 1971, a *Collected Poems*, a *Selected Poems*, a biography and an academic study have all been published; yet it is still true to say that he has 'fit audience though few' (as Milton said of *Paradise Lost*). In addition, his old friend Leslie Norris compiled and introduced *Andrew Young: Remembrance and Homage* (a collection of 13 poems by friends, including John Arlott, George MacBeth and Edmund Blunden), published by The Tidal Press in 1978, echoing Leonard Clark's *Prospect of a Poet* of twenty-one years earlier. John Arlott commented that he 'loved him without understanding him', a comment that could doubtless have been echoed by many of his family and friends.

It is certainly time for a reassessment of his place in 'tradition' (i.e. literary history); of his 'individual talent' (i.e. idiolect and style); and of his significance as a poet, nearly half a century after his death. Literary taste and critical thinking have changed greatly during this time: poetry is less formal; relatively free of verbal tropes; less distinct from prose than previously; incorporating text-speak, rap, ethnically diverse expressions, ungrammatical idiom (e.g. 'I was, like, gutted'; '*Can I get* a latte?'). In an age which dislikes elites, *accessibility* is paramount, so Pam Ayres is 'popular' rather than Geoffrey Hill; and creative writing classes encourage the view that anyone can write anything.

Criticism has moved on from ideas of a great tradition in prose, or a 'continuous literary decorum' in poetry. Practical criticism, or in-depth study of the free-standing text (as learned by generations of English graduates from I.A. Richards) has given way to texts in context, with greater emphasis on social, historical, biographical and psychological background. Structuralism has given way to post-structuralism; feminism, formalism, and so on and so on, have also had their day and linger on in odd corners.

If Eliot was right that poets must *not* be judged 'by the canon of dead critics',[3] (himself included), is there, or can there ever be, a form or system of critical assessment which is valid across time and is not merely a set of subjective value judgements?

Andrew Young wrote his significant poetry in the mid-twentieth century (1930-1960), but should he therefore be 'judged' (i.e. evaluated) by the common critical consensus of that time? In any case, literary history tells us that many poets, famous in their time, become quickly forgotten, e.g. who reads Gordon Bottomley now, or has ever heard of Laurence Hope? Charles Doughty? Ted Walker? All well-known, praised, anthologised poets once. Literary history is tidal in nature, with its ebbs and flows.

---

3.   Essay 'Tradition and the Individual Talent' in *The Sacred Wood*, 1920.

Whilst critically appreciated by some (Geoffrey Grigson, for example) in his own time, Andrew's marked disdain for most trends in twentieth-century poetry, made him an 'outsider' and an 'unknown' to many of the poetry-reading public of his own day. Novelty was never his middle name: he respected traditional forms (but then, so did Larkin); on the whole disliked innovators, such as Hopkins, T.S. Eliot, Yeats, Auden; often overestimated minor contemporary figures such as de la Mare or John Freeman; and resolutely kept apart from schools, groups or movements in poetry. He probably believed that, as a poet, he was preserving the traditional verities from decay; that *he* was mainstream, whilst others were merely 'trends'. To some extent he was right.

LINES OF DESCENT

Andrew owes a debt to a number of his predecessors, whom he emulated, from whom he learned, or indirectly *derived from,* without being *derivative*, since his own developed idiolect *is* his own and matured with him. In poetry, his formative influences may be summarised as: the English 'dream vision' poets, Langland and the anonymous 'Gawain poet', especially perhaps *Pearl* with its child guide in the next world; Dante's *Divine Comedy;* the poets of the English pastoral tradition, particularly: Clare, Vaughan, Wordsworth, Hardy, Edward Thomas, Robert Frost; and from the beginning, the metaphysicals, especially Marvell and Donne and the use of the 'conceit'. He also belongs to the tradition of parson poets, including: Herbert, Crabbe, Crashaw, Herrick, and R.S. Thomas; and the diarist, Parson Woodforde.

He outgrew early the influences of Swinburne and most of the 'Georgians', and as Sell said, managed to reinvent himself as he went along.

As a prose stylist he 'descends' from, or is in the tradition of: Izaak Walton, Gilbert White, Thomas Browne, Michael Drayton, Francis Kilvert, John Bunyan and W.H. Hudson, but created his own inimitable poetic prose style and amiable persona, especially in the two flower books. He studied, reread and extensively annotated these writers and seems to have deliberately emulated them.

MODES OF VISION

Andrew's main themes as a poet were *mortality* in all its forms, e.g. dead animals (birds, mole, crab, sparrow, shot magpie etc); natural changes: such as seasons, weathers and places; immortality and the hereafter (*Out of the World and Back*), and religious or spiritual aspects of life. Like Webster, he 'saw the skull beneath the skin', and as George

Szirtes remarked,[4] he had 'a Jacobean appreciation of the macabre'; yet he also shows a constant sense of awe/wonder (e.g. in poems like *The Ventriloquists*).

Andrew's style became increasingly complex, including his use of irony, paradox, juxtaposition, wit, humour, personification, apt or startling imagery, pathetic fallacy and powers of understatement. His prosody was mostly conventional, e.g. rhyme, iambic pentameter, no free verse. He replicates the 'dream vision' poems in modernised form in the final two poems, on which his ultimate reputation rests. He shows marked powers of precision, exactitude and erudition yet simplicity.

Originality is not a matter of saying what has never been said before, but of saying it in a new way that has not been done before; that is, of creating a unique artefact; or, as Wordsworth said in 1815:

> Of genius the only proof is, the act of doing well what is worthy
> to be done, and what was never done before.

Andrew's descriptive powers were outstanding, especially in his cultivation of the conceit; his pastoralism was unsentimental, bold, vivid; his wit was finely-edged, like a scalpel; his imaginative scope, especially in the last two poems, was panoramic – involving, for example, flight, claustrophobia, invisibility and physical disintegration, as well as spiritual encounters. *Into Hades* is a dream vision with nightmarish aspects! His two flower books are knowledgeable without pedantry, written in an entertaining and engaging style, and are classics of their kind, worthy to stand alongside the prose of those English writers whom he most admired.

ANDREW YOUNG'S 'CLAIMS TO FAME'

As we no longer have defined 'canons' of English literature, in poetry or prose, it is difficult to 'place' Andrew in either English, Scottish or twentieth-century literature. He is simultaneously a moral philosopher, a pastoral realist, a theist and a pantheist, a mystic, an ironist and a wordsmith. Like his poetic ancestors, the metaphysicals, he integrated the intellectual component into his poetry, juxtaposing incongruities into new wholenesses.

A poet of lasting significance should be of his time, yet somehow timeless; both referring backwards yet pointing forwards; having an intrinsic worth, always perceptible, even when the circumstances in which it was produced change radically. The poetry of Langland, Wyatt, Herbert, still speaks to us, despite time and change. Will Andrew's do the same, in another fifty years' time, and beyond?

---

4.   In *The Literary Review,* March 1985.

He was 'written off' as a 'minor' poet of the natural world by some critics and reviewers in his own day; later, Roger Sell made a claim for him as a 'major' poet; it is also arguable that he is, in his best short poems and in his two long poems, a *great* poet, who incorporates the timeless qualities of:

- clarity
- economy
- precision
- euphony
- wit
- spaciousness
- resonance

and ultimately,

- transcendence

from the limitations of language itself.

It is doubtful that he will ever become 'popular': but then again, he never was; but his intrinsic worth is self-evident to serious readers, or students of twentieth-century poetry.

Often called 'a poet's poet', he adds to our understanding of ourselves and of the world, embodying aspects of universal truth in a perfect unity of form and lexis.

Eliot said, over 80 years ago – and it is as true today as it was then – that 'no honest poet can ever feel quite sure of the permanent value of what he has written: he may have wasted his time and messed up his life for nothing'.[5]

I don't believe that Andrew did.

---

5.   *The Use of Poetry and the Use of Criticism*, 1933.

Bibliography

Balfour, G.F., *The Life of Alexander Whyte* (London: Hodder & Stoughton, 1924)

Barr, James, *The United Free Church of Scotland* (Oxford: Allenson, 1934)

Cheyne, A.C., *The Transforming of the Kirk: Victorian Scotland's Religious Revolution* (Edinburgh: St Andrew Press, 1983)

Church, Richard, *Over the Bridge* (Portsmouth NH: Heinemann, 1955)

Clark, Leonard, *Andrew Young: Prospect of a Poet* (London: Hart-Davis, 1957)

Edel, Leon, *Literary Biography* (London: Hart-Davis, 1957)

Hollis, Matthew, *Now All Roads Lead to France: The Last Years of Edward Thomas* (London: Faber & Faber, 2011)

Kohfeldt, Mary Lou, *Lady Gregory: The Woman Behind the Irish Renaissance* (London: Andre Deutsch, 1985)

Lowbury, Edward and Young, Alison, *To Shirk No Idleness* (Salzburg: University of Salzburg Press, 1997)

Mendelson, Edward, *W.H. Auden: Selected Poems* (London: Faber & Faber, 1979)

Norris, Leslie (ed.), *Andrew Young: Remembrance and Homage* (London: Tidal Press, 1978)

Sell, Roger D., *Trespassing Ghost: A Critical Study of Andrew Young* (Turku, Finland: Åbo Akademi, 1978)

Woolf, Virginia, *The Death of the Moth and Other Essays* (London: Penguin, 1942)

Young, Andrew
Poetry

Memorial Verses, 1918
Boaz and Ruth and Other Poems, 1920
The Death of Eli and Other Poems, 1921
Thirty-One Poems, 1922
The Bird Cage, 1926
The Cuckoo Clock, 1928
The New Shepherd, 1931
Winter Harvest, 1933
The White Blackbird, 1935
Collected Poems, 1936
Speak to the Earth, 1939

The Green Man, 1947
Collected Poems, 1950
Into Hades, 1952
Out of the World and Back, 1958
Collected Poems, 1960
Complete Poems, 1974
The Poetical Works, 1985
Selected Poems, 1998

PLAYS

The Adversary, 1923
Rizpah, 1923
Nicodemus: A Mystery, 1937
The Sirens (unpublished), 1939–40

PROSE

A Prospect of Flowers, 1945
A Retrospect of Flowers, 1950
A Prospect of Britain, 1956
The Poet and The Landscape, 1962
The New Poly-Olbion, 1967
The Poetic Jesus, 1972
Parables, 1985

INDEX

9 7 8 0 7 1 8 8 9 5 1 3 6

An environmentally friendly book printed and bound in England by www.printondemand-worldwide.com

PEFC Certified

This product is
from sustainably
managed forests
and controlled
sources

www.pefc.org

PEFC/16-33-415

This book is made of chain-of-custody materials; FSC materials for the cover and PEFC materials for the text pages

Reprint of # - C0 - 234/156/11 - PB - Lamination Gloss - Printed on 14-Sep-18 05:30